Security or Armageddon

Other Books by Louis René Beres

The Management of World Power: A Theoretical Analysis (1973)

Reordering the Planet: Constructing Alternative World Futures, with Harry R. Targ (1974)

Transforming World Politics: The National Roots of World Peace (1975)

Planning Alternative World Futures: Values, Methods and Models, with Harry R. Targ (1975)

Terrorism and Global Security: The Nuclear Threat (1979)

Apocalypse: Nuclear Catastrophe in World Politics (1980)

People, States and World Order (1981)

Mimicking Sisyphus: America's Countervailing Nuclear Strategy (1983)

Reason and Realpolitik: U.S. Foreign Policy and World Order (1984)

Security or Armageddon

Israel's Nuclear Strategy

Edited by
Louis René Beres

Lexington Books

D.C. Heath and Company/Lexington, Massachusetts/Toronto

Library of Congress Cataloging in Publication Data
Main entry under title:

Security or Armageddon.

Includes index.
1. Israel—Military policy. 2. Nuclear weapons—Israel. I. Beres, Louis René.
UA853.I8S42   1986   355'.0335'5694   84-48505
ISBN 0-669-09566-4 (alk. paper)
ISBN 0-669-11131-7 (pbk. : alk. paper)

Published simultaneously in Canada
Printed in the United States of America
Casebound International Standard Book Number: 0-669-09566-4
Paperbound International Standard Book Number: 0-669-11131-7
Library of Congress Catalog Card Number: 84-48505

The paper used in this publication meets the minimum requirements of American National Standard for Information Sciences—Permanence of Paper for Printed Library Materials, ANSI Z39.48-1984. ∞™

*For all who would spread the Tabernacle of Peace
over Jerusalem*

Contents

Acknowledgments

In this third happy alliance between author and publisher, I am again greatly indebted to the sympathetic and sustaining staff at Lexington Books. Special gratitude goes to my editor, Jaime Welch-Donahue, who makes everything possible. Combining understanding with a persistently lively intelligence, she has made an important contribution to this book. I am also grateful to Susan Cummings for her conscientious shepherding of the manuscript through the production stage. This book has benefited from the marketing efforts of Pamela J. Walch-Constantine and Eileen Young—efforts that are both skillful and heartfelt—and from Martha Cleary's capable production assistance. Cynthia Insolio Benn deserves praise for once again making a positive mark as a creative and insightful copy editor. Finally, I thank my friends and colleagues in Israel and America who contributed to this volume and who thereby share my concern about a subject of terrible urgency. In this connection, it should be understood that the views expressed herein by each contributor are those of an individual scholar and do not necessarily represent the positions of particular institutions or governments.

Louis René Beres

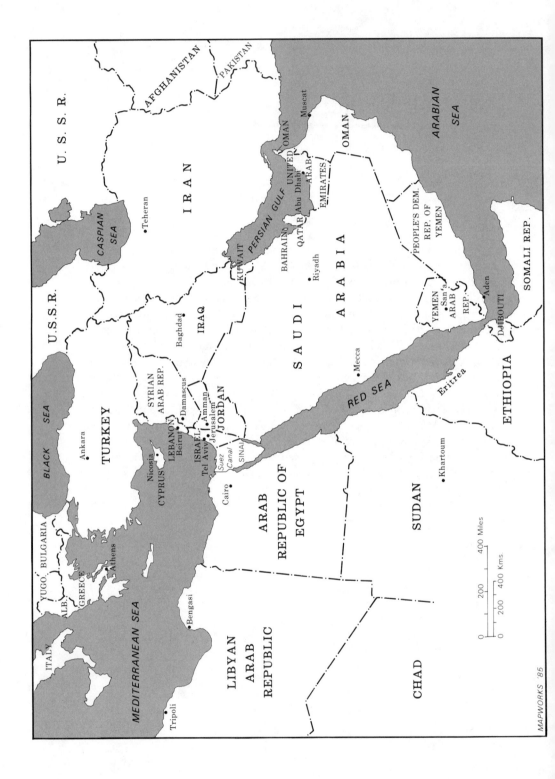

MAPWORKS '85

1
Introduction

Louis René Beres

Medieval maps often portrayed Jerusalem at the center of the world. From the perspective of nuclear strategy and world order, such a portrayal might have particular validity today. Confronted with enormously difficult choices concerning military posture and effective deterrence, Israel's decision on the nuclear option will have far-reaching implications for regional peace and stability. And since world order is strongly affected by what happens in the Middle East, this decision will have planetary consequences.

What, exactly, should Israel choose? If there is a "bomb in the basement," an undisclosed force of nuclear weapons or components that could be assembled rapidly into such weapons, should it remain there? Or would Israel be better served by moving beyond its current policy of deliberate ambiguity[1] to one of an explicit declaration of nuclear capability? If, as some scholars suggest,[2] Israel has never actually moved to implement a nuclear weapons option, should it now exercise that option? And if it does, should the necessary steps be taken under the mantle of obscurity, or should they be accompanied by public disclosure?

With these questions in mind, the contributors to this book have sought to trace the contours of Israel's security needs at a time of great uncertainty. Informed by four decades of nuclear deterrence doctrine operating among the major powers, they have applied this understanding to Israel's special circumstances. The result, it is hoped, will support the Talmudic observation that "scholars build the structure of peace in the world."[3]

There are no easy answers. Although each contributor seeks to spread the tabernacle of peace over Jerusalem, there is no general agreement upon how this might best be accomplished. We must do everything to prevent the destruction of the Third Temple, but the hazardous flux of world affairs may make a mockery of even the most cherished military doctrines.

At one level, the protracted nuclear stalemate between the superpowers since the dawn of the atomic age suggests optimism about nuclear deterrence. The "delicate" balance of terror has held for almost forty years. Why, then, shouldn't it continue to hold? And why shouldn't it be extended purposefully to the Middle East?[4]

In response, we must understand that it is much too soon to claim success for nuclear deterrence between the United States and the Soviet Union.[5] The fact that it has "worked" thus far (a characterization that leaves out the overwhelming economic and ethical costs of nuclear deterrence) is no more reassuring than the case of the cigarette smoker who has been puffing for twenty years without getting cancer. If that smoker dies in his twenty-first year of smoking, the final calculation of costs and benefits will certainly be negative.

With the atomic secret torn from nature, the existing nuclear powers have done little more than defer a remorseless judgment. At one time or another, in one way or another, the manifestly catastrophic possibilities now latent in nuclear weapons are almost certain to be exploited. Whether by design or by accident, by misinformation or miscalculation, by lapse from rational decision, or by unauthorized decision, the system of "deadly logic" will fail.

Consider the possibilities. A nuclear war could come about inadvertently through the outcome of competition in risk-taking. It might begin by the seizure of nuclear weapons by allied countries. It might be provoked by a smaller power (catalytic war) or by war between smaller powers.[6]

It might take place because of errors in calculating the outcomes of various anticipated courses of action. Or, it might even take place as a consequence of irrationality, through use by unauthorized personnel, or by mechanical, electrical, or computer malfunction.

In considering these possibilities, we must keep in mind that nuclear deterrence is a dynamic process, one that changes continually with serious and unforeseen effects. Exhibiting a complex momentum unplanned by legions of strategic theorists, the current superpower arms race bears little resemblance to its early form. Instead of the relatively unthreatening pattern of "mutual assured destruction" (MAD), nuclear deterrence between the superpowers now rests upon the capacity to fight a potentially "protracted" nuclear war via "nuclear utilization theory" (NUT). With this fundamental shift in deterrence logic, the United States, the Soviet Union and other nuclear powers plan to deploy a variety of weapons that are unsuitable for anything but an initial move of war.

These developments have an important bearing upon Israel's nuclear strategy. Even if Israel were to develop a "countervalue" nuclear strategy, a strategy without the provocative elements now present in superpower nuclear relations, there is no assurance that it would not evolve (as it did between the superpowers) into a "counterforce" strategy.[7] Moreover, the subtle intellectual distinctions between "countervalue" and "counterforce" may have little meaning in the Middle East, where distances are close and intentions often undecipherable. Indeed, a counterforce strategy in this theater could lack credibility because "collateral damage" might destroy entire populations.

Some argue that Israel's security would be high as a nuclear power even if it coexisted with several adversary nuclear powers in the region.[8] This is the case, it has been alleged, because there would be little reason to strike first in a nuclear crowd. In Shai Feldman's words: "Since nuclear weapons enjoy a high cost-exchange ratio against answering or neutralizing weapons, the incentives for preemption have drastically decreased."[9]

But why? Even if preemption could not prevent an overwhelmingly destructive retaliation, it could have (or appear to have) some damage-limiting benefits. Hence, it might well be rational for nuclear armed states to preempt other nuclear states if they believe the only alternative is to be struck first—an alternative that could never be dismissed in a nuclearized context, especially where counterforce strategies are augmented by defensive measures.[10]

And what about *rationality?* The durability of any system of nuclear deterrence is always contingent upon this assumption. Can we assume that leadership in the Middle East is immune to irrationality? If not, then there can never be any long-term security in nuclear proliferation.[11] Should a new nuclear weapons state fall under the leadership of a person or persons suffering from madness, severe emotional stress, or major physiologic impairment, this state might initiate nuclear first strikes against other nuclear states even though enormously destructive retaliation could be anticipated. Since the logic of nuclear deterrence is based upon the assumption that states consistently value self-preservation more highly than any other preferences, the appearance of irrational national leaders would immobilize that logic. The strategy of nuclear deterrence would not work in the face of irrational leaders with nuclear weapons. This, of course, was one of the concerns expressed by Israel in justifying its attack on the Iraqi nuclear reactor.

This fact is particularly disturbing when it is understood that instances of irrationality at national leadership levels are well known in world politics. And it is even more disturbing when it is recognized that dictatorship, which is led by the most reckless of personality types, is the prevailing form of government among Israel's adversaries.

It would, however, be a mistake to identify the problem of irrationality exclusively with the "crazy leader" scenario. This is not the heart of the irrationality problem. Rather, irrationality—as was demonstrated by President Kennedy during the 1962 Cuban missile crisis, can be displayed by perfectly cool, calm, intelligent, and self-preservation minded leaders. Kennedy, we must recall, imposed his quarantine on the assumption that it carried a 50/50 chance of nuclear war.

The central problem of rationality lies in the nature of nuclear deterrence itself. Nuclear strategy is a game that sane national leaders may play, but it is one that frequently requires extraordinary risk-taking to maximize near-term security. The results of these required ventures in escalation and committal are never known in advance. Under certain conditions, they could include an all-destructive nuclear war.

Significantly, Israeli considerations of rationality and irrationality are likely to be based upon the traditional Western concept embraced by American nuclear strategists. For example, Feldman notes: "Israel's destruction would bring them (Arab adversaries) little joy if they are destroyed in retaliation."[12] But he may be quite wrong! Using different standards of rational judgment (the "liberation" of "Palestine" as an overriding value for one), the expected benefits of attacking Israel might be judged to exceed the expected costs *whatever the anticipated retaliatory consequences*. In this connection, it is sobering to recall U.S. miscalculations of enemy rationality in Vietnam.

In his book on the subject of Israeli nuclear deterrence, Shai Feldman identifies an important variable in adversary power relationships: relative willingness to absorb punishment.[13] A variant of the rationality problem, this factor suggests that even if Israel were to achieve a significant nuclear weapons capability, its nuclear deterrent could be undermined by enemies with a greater willingness to absorb punishment. Indeed, confronted by the forces of *jihad* or holy war, Israel might confront a situation where no level of threat would be adequate to prevent a devastating attack on Israel. In such a situation, its only alternative to preemption (possibly against several adversaries simultaneously) might be judged an all-out nuclear war.

Much of the optimism surrounding the argument for Israeli nuclear deterrence neglects to take account of the adversaries' *perceptions*. In the United States, our error is that we cannot conceive of the Russians viewing us as an aggressor. After all, we suggest, it is perfectly obvious that this is a Manichean struggle between ourselves and the Soviet Sons of Darkness. Looking over the Reagan administration's nuclear strategy, much of it might have been drawn from the Good versus Evil polarity of the Dead Sea Scrolls.

But what does the struggle look like from the Soviet vantage point? They see a United States that is the only country ever to have used atomic weapons—and used them against unprotected civilian populations. They see a United States that speaks of "prevailing" in a "protracted" nuclear war, and that augments this doctrine with first-strike weapons and elaborate, preemption threatening, schemes for defense. They see a United States that blocks all attempts at arms control and that continues to rely on the policy of "first use" of nuclear weapons. They see, in other words, an adversary that is making plans to strike first. As a result, whether or not they are correct in their perceptions, they are more and more likely to strike first themselves.

There is a lesson in all of this for Israel. The lesson is that not all of her adversaries will judge her incapable of aggression. However sincere Israel might be about using nuclear weapons only for retaliation, there is no way to convince all of her adversaries of this sincerity. As a result, a nuclear arms race in the Middle East carries the same perils as the superpower *folie à deux*.

In this connection, some scholars believe that an Israeli nuclear deterrent would benefit from that country's exclusive concern for self-defense. As Shai Feldman suggests, since the "willingness to defend one's state will be greater than the willingness to conquer another state," there should be no nuclear attack against Israel.[14] Since Israel's commitment to self-preservation will always exceed its adversaries' commitments to destroy Israel, it is argued, Israel's nuclear deterrent should be credible.

But there are serious problems with this reasoning. Even if we leave aside the issues of irrationality and relative willingness to absorb punishment, it is unlikely that Israel's adversaries will always perceive safety from first-strike attack. In the real world, the line between self-defense and aggression may not be so neatly drawn, and adversary states may judge self-defense to require a preemptive strike. The objective of such a strike would not be conquest per se, but rather national security through prophylaxis.

The likelihood of such strikes would be greatest where adversaries coexist amid conditions of great uncertainty and where each state fears preemption by one or several others. It follows that the alleged benefits that would accrue to an Israeli nuclear deterrent because of its association with self-defense are illusory. Ironically, this should be especially apparent to Israeli strategists, for whom the notion of anticipatory self-defense has long been accepted practice.

This brings us to the problem of accidental nuclear war and nuclear weapons accidents. The reason for this problem is not simply a function of number (by which the more nuclear weapons states, the greater the number of existing risks), but it is also a consequence of the need to compensate for vulnerable nuclear forces by utilizing risky command and control measures. In addition, new nuclear powers are unlikely to invest the time and expense needed to equip the nuclear weapons themselves with interlocking safety mechanisms.

Today, U.S. and Soviet nuclear forces are safeguarded from accidental firings by a considerable array of features built into both the chain of command and the weapons themselves. These features are highlighted by the "two-man" concept whereby no single individual has the capability to fire nuclear weapons; by a control system whereby each individual with a nuclear weapons responsibility has been certified under the Human Reliability Program; by the use of secure codes; by the employment of coded locking devices which prevent firing in the absence of specific signals from higher command; and by the use of environmental sensing devices which prevent unwanted detonations through the operation of switches that respond to acceleration, deceleration, altitude, spin, gravity, and thermal forces.

It would be the height of folly to expect all new nuclear powers in the

Middle East to undertake similar precautions against inadvertent firings of nuclear weapons. To be effective, safety measures would have to apply to all available nuclear weapons and to all pertinent nuclear weapons operations throughout the stockpile-to-target sequence, that is, to storage, maintenance, handling, transportation, and delivery. Moreover, specific provisions would be needed for all unique nuclear weapons system operations, including alerts, operational posturing, maneuvers, exercises, and training.

When one considers both the complexity and cost of such safety systems and the fact that new nuclear powers will find it necessary to disavow certain safeguards in the interest of preventing preemption, the prospect of accidental nuclear war is undeniably very significant in a proliferated region. This prospect is magnified by the specter of catastrophic accidents which do not give rise to nuclear war but which still produce a nuclear yield. Since the U.S. record of nuclear weapons accidents has included a number of very close calls, one can't help but anticipate a new rash of such broken arrows among forces of new nuclear powers. What will happen when their bombers crash; when the nuclear payloads they carry are accidentally dropped or intentionally jettisoned; or when these nuclear bombs or missiles are burned in a fire on the ground? With the proliferation of nuclear powers in the Middle East, such accidents can be expected to occur at an increased rate.

As with accidental nuclear war and nuclear weapons accidents, regional nuclear proliferation would also increase the probability of the unauthorized use of nuclear weapons. This is the case, again, not only because of the expanded number of existing risks, but because the new nuclear powers would almost certainly lack the safeguards now in place in superpower arsenals. In response to the need for a quick-reaction nuclear force which can be fielded as soon as possible, new nuclear powers will inevitably turn to automatic or nearly automatic systems of nuclear retaliation which are not encumbered by complex and costly command and control checks.

The new nuclear weapons states will also be likely to increase the number of national decisionmakers who are properly authorized to use nuclear weapons. As long as their early warning networks are not good, and as long as concern exists that field commanders might not be able to respond to a first-strike attack if central authorization is required, these secondary nuclear powers may predelegate launch authority to selected field commanders. Such launch-on-warning strategies would increase the probability of all forms of both authorized and unauthorized nuclear attacks. In this connection, we must include the prospect of *intra*national nuclear weapons seizure via coup d'état, a prospect that has particularly ominous overtones in such coup-vulnerable potential proliferators as Iraq, Iran, and Pakistan.

The probability of unauthorized use of nuclear weapons that accrues from nuclear proliferation can also be expected to increase because of premeditated false warnings. The larger the number of nuclear weapons states, the greater the likelihood that personnel who man early warning satellite or radar systems will deliberately falsify information about hostile action, especially since the new nuclear powers may enforce less than the highest standards of human and mechanical reliability. The results of such falsification, of course, might well be nuclear first strikes that are disguised as retaliation.

But what if regional proliferation is inevitable? What, then, should be Israel's strategy? Under such conditions, can Israel be expected to hew to a policy of "deliberate ambiguity"?[15]

These are very serious questions. In the aftermath of Israel's raid on Iraq's nuclear reactor on June 7, 1981, Iraq's President Saddam Hussein urged "all peace-loving countries [to] help the Arabs obtain the nuclear bomb in order to confront Israel's existing bombs."[16] There is considerable evidence that a number of Israel's adversaries have not hesitated to heed Hussein's call. In this connection, Stephen M. Meyer speaks of "hard-core proliferants"— countries that have already made the decision to become nuclear powers; countries whose intensity of "motivational profiles" is such that "no matter how many technology barriers are thrown up in their paths, they will continue to pursue a nuclear weapons capability" (as have Pakistan, Iraq, and Libya).[17]

In considering the likelihood of Israel's adversaries "going nuclear" apart from any direct response to Israeli actions, we must also take into account other adversary relationships in the region. Since there are many axes of conflict in the Middle East (Iran and Iraq; Egypt and Libya; Libya and Sudan), Israel's enemies may have substantial incentive to proceed with nuclear weapons technologies irrespective of Israel's strategic posture. It follows that fully effective measures to deal with regional proliferation would have to focus on the entire range of area rivalries, and not merely on the Arab–Israeli disputes.[18]

The value of nuclear forces has already been openly recognized by several pertinent actors in the region. Several years ago, Ismail Fahmi, President Sadat's minister of foreign affairs, suggested that nuclear status would not only neutralize the ever-present possibility of Israeli nuclear threats, but it would also neutralize the possibility of threats from other nuclear states in the area (such as Libya and Iraq). Moreover, noted Fahmi, such status would lead to a technological, scientific, and strategic revolution in Egypt, making it a leading power in that part of the world.[19]

A special problem area is the Gulf. This is one of the few areas in the developing world where surplus funds exist to support proliferation or to purchase nuclear weapons from a third party. Perhaps just as significantly, the Gulf states are exceptionally vulnerable to a nuclear attack. According to Anthony H. Cordesman: "One well-placed bomb on a capital could destroy the national identity and recovery capability of most of the smaller southern Gulf states, and only five to seven such strikes could probably destroy the national identity of Iraq, Iran or Saudi Arabia. This makes the Gulf states vulnerable to both nuclear attack and nuclear blackmail."[20]

If a nuclearized Middle East becomes a fait accompli, Israel would, of course, have little choice. It would be compelled to adopt an open strategy of nuclear deterrence. Should such a point be reached, it would not make nuclear war inevitable, but it would require extraordinary forms of regional power management.

In the first place, steps would need to be taken to slow down the *rate of proliferation.* As long as a number of potential proliferants had not yet attained membership in the nuclear club, efforts would have to be undertaken to inhibit further nuclear proliferation.

In the second place, steps would have to be taken to ensure the stability of nuclear power relationships and to spread information and technology pertaining to nuclear weapons safeguards. This means that an all-out effort would have to be mustered to prevent intense crises in the region and that such an effort would have to be supported by technical assistance to Nth country nuclear forces. Since many, if not all, of the new nuclear weapon states would be especially vulnerable to accidental, unauthorized and preemptive firings,[21] the superpowers would have to take seriously the prospect of helping these states to develop safe weapon systems and reliable command, control, and communications procedures.

The need for such assistance would be dictated by a number of factors. For one, new nuclear powers, in response to the need for survivable forces, would almost certainly turn to quick-acting systems of retaliation. For another, new nuclear powers would be unlikely to invest the enormous amounts of money needed to equip the nuclear weapons themselves with trustworthy safety design features. It would be essential, therefore, in the event of regional proliferation of nuclear weapons, that the superpowers share many of their safeguard strategies with the newer members of the nuclear club. At a minimum, such sharing would have to include information about (1) making accurate identification of an attacker, (2) rendering nuclear forces survivable for a second strike, (3) ensuring human reliability in the command and control setting, and (4) ensuring weapon-system reliability through such means as coded locking devices and environmental sensing techniques.

In addition to offering technical assistance to Nth countries, the superpowers would also have to influence the strategic doctrines of these new nuclear weapon states. At a minimum, such efforts would have to be directed at underscoring the deterrence function of strategic force, reinforcing the idea that nuclear weapons must not be considered for actual war-waging. Special emphasis would have to be placed on the centrality of "minimum deterrence" and on the disavowal of first-strike options and capabilities.

It goes without saying, however, that it would be best for all concerned in the region to prevent nuclear proliferation in the first place. If there is still hope for a nuclear weapon free zone in the Middle East, Israel and all other regional powers would do best to bring it into existence.[22] In the bad dream of living in a nuclear crowd, there would be myriad sources of instability:

The expanded number of nuclear powers could wreak havoc upon the idea of a stable balance of terror in world politics. There would simply be too many players, too much ambiguity, for any sense of balance to be meaningful.

The expanded number of nuclear powers would shatter the relative symmetry of strategic doctrine between nuclear weapons states. Some of the new nuclear powers would shape their strategies along the lines of assured destruction capabilities. Others would seek more ambitious objectives, including a nuclear war-fighting or counterforce capability. As a result, nuclear weapons might lose their image as instruments of deterrence, a situation that would surely be accelerated by the first actual use of nuclear weapons by a secondary nuclear power. If, for example, the nuclear "firebreak" were actually crossed, whether by Israel or by an Arab state, other pairs of antagonistic states would be more likely to think the unthinkable. A ripple effect would begin to be evident, with perhaps Libya contemplating preemption against Egypt, or Iran thinking seriously about a nuclear strike against Iraq.

The expanded number of nuclear powers would ultimately create the conditions whereby first-strike attacks could be unleashed with impunity, whatever the condition of the intended victim's willingness to retaliate or the security of its retaliatory forces. This is the case because in a region of many nuclear powers, it would become possible for a nuclear-armed aggressor to launch its weapons against another state without being identified. Unable to know for certain where the attack originated, the victim state might lash out blindly. In the resulting conflagration, a worldwide nuclear war enveloping even the superpowers might ensue.

The expanded number of nuclear powers would create the conditions for a chain reaction of nuclear exchanges. Even before it becomes possible to launch a nuclear strike anonymously, a strategic exchange might take place between two or more new nuclear weapons states that are members of opposing alliances. Ultimately, if the parties to such a clash involve clients of either or both superpowers, the ensuing chain reaction might consume the United States and the Soviet Union along with much of the rest of the world.

The expanded number of nuclear powers would create the conditions whereby microproliferation, the spread of nuclear weapons capabilities to insurgent groups, might be accelerated. A possible outcome of such microproliferation might be not only nuclear terrorism, but also an anonymous terrorist detonation that could be mistakenly blamed upon another state by the attack victim. In this way, microproliferation could actually spark regional or systemwide nuclear war between states.

The expanded number of nuclear powers would create major asymmetries in power between rival states. Where one rival would find itself in possession of nuclear weapons, and another rival would be denied such possession, the new nuclear state might find itself with an overwhelming incentive to strike. The cumulative effect of such inequalities of power created by the uneven spread of nuclear weapons could be an elevated probability of nuclear aggression against nonnuclear states.

It should not be assumed, however, that an Israeli nuclear monopoly in the Middle East would necessarily produce safety. Even if it were to adopt a policy of nuclear disclosure as the only regional nuclear power, this posture might have little or no deterrent effect on "small" incursions or assaults upon Israel or its interests throughout the world. This is because the prospective aggressors (state or subnational) would be unlikely to believe Israel's willingness to use nuclear force under any but the most urgent (nation-threatening) conditions.[23]

In this connection, one must also understand that Israel's nonnuclear enemies might achieve significant counterdeterrent effects by means of other highly destructive weapons technologies—chemical, biological, or nerve weapon systems, technologies well within the grasp of every adversary of Israel. For example, a nonnuclear adversary of Israel might, after absorbing an Israeli nuclear assault, be able to retaliate against Israeli cities with chemical or biological weapons. Knowing this, would Israel's threat to make use of its nuclear weapons be credible?

It is conceivable, of course, that Israel might move to accompany its nuclear disclosure with a parallel weakening of its conventional forces, a move designed to signal a heightened Israeli willingness to resort to nuclear weapons. Although such a move would also carry significant economic benefits, it would have the effect of reducing Israeli options to calamity or capitulation. Hence, it would be profoundly contrary to Israel's security interests.[24]

In assessing Israeli deterrence under conditions of a nuclear monopoly, one must also consider world public opinion. Although Shai Feldman has argued that the enormity of the nuclear threat makes nuclear deterrence credible, it is precisely that enormity that could render nuclear threats *incredible*. After all, how likely is it that Israel could ignore public reaction to its use of nuclear weapons against nonnuclear adversaries? Could Israel defend the morality of such use? Could it expect to undertake such use without suffering an incalculable loss of global esteem and support? Would the terrible historical irony of a Jewish State visiting nuclear holocaust upon others be lost upon Israel's decisionmakers?

It is also apparent that the physical and biological effects of Israeli nuclear attacks could harm Israel as well as its target populations. On the basis of an ever-expanding body of knowledge concerning the consequences of nuclear explosions, it is likely that the expected costs of fallout returning to Israel's cities and countryside would outweigh any expected benefits of attack. Hence, Israel could be self-deterred.[25]

In the final analysis, everything points to the imperative avoidance of nuclear attacks. Although we can conceive of circumstances in which the only choice available to Israel is nuclear attack or the physical destruction of Israel, there would in fact be no real choice. If the attack were directed at nonnuclear adversaries, Israel might avoid immediate physical destruction, but her long-term continuance as a member of the community of nations would be untenable. If the attack were directed against one or more nuclear enemies, the entire region would lay in rubble. For any semblance of a livable species to be born out of the radioactive ash of such a war, a gravedigger would have to wield the forceps.[26]

Even the most limited nuclear exchange would signal unprecedented catastrophe. The immediate effects of the explosions—thermal radiation, nuclear radiation, and blast damage—would cause wide swaths of death and devastation. Victims would suffer flash and flame burns. Retinal burns could occur in the eyes of persons at distances of several hundred miles from the explosion. People would be crushed by collapsing buildings or torn by flying glass. Others would fall victim to raging firestorms and conflagrations. Fallout injuries would include whole-body radiation injury, produced by penetrating, hard gamma radiation; superficial radiation burns produced by soft radiations; and injuries produced by deposits of radioactive substances within the body.

In the aftermath, medical facilities that might still exist would be stressed beyond endurance. Water supplies would become unusable as a result of fallout contamination. Housing and shelter would be unavailable for survivors. Transportation and communication would break down to almost prehistoric levels. And overwhelming food shortages would become the rule for at least several years.

Since the countries involved would have entered into war as modern industrial economies, their networks of highly interlocking and interdependent exchange systems would now be shattered. Virtually everyone would be deprived of a means of livelihood. Emergency fire and police services would be decimated altogether. Systems dependent upon electrical power would cease to function. Severe trauma would occasion widespread disorientation and psychological disorders for which there would be no therapeutic services.

In sum, normal society would disappear. The pestilence of unrestrained murder and banditry would augment the pestilence of plague and epidemics. With the passage of time, many of the survivors could expect an increased incidence of degenerative diseases and various kinds of cancer. They might also expect premature death, impairment of vision, and a high probability of sterility. Among the survivors of Hiroshima, for example, an increased incidence of leukemia and cancer of the lung, stomach, breast, ovary, and uterine cervix has been widely documented.

Such a war could also have devastating climatic effects. It is now widely understood that even the explosion of a mere 100 megatons (less than 1 percent of the world's arsenals) would be enough to generate an epoch of cold and dark nearly as severe as in the 5,000-megaton case. As we have learned from Carl Sagan, the threshold for the nuclear winter is very low.[27]

The idea that the concept of victory has no place in a nuclear war is as old as the nuclear age. It is an idea that should be reaffirmed by all parties to conflict in the Middle East. Even before the nuclear age, Machiavelli, in the *Discourses*, recognized the principle of an "economy of violence" which distinguishes between creativity and destruction.

Still another problem with the idea of victory in a nuclear war is the arbitrariness or unpredictability intrinsic to such dimensions of violence.[28] Contrary to the anesthetized expectations of strategists who anticipate near perfect symmetry between human behavior and their own rarified plans, nuclear war harbors within itself an ineradicable element of the unexpected. National leaders must learn to appreciate how little humankind can control amid the disorderly multitude of factors involved in nuclear war. They must learn to understand what presumptuous hazards are associated with a strategy that seeks to impose order on what must inevitably be a form of chaos.

To counter the encroachment of Armageddon, statesmen in the Middle East would do well to reconsider Thucydides' account of the Peloponnesian War. There they would learn that the wellsprings of strategic behavior lie in the irrational and impulsive recesses of the human psyche. There they would encounter a memorable recitation of events in which the blind drives of honor and recklessness take precedence over considerations of safety and survival, a recitation that prefigures the consequences of excessive faith in rational models of nuclear warfare.

The conditions that arose in Classical Greece after the death of Pericles and the ascent of Cleon and Alcibiades in Athenian affairs have been repeated in countless episodes of human history. Understood in terms of a purposeful nuclear strategy, these conditions point to an overweening pride and arrogance in counseling preparations for nuclear warfare, a pattern of hubris that underscores the urgency of Albert Einstein's warning that the unleashed power of the atom has changed everything except for our thinking.

Israel's path to security will continue to be treacherous. Burdened by the corrosive economic effects of military spending and the difficulties of maintaining conventional superiority,[29] it will be tempted by the apparent benefits of an openly declared nuclear strategy. Reminded of the laments of ancient King Pyrrhus, whose successive victories with a small army finally led him, after one such victory, to declare: "One more such victory and all is lost," Israel knows that it must choose between the sheer rock of Scylla and the whirlpool of Charybdis.

But choose it must! As the following essays suggest, a number of specific steps can be taken to protect national security without enlarging the risk of nuclear war. In the final analysis, all of these steps point in one way or another to a political settlement of differences in the region. Only this sort of settlement can provide enduring safety for Israel.

In an important book, *The Bar Kokhba Syndrome: Risk and Realism in International Politics*, Yehoshafat Harkabi, a former chief of Israeli military intelligence, speaks about the grave dangers that lurk in unrealistic assessments of historical and political circumstances. Drawing upon the lessons of the Bar Kokhba Rebellion in 132 A.D., which pushed the Jewish People to the very margins of history, Dr. Harkabi concludes that public policy must never place the nation's very existence in jeopardy. Understood in terms of Israel's decision on the nuclear option, the author's wisdom suggests extraordinary caution to ensure that Israel does not behave suicidally. Just as Bar Kokhba transgressed *ahavat Yisrael* ('love of Israel') by choosing rebelliousness detached from responsibility, so might the leadership of modern Israel make ill-considered choices with irreversible consequences. In his own words, the "operative guidance" that springs from the Bar Kokhba Rebellion is as follows:

> In choosing a style of fighting, be wary of warfare in which the reaction required of the enemy, from the enemy's point of view, may lead to an action detrimental for you. This is a difficult demand, but the instance of Bar Kokhba makes it vivid: the challenge to Rome by the Jewish guerrilla defenses could be overcome by the Romans only by extermination warfare. This is an important lesson in nuclear circumstances: refrain from a provocation for which the adversary may only have one response, nuclear war.[30]

Violence is not power. Sometimes they are opposites. Understood in terms of the requirements of peace in the Middle East, Israel and her adversaries must soon begin to recognize the essential interdependence of all actors in the region. By substituting the dignity of cooperation for the folly of mortal competition, these state and nonstate actors could create the conditions for a general and graduated process of deescalation and conflict reduction.[31] Rejecting the self-defeating lure of relentless hostility, they could embrace a new kind of lucidity, a pattern of coexistence replacing predatory imaginings with pragmatic partnership.

In the words of *Ecclesiastes,* "Vain hopes delude the senseless and dreams give wings to a fool's fancy" (34:1). Seizing the moment, the nations of the Middle East still have an opportunity to choose life. Vitalized by genuine understanding rather than the desolate communion of military force and coercion, they could begin to act as members of a single society. There is no other way.

2
Going Public with the Bomb: The Israeli Calculus

Alan Dowty

et us suppose for the moment that we know nothing about the actual state of Israeli nuclear weapons programs. Looking simply at Israel's situation and the options available, what kind of program would we predict as the most likely course of action? In other words, what seems to be the logical perspective on nuclear weapons for a state with Israel's security problems, capabilities, and international standing?

This question can be divided into two specific issues. First, what aims might be served by an Israeli nuclear weapons program? Second, given these aims, what kind of program, if any, seems most appropriate—and should it be kept quiet or disclosed publicly? Answers to these questions will provide an instructive perspective from which to review, in concluding, what we do know about actual Israeli nuclear weapons policy.

The Possible Aims of a Weapons Program

The minimal aim of any Israeli nuclear weapons program would be to *offset an Arab nuclear force,* should such a force come into being. Barring an effective renewal of the Iraqi crash program, this seems to be several years in the future; in fact, the estimated lead times of most Arab nuclear weapons programs have not decreased much over the last two decades. There is also the possibility of nuclear arms transfers to an Arab state, though this seems unlikely as long as Israel remains nonnuclear. In sum, the danger of Arab nuclear weapons development does not seem to justify actual Israeli nuclear weapons development at present, though it is grounds for keeping available an option, with an appropriate lead time.

Danger from Arab conventional arms is a much more likely motivation for nuclear development. Despite commitments from the United States, Israel is protected by no formal alliances or guarantees. Moreover, Arab conventional superiority could conceivably develop with less advance warning than an Arab nuclear capacity, requiring a shorter nuclear option. Israeli decisionmakers would be remiss if they did not consider what "ultimate" or "last resort" deterrent might be employed if successful invasion by Arab armies seemed imminent.

As an extension of this, policy makers might want to *prevent extensive casualties to Israeli cities,* should they be faced with loss of air superiority, development of substantial Arab missile capability, or the threatened use of unconventional weapons (chemical or biological agents, for example). This might require an option with a shorter lead time, but like the "last resort" deterrent, would not necessarily require disclosure before the threat actually materialized.

One might also consider the use of nuclear weapons in *ordinary military circumstances,* to offset Arab advantages in numbers or otherwise improve Israel's fighting capability. There are some plausible scenarios involving the tactical use of nuclear weapons on the battlefield.[1] Even advocates of Israeli nuclear status, however, tend to discount the wisdom of introducing tactical or battlefield nuclear weapons, as this would cast doubt on the resolve behind strategic threats, and (given the relative vulnerability of tactical weapons) would increase incentives to preempt.[2] From a purely military perspective the disadvantages of introducing nuclear weapons into the conflict would seem to far outweigh any advantages, except under last resort conditions. So long as Israel possesses an adequate nonnuclear response to nonnuclear threats, nuclear weapons would not increase security but would probably be immediately offset by nuclear counterthreats, and would in addition trigger an international reaction endangering needed outside support of Israel's conventional capability (see the discussion in the next section).

It has also been suggested that an Israeli nuclear force could *deter limited provocations.* But the weight of evidence in the nuclear era is that nuclear weapons have been singularly ineffective on this level of deterrence. They were of no notable value to the United States in Korea or Vietnam, to the Soviet Union in Afghanistan, or to China against the Vietnamese, and there is no reason to suppose they would be of greater use to Israel in deterring terrorism or Syrian artillery bombardments.

Shai Feldman argues that nuclear weapons could deter low-level harassment under certain conditions, since it would be clear that Israel was defending its existence and that the risks of escalation were therefore quite real. For related reasons, terrorism would be dampened; the Palestine Liberation Organization's strategy of instigating general Arab–Israeli wars would no longer work if Arab states were deterred from such wars.[3] But unwillingness to risk a general war would not totally inhibit determined foes from low levels of testing or from a strategy of gradual encroachment, any more than it has inhibited the superpowers from testing each other in sensitive areas. And not all violence is so carefully calculated; terrorism may as often be a matter of catharsis, of competition between different organizations, or of other such motives, as of a carefully formulated strategy responsive to logical considerations.

Nuclear weapons may indeed induce greater caution against the *escalation* of low levels of violence, but their very presence, by deterring full-scale wars, has paradoxically brought about a proliferation of limited and irregular warfare. In any event, as one observer notes, "it is not at all clear . . . why Israel's nuclear threat should inhibit small, fanatical, and largely uncontrolled groups from terrorist attacks on Israel . . . while Israel is supposed *not* to be deterred from its reprisal raids by Arab nuclear missiles aimed at Jerusalem and Tel Aviv."[4]

Another conceivable motivation for an Israeli nuclear weapons force is to *deter Soviet threats* that might endanger Israel's existence. The argument is that even a very limited capability against the Soviet Union might be effective and credible, if Israel were indeed in desperate straits.[5] But it seems unlikely, by all indications, that Israeli policymakers could seriously consider deterrence of the Soviet Union a plausible aim.

Soviet air defenses are the most formidable in the world. It is doubtful that Israel could credibly threaten Soviet targets, even on a minimal scale and after considerable expenditure; most proponents of an Israeli nuclear force have reached this conclusion.[6] The best counter to a Soviet threat is the instinctive American reaction to it and the mutual deadlock between the superpowers, as demonstrated in the "nuclear alert" during the 1973 Middle East war.

Aside from security goals, is maintenance of nuclear weapons or a nuclear option convertible to *gains in political, diplomatic, or other nonmilitary arenas?* Nuclear powers have often found it difficult to translate their strategic superiority into concrete gains in influence and control; consider the United States and Cuba, or the Soviet Union and Albania. Regarding Israel, it has been argued both that a public nuclear deterrent would "freeze" the post-1967 territorial gains and help impose peace on Arab states, and that it would "unlock" the territorial question, making it both necessary and possible for Israel to withdraw from territories occupied in 1967.[7]

The same conclusion—that disclosed nuclear weapons status would be in the Israeli interest—is thus reached from opposite assumptions regarding the preferred aims of Israeli policy and the impact of nuclear weapons in the Middle East. In truth, it seems to me that there is no necessary connection either way; Israeli policy on the West Bank and Gaza is not simply a function of the level of weaponry, but is a highly charged emotional and political issue, with its own dynamic, that has divided Israeli society since 1967.

It is even more doubtful that nuclear weapons would compel the Arabs to make peace. Given the history of the conflict and past reactions, it seems more plausible that open acquisition of nuclear weapons by Israel would only make its enemies more hostile and more desperate. Certainly there is nothing in the history of the nuclear era elsewhere that would give comfort on this score. Nuclear weapons may have deterred major wars, but they have been less effective against lesser forms of attack, and even more useless in trying to compel other states to take a given course of action. This is true even in cases where a nuclear superpower faced far weaker and less hostile rivals than the Palestinian organizations and Arab states in relation to Israel.[8]

In a more limited vein, it can be argued that an Israeli nuclear force would help *deter further Soviet involvement* in the Middle East by raising the stakes of the game (this should be distinguished from deterrence of Soviet military threats, discussed previously). But the Soviet Union has more than one possible response to an Israeli bomb, and it might be that a more likely reaction would be deeper involvement rather than disengagement. Certainly one clear result of overt Israeli nuclearization would be Arab pressure on the Soviets to counter the Israeli move in some way. And it would be rash to expect the Soviets to respond more circumspectly than they did to the British and French bombs in Europe or the Chinese bomb in Asia.

One limited political aim that should be kept in mind, however, is *strengthening Israel's bargaining position* internationally and in bilateral relations with the United States. Israel is considered a key country in efforts to prevent nuclear proliferation, and the dangers of a nuclearized Middle East are of special concern to the superpowers. Israel is therefore in a good position to win important concessions by playing on the possibility of "going nuclear" if its situation becomes desperate. One assumes that this consideration plays an important role, spoken or unspoken, in negotiations over conventional arms supplies.

It has also been suggested that in order to *reduce dependence* on the United States, Israel should "change from its present policy of maintaining a 'nuclear option' to a policy based on a known nuclear deterrent."[9] In this view, an Israeli nuclear weapons capability would be a viable means of reducing the risks on both sides and stabilizing the local environment by demonstrating Israel's permanence, with or without U.S. aid. But a public nuclear status would not solve the problems of dependence in areas of advanced conventional technology, nor would it enable Israel to survive financially without U.S. assistance. In fact, by undercutting U.S. assistance to Israel and spurring an increase in Soviet assistance to Arab states, Israeli nuclearization might well contribute to the very deterioration of the conventional military balance that it was designed to offset. Whatever the problems of reliance on outside support, continued dependence on the United States would seem very preferable to this kind of independence.

Finally, in other "threshold" countries the nonmilitary motives of *status, prestige, and equality* have sometimes played a role in favor of weapons programs. It is unlikely, however, that these considerations are of much importance in Israeli nuclear policy. Issues of security dominate Israeli thinking to such an extent that status-climbing in international society hardly seems relevant. In a nuclear context, it must certainly give way to other priorities.

In sum, it seems that last resort deterrence of Arab conventional arms is the most plausible aim of an Israeli nuclear weapons program. This might be expanded to include deterrence of lesser but still critical threats such as massive destruction of Israeli cities; the force needed for this purpose would in any event be the same as that needed for the last resort. The possibility of an Arab nuclear force seems important largely as a reason for keeping the nuclear option open rather than closing it off altogether, and the deterrence of Soviet military threats seems an implausible basis for a weapons program. The main nonmilitary use of nuclear capability would seem to be in strengthening Israel's bargaining position, in particular in relations with friendly states (this does not, of course, necessitate actual weapons development). Other nonmilitary aims—political and diplomatic influence, reduction of dependence, status—seem problematic or irrelevant.

Decisions on Development and Disclosure

The Israeli government basically has two decisions to make regarding nuclear weapons: whether to produce such weapons, and whether to reveal whether it has produced such weapons. As we shall see, neither of these is actually a simple either–or decision, but taken for the moment as though they were, the two choices produce four basic alternative policies.

1. No utilization of the nuclear option, and full disclosure. This would presumably involve some open commitment not to manufacture nuclear weapons, such as adherence to the Non-Proliferation Treaty.
2. Utilization of the nuclear option, and full disclosure. Announcement of the existence of nuclear weapons would probably come after completion of the development program, signaled perhaps by a successful test.
3. No utilization of the nuclear option (for the time being), and no disclosure of intentions. This is the "nuclear option" posture, keeping the possibility of weapons production alive and keeping others guessing about whether weapons have been produced or not.
4. Utilization of the nuclear option, and no disclosure of intentions. This means, in essence, secret weapons development, or a "bomb in the basement."

In light of the probable aims of Israeli nuclear policy as analyzed thus far, which of these alternatives is likely to be preferred?

1. A Disclosed No-Bomb Status. This assumes a "best-case" analysis in which the contingencies for an Israeli weapons program (especially the last-resort case) would not arise, or if they did, outside guarantees would prove adequate. Reliance on outside assurances, at a time when even commitments within established defense alliances are openly doubted, seems highly doubtful in view of Israel's general lack of confidence in guarantees. Futhermore, no nation has offered Israel a guarantee against conventional attack, which is precisely the danger most feared. And even if offered, such a guarantee might be neutralized by a superpower supporting the Arab states, leaving conventional warfare in the Middle East to run its course.

Even if we assume no present need for a weapons program, closing off future options would involve accepting unknown future risks in return for marginal present profit. Commitment to nonmanufacture of nuclear weapons might win a few immediate political gains, but it would also mean loss of an important bargaining counter, since once surrendered the nuclear option would win no further concessions. The advantages of ambiguity, in bargaining and in creating uncertainty among Israel's foes, would be lost. In addition, Israeli policymakers would not want to establish a precedent of accountability to the world in strategic decisions of great importance to Israeli security.

This is not to say that Israel would never consider this option. If it transpired that a mutual commitment to nonmanufacture of nuclear weapons would effectively curtail Arab nuclear weapons programs, any responsible Israeli government would have to consider it seriously. Israel in fact has a standing offer to the Arab states, for a regional nuclear-free zone, which will be discussed later. Needless to say, the prerequisites for the success of such an agreement are, in present circumstances, highly unlikely to be met. And such an arrangement would leave Israel with the problem of how to cope with the last-resort case. But only a rash government would close the door completely to the possibility of keeping nuclear weapons out of the Arab–Israeli conflict.

2. A Disclosed Nuclear Weapon Status. The classic arguments against a standing Israeli nuclear deterrent force are as follows:

a. An Israeli nuclear force would be neutralized immediately by Soviet counterthreats or transfer of weapons to Arab states, and eventually by development of Arab nuclear weapons.

b. An Israeli nuclear force would unite the Arab world against Israel as almost no other single step could.

c. The political costs of going public with such a force would be enormous, especially regarding the impact on U.S.–Israeli relations.

d. In a mutually nuclearized situation, an Israeli nuclear deterrent would in any event be ineffective against limited provocations.

e. In a mutually nuclearized situation, the vulnerability of both sides and the ease of delivery would provide a constant temptation for preemptive strikes.

f. In case of actual nuclear war, Israel would be at a disadvantage because of her size and concentration of population, and foreknowledge of this would undercut the nuclear deterrent.

g. The most Israel could hope to achieve would be a stalemate on the nuclear level, with the likelihood of huge civilian casualties in any encounter.

Some of these arguments tend to transfer the logic of superpower nuclear deterrence to the Middle East; the argument about unequal vulnerabilities, for example, would not be of great importance if an Israeli nuclear force were designed to supplement conventional superiority and were aimed at enemy armed forces rather than cities. Nor is unequal vulnerability crucial in the basic, last-resort case. But on the whole, these arguments constitute a strong prima facie case against disclosed nuclear status in any but the most desperate circumstances.

For a number of years, these "common sense" arguments tended to dominate debate (or at least the public debate) over Israeli nuclear weapons. Over the last decade, however, a number of analysts, Israeli and non-Israeli—Fuad Jabber, Robert Tucker, Shlomo Aronson, Steven Rosen, Shai Feldman—have argued that a disclosed Israeli nuclear weapons status might, to the contrary, stabilize the volatile Middle East arena. The argument is, in essence, that the stable nuclear deadlock between the superpowers can be copied on the regional level.

For such a balance to be stable requires, first, that nuclear forces not be vulnerable to preemptive attack, and that each side have the capability to retaliate even after such an attack. Feldman recognizes that "in the absence of second-strike capability, a Middle East balance of terror would be extremely unstable."[10] Maintenance of this capability depends on a series of ever-changing technological equations, continuously subject to new challenges, equations which are a source of constant concern on the superpower level.

Proponents of overt nuclear deterrence claim that an Israeli nuclear force could be so protected, against both conventional and nuclear surprise attack. This is not the place to review the technical arguments on the issue; I shall merely note that many technically oriented writings on the topic dispute this claim.[11]

Of course it is not necessary to protect all nuclear weapons, but only enough to preserve a threat of retaliation. Feldman concedes that all the measures of protection "may not guarantee that the majority of Israeli weapons would survive an Arab counterforce attack," but the probability of a minority surviving would prevent the attack being launched.[12] But if it is this difficult to protect the greater part of the Israeli force, how can Arab states, facing the Israeli air force, hope to achieve a reasonably secure second-strike force?

Most of the analyses of stable "mutual" deterrence in the Middle East focus on the force requirements for Israel alone. But one must assume that a public Israeli bomb would be followed by Arab crash programs, and it would hardly contribute to peace of mind if Israel managed to build an invulnerable nuclear force, but Arab states possessed nuclear weapons that could be destroyed unless they were used first, in a surprise attack. Finally, there is also the problem of the transition; even if mutual invulnerability is ultimately achievable, at certain points along the path there will be situations of relative vulnerability in which one side or the other will have a strong urge to strike while it still has the chance.

But even if all these problems are overcome, we have not yet established the stability of a nuclear balance in the Middle East. It is a habit of superpower deterrent analysis to equate invulnerability with stability, but vulnerability of nuclear forces is not the only reason a state might feel impelled to try a preemptive attack. Nuclear stability is not just a technical problem.

Given the small number and size of nuclear weapons in a nuclearized Middle East, the constant preoccupation with surprise attack, and the demonological assumptions on both sides regarding the behavior of the other, the U.S.–USSR model of "mutual assured destruction" hardly seems applicable. It seems quite possible that a "damage-limiting" preemptive blow will at one time or another appear as the most viable way out of a tense situation, given the doubt on both sides regarding the certainty of an overwhelming second strike and the assumption that war is unavoidable.

Middle East states have regularly fought wars with one another, unlike the United States and the Soviet Union. The threshold on decisions involving force is considerably lower than the institutionalized inhibitions that bind the superpowers. The idea of anticipatory self-defense is commonly espoused and practiced. There are numerous precedents for surprise attack, and indeed each side attributes past "failures" (the Arabs, 1956 and 1967; the Israelis, 1973) to being surprised. It is not at all difficult to devise dozens of scenarios in which one state or another would find itself in a situation in which—out of a sense of honor, desperation, fatalism, or misjudgment—a preemptive nuclear attack appeared to be the only option, even though some level of retaliation seemed unavoidable.

Nor is it particularly comforting to be told that such behavior as Nasser's

challenge to Israel in 1967 is no worse than similar foolhardy actions elsewhere. In a nuclearized Middle East, such reckless regard for consequences
may have much more devastating results than elsewhere. This has often been
stated as an issue of "irrationality," and indeed the stability of nuclear deterrence does depend on both sides being guided by a rational appreciation of
the costs of failure.

But it is more than simply "sensitivity to costs," as Feldman puts it;[13] one
can be sensitive to costs, and yet accept them willingly because of other values
that are involved. Are the Shi'ite suicide bombers in Lebanon unaware of the
high costs that their missions entail? And what can one say of a government
that deliberately levels one of *its own* cities, killing thousands of innocent
inhabitants, in order to suppress internal dissent—as the Syrians did in Hama
in 1982? Have the restraints practiced by Iran and Iraq in their war demonstrated a great "sensitivity to costs"?

Nor does this exhaust the sources of irresponsibility and miscalculation.
Many Middle Eastern states are, unlike the present nuclear weapons states,
quite unstable. Apart from bringing extremists to power, this instability provides incentives for dramatic gestures and breaks down internal discipline.
Unauthorized flights by Arab fighter aircraft have occurred more than once.
In a situation of internal upheaval, the risk of war by loss of control, or by
some other inadvertent path, increases dramatically.

Aside from the risks of an openly nuclearized Middle East, the political
costs of a public Israel bomb would also be tremendous. First of all, the 1977
U.S. International Security Assistance Act cuts off all American aid to any
nonnuclear country conducting a nuclear test. But even if this were finessed,
the impact on U.S.–Israeli relations would in all likelihood be devastating,
given the strong stands taken by every U.S. administration against nuclear
proliferation and against an Israeli bomb program in particular. The motivation for helping Israel maintain its edge in conventional weaponry, at great
cost to the American taxpayer, would be undercut. Israel would also forfeit
the bargaining leverage enjoyed as a potential nuclear power that could be
persuaded by suitable concessions not to build weapons.

It has already been argued that the political gains of "going public"
would be nil, and that overt deterrence would not freeze the status quo in
Israel's favor. Nuclear deterrence is unlikely to help much against limited
provocations—and to the extent that it does, it may not depend on the deterrent being publicly declared. In fact, of all the aims Israel might hope to
achieve by manipulation of nuclear capability, none of them depend on disclosing possession of nuclear weapons, prior to last-resort conditions. In particular, the political uses of rumored capability seem decisively superior to
the balance of political costs and gains resulting from disclosure.

The advantages of disclosing the existence of a nuclear weapon force, as
opposed to keeping it secret, have been developed in most depth by Shai

Feldman.[14] Feldman argues that a deterrent is more credible when it is certain, when its existence is stated clearly and precisely. He also believes that a public posture makes possible a better development of doctrines and procedures, helping to avoid miscalculations, and creates an open dialogue between adversaries that prevents misunderstanding.

These arguments would all appear to have weight in the abstract, or in the superpower setting. For example, the need to work out clearly understood doctrines on the use of nuclear force is essential in the complicated U.S.–USSR strategic balance, with thousands of planners, policymakers, and implementers involved. It is not that certain that the arguments have such weight in the Middle East, where the scale and context are altogether different. Surely top decisionmakers would want to keep tight control over the few weapons available, and operational planning would be ad hoc. Dialogue between adversaries would not be the same; in fact, knowing more may lead to a better directed effort to neutralize the enemy force, rather than to sharing understandings. In some contexts, the unknown or uncertain may deter as well as, or even better than, a known quantity.

The analysis of the first two alternatives leads to the conclusion that *disclosure is the worst strategy* in either case, whether or not weapons are developed. This is consistent with our discussion of aims: in the contingencies most likely to require nuclear weapons (the last resort), no prior announcement—no standing, publicized deterrent on the superpower model—is needed. Other aims that would require disclosure, such as status and political gains, are secondary at best. As for Israel's bargaining position, revelation of a final decision either to produce or not to produce weapons would effectively undercut it, while either of the ambiguous alternatives would preserve it.

What remains, then, is to compare alternatives 3 and 4. In both cases, the advantages of bargaining and ambiguity remain; the difference lies in the utility of actually producing secret weapons.

3. Ambiguous Status, without Weapons Development. Supporters of this alternative argue that the circumstances requiring an Israeli nuclear capability are not likely to develop without sufficient warning. There will therefore be time, before the last-resort case arises, to exercise the nuclear option. Developing weapons before that point would merely run the risk of discovery, which is substantial in an age of sophisticated intelligence. Israel would then pay the full price of public disclosure, including Soviet counterthreats to Israeli nuclear deterrence and instigation of a more serious Arab nuclear program—the very thing Israel wants to avoid, as it would undercut the effectiveness of the last resort deterrent. One could still, of course, reduce the nuclear option to a minimal period of time so that the risk from a rapid loss of conventional superiority is minimized, though this might require steps that themselves risk discovery.

4. Ambiguous Status, with Secret Weapons Development. It can be argued that, since all weapons work must be secret anyway, there is no point in stopping short of the final product. As for the risk of discovery, the discoverers might not disclose what they know because of their own interest in Middle East stability (this could be said of the United States, and perhaps even of the Soviet Union). In any event, a flat Israeli denial of actual weapons production would be hard for foreign sources to disprove, whatever the truth of the matter.

Needless to say, there are those who feel that the quick pace of events in the Middle East makes it imperative to have a bomb actually on hand, as last-resort conditions might develop unexpectedly. And once a state has reduced the length of its nuclear option to a certain point—months or weeks—it might feel compelled to complete the process, since discovery at that stage of progress would invite preemptive attack more than revelation of the finished product would.

As this indicates, the line between alternatives 3 and 4 is not always very clear. In fact there are choices along a continuum, and what constitutes "possession of weapons" is sometimes a matter of definition. Since testing is not considered absolutely essential, an option of varying length—from months to minutes—could be maintained, depending on decisions regarding the design and assembly of weapons. Is an assembled or almost assembled, but untested, primitive nuclear device a weapon?

Israel's "logical" nuclear policy seems to fall, then, somewhere on this continuum, between a nuclear option of one or two years and possession of untested nuclear devices. The exact point at which it falls will probably remain undisclosed for the foreseeable future and will depend to some extent on technical issues that have not been discussed here.

The Unambiguous Case for Ambiguity

Some years ago I wrote the following about the "evidence" that Israel has nuclear weapons:

> Given the deliberately created fog that envelops the subject, it is hardly surprising that experts must speculate, but the inventiveness of the speculations is sometimes astounding. Problems of evidence are solved by citing other expert opinions, which in turn are based on other unconfirmed reports, creating a "preponderance" of opinion. "Israel apparently has been actually building nuclear weapons," says one typical recent study that was widely publicized as a scholarly finding. On closer examination the "evidence" is the same body of speculative literature (to which this study will no doubt be added, and cited by others).[15]

The situation is essentially unchanged today. One recent book, arrestingly entitled *Israel's Nuclear Arsenal,* performs the same legerdemain of turning surmise and estimate into presumed fact.[16] Nevertheless, there are a few additional pieces of solid evidence. A leaked U.S. Central Intelligence Agency memo says, "We believe that Israel has already produced nuclear weapons."[17] The former head of the French Atomic Energy Commission has confirmed that the French nuclear assistance to Israel, in the 1950s and 1960s, included a facility for plutonium separation.[18] And in 1981, after the Israeli destruction of the Iraqi reactor, Moshe Dayan provided the clearest authoritative statement to date of Israel's status: "We don't have any atomic bombs now, but we have the capacity, we can do that in a short time."[19]

Yet the official position remains ambiguous, despite the revelations. For almost twenty years, through the governments of six different Israeli prime ministers of varying political persuasions, Israel has resisted the argument that going public with the bomb would be a good thing. Such consistency in resisting the advice of experts should tell us something.

It seems that so far no Israeli government, no matter how hawkish its complexion, has found a policy of overt deterrence preferable to the status quo. Ambiguity may have its drawbacks, but it seems to offer most of the advantages that an overt deterrence might confer, without the considerable risks and costs that going public would entail. One of these costs, unknown to an outsider but potentially quite decisive to decisionmakers, is exactly what sanctions the United States has threatened—and what promises it has made—to keep Israel committed to a posture of calculated ambiguity (an ambiguity with which the United States can cope much more easily than an official Israeli nuclear weapon status).

Policymakers also tend to prefer the known to the unknown, the "devil you know" to the one you don't. The debate on the implications of an overt deterrent (including much of what is written in this chapter) is necessarily speculative. The optimists who favor such a deterrent may be entirely correct in their estimates of its impact, but they cannot prove that they are better seers of the future than the pessimists. In the meantime, the current situation is comprehensible, familiar, and—in a sense—secure.

Furthermore it can be argued that the *possibility* of Israeli nuclear weapons, or what we might call the "shadow effect" of presumed bombs in the basement, is already playing a role in the Arab–Israeli conflict. It is argued, for example, that in 1973 both Egypt and Syria failed to exploit initial successes because they had no plans to threaten the Israeli heartland, partly out of apprehension of a nuclear response.[20] If this is the case, it is an argument that disclosure of nuclear weapons is superfluous (if not counterproductive), as the deterrent effect already exists. In any event, it is quite conceivable that Arab states can be quietly brought to a realization that all-out efforts to destroy Israel are no longer feasible, without the need to publicly unveil the weaponry that undergirds this fact.

Policymakers undoubtedly also appreciate the fact that ambiguity still leaves further options open, while going public may be irreversible. Israel can still choose to disclose more, should that seem a wise thing to do. But no nation adopting a public nuclear weapons posture has ever retraced its steps. Among other things, the door to potential denuclearization of the area would be closed, as Arab states would inevitably follow Israel's lead. In this regard, some attention should be paid to Israel's denuclearization proposals.

Israel made a dramatic and important new departure in October 1980, when it proposed a conference to negotiate a nuclear-free zone in the Middle East, on the model of the Latin American Treaty of Tlatelolco. During the same United Nations session, Israel voted in favor of an Egyptian resolution favoring a nuclear-free zone in the Middle East.[21]

There is a tendency to dismiss such gestures as window dressing, but the Israeli government clearly viewed it as a serious step. The new policy was preceded by a long internal debate, and was framed in as acceptable a form as possible (dropping, for example, preconditions such as negotiation of a peace treaty). The Israeli proposal differed from the Egyptian resolution primarily in proposing actual procedures to bring a binding nuclear-free-zone treaty into effect. In the background was a growing Israeli concern over nuclear programs in Iraq, Pakistan, and Libya that was apparent to any close observer long before the attack on the Iraqi reactor.

Far from avoiding safeguards, the Israeli proposal would have gone beyond the Non-Proliferation Treaty, whose verification provisions Israel does not trust (as seen in the Iraqi case). Israeli advocacy of a binding regional treaty and its criticism of existing safeguards deserve to be taken more seriously. There is no doubt that Israel would ideally like a treaty that would allow retention of as much of a nuclear option as possible, while keeping Arab states from developing weapons at all—but even if forced to accept a very low-level option to accomplish the latter, the bargain might be worthwhile.

The point is that Israeli leaders do not think of the stability of a nuclear balance in the abstract. For them, nuclear proliferation means Arab regimes with nuclear weapons. There are few priorities higher than keeping such weapons out of the hands of regimes like Iraq—and this effort would be burdened considerably if Israel itself went publicly nuclear. Other Arab states, Egypt in particular, have been content to move slowly in the nuclear field, so long as they were not goaded by a public Israeli bomb. Israel has no interest in disturbing this repose. In all the discussion, the likely Arab reaction to a disclosed Israeli bomb has been greatly understated as a touchstone for Israeli policymakers.

In concluding his argument for an overt deterrent, Feldman says Israel should avert the political costs of such a move by attempting to postpone the step "until a few more states have gone nuclear."[22] Even better, he adds, to wait until the day an Arab or Moslem state has the bomb. This course does not differ, however, from the minimal program laid out here, or, by all evidence, from the present attitude of Israeli policymakers. All that need be added is the wish that that day be, and remain, as far away as possible.

3

Deliberate Ambiguity: Evolution and Evaluation

Gerald M. Steinberg

I n discussions of nuclear proliferation, Israel is consistently included among the countries with the technical capabilities and political incentives necessary to deploy nuclear weapons. For many years, Israel has been considered by many analysts as the most likely candidate to join the nuclear "club." The technical basis for the manufacture of nuclear weapons clearly exists, and the continuing threat to Israel's existence provides sufficient political motivation.

Yet, over the past decade, as India has demonstrated its nuclear "device" and Pakistan moves inexorably closer to its own nuclear weapons, Israel's nuclear posture has not changed. Israeli nuclear capabilities continue to be highly ambiguous and successive Israeli governments have avoided altering this policy significantly in any direction. Rather, the policy of deliberate ambiguity carefully crafted under Ben-Gurion continues to be maintained and even reinforced.

Nevertheless, in the past decade, this policy has been challenged and debated within Israel for the first time. In the mid-1970s, while between cabinet posts, the late Moshe Dayan publicly called for an overt demonstration of Israeli nuclear capabilities.[1] His call was echoed by some analysts and academics, most notably, Shai Feldman of the Institute for Strategic Studies at Tel Aviv University.[2] Other political leaders, such as Prime Minister Rabin, Chief of Staff Mordechai Gur,[3] and the late Yigal Allon[4] (then foreign minister), publicly rejected Dayan's proposals and reiterated their support for the policy of deliberate ambiguity. While the policy has not changed, this debate has led to a reassessment both in and outside Israel, and the debate has yet to run its course.

I would like to thank Ayelet Bar-On for research assistance.

The Technical Basis for Ambiguity

In a technical sense, efforts to acquire nuclear weapons can be divided into two groups: (1) those like the nuclear powers (the United States, the Soviet Union, the United Kingdom, France, the People's Republic of China) which are based on facilities "dedicated" to the production of weapons, and (2) those of most "Nth" countries such as India, Iraq, Iran, and South Africa, which proceed, as least ostensibly, via civil nuclear power or research programs. Direct "dedicated" weapons programs are generally quite visible and unambiguous, but the latter efforts are, by their very nature, unclear and subject to efforts to disguise and hide the diversion of facilities and materials from civil to military purposes.

Each such Nth country effort is subject to its own type and degree of ambiguity. Reactors that are designed or can be readily modified and operated to produce large amounts of weapons-grade plutonium (or which use highly enriched uranium or reprocessed plutonium as fuel and which allow for the diversion of this fuel) are most clearly useful for weapons production. Countries in which plutonium separation facilities or uranium enrichment facilities exist are more capable of producing weapons than countries without such facilities.

In this sense, the ambiguity surrounding Israel's nuclear weapons capability is particularly salient. The Israeli effort to acquire nuclear weapons began in the mid-1950s, when construction began on a French-designed reactor near Dimona in the Negev desert. This reactor, like many others, can be considered dual purpose, in that it can provide power as well as be used to make nuclear weapons. Compared to other such dual-use reactors, however, its design is particularly useful for the manufacture of weapons and generally ill-suited for power production.

Despite the great secrecy that surrounded the construction effort, it soon became clear that the highly secret and heavily guarded "textile" plant in the desert was really a nuclear reactor. By the late 1960s, it was generally acknowledged that Israel had the technical capability to produce fissile material (plutonium). At the same time, however, evidence of other aspects of a nuclear weapons capability has been notably difficult to ascertain. Despite occasional press reports and quasi-academic speculations regarding the existence of an Israeli reprocessing facility (to convert the spent nuclear fuel into weapons-grade plutonium), no reliable evidence regarding the existence of such a facility has been published.[5] Similarly, speculations linking Israeli nuclear tests to mysterious explosions off the coast of South Africa have also been short on evidence. (Indeed, the weight of the evidence suggests that the flashes detected by U.S. satellites were not caused by nuclear explosions.[6])

Potential Israeli delivery vehicles have also been the subject of various rumors. While, in theory, Israeli combat aircraft could deliver nuclear warheads to most if not all potential targets in the region, the development of more secure and accurate systems such as short- and intermediate-range ballistic missiles has been suggested in the press. (Thus, the 1979 *Jane's Weapons Systems* listed the Jericho missiles, and other reports speak of the Zeev, or Wolf, although the latter has also appeared in the press as a short-range tactical missile.)[7]

Israeli sources have not "cooperated" in decreasing the ambiguity which surrounds these systems and facilities. No nuclear weapons tests have been announced or acknowledged, and no tours of reprocessing facilities have been arranged. The U.S. inspections which have taken place were highly circumscribed and, if anything, increased ambiguity. While Israeli-made tanks, aircraft, patrol boats, and ammunition are widely advertised and, in the effort to recoup research and development costs, sold internationally, there is no hint of the Jericho (and even *Jane's* has dropped references to this item).

Political Contributions to Ambiguity

While the technological components may have provided the basis for ambiguity, the Israeli nuclear posture is the result of political choice. The political basis for ambiguity was set in the secrecy which surrounded the Israeli effort to develop nuclear weapons. In the beginning, Israeli leaders had every incentive to keep the effort secret and to avoid, to the extent possible, all publicity—at least until the Dimona reactor had produced significant quantities of plutonium. During this period, which can be estimated at ten years (1956–1966), the facility was particularly vulnerable to a preemptive attack that might have prevented Israel from obtaining a nuclear capability. Indeed, Arab leaders actually threatened to take actions to stop the Israeli nuclear program before it became operational. In 1969 Nasser threatened to send "millions of soldiers" to destroy Israel's nuclear potential.[8]

Despite efforts to maintain the secret, however, the construction at Dimona was too massive to hide completely. As a result, even while the reactor was still in construction, the U.S. government began to raise questions. Some of the intelligence information which reached Washington, as well as other capitals, spilled over into the press.

The Israeli response was one of avoidance and denial. Thus, the reactor was first publicly passed off as a textile plant (at the same time, the Central Intelligence Agency headquarters outside Washington was labeled as the Department of Transportation). The combination of queries from Washington and denials from Israel surrounded the Israeli nuclear effort in uncertainty and ambiguity.

In December 1960 the outgoing Eisenhower administration focused international attention on the Dimona reactor by publicly suggesting that the facility was designed to produce nuclear weapons. This revelation led to an angry response by Ben-Gurion. When asked about the Israeli program, he cited Egyptian nuclear activities, which included operation of a Soviet research reactor, plans to purchase a larger reactor from Britain, and the ongoing missile development supported by German scientists. Ben-Gurion emphasized that relative to these Egyptian activities, Israeli efforts were benign, and he denied that Israel was pursuing a nuclear weapons option.[9]

Subsequently, the incoming Kennedy administration repeated these concerns, although with less publicity and in the context of a wider regard for the consequences of nuclear proliferation. As a result, the U.S. government demanded that Israel open the Dimona reactor for inspection to ensure that, as claimed by Israel, the reactor was to be used strictly for civil purposes. (U.S. demands for inspection were coupled with pressure on Egypt to abandon its missile construction program.)[10] Israel's initial response to the U.S. demands for inspection was to reiterate the claims and statements as to its civilian purpose. As pressure grew, Ben-Gurion, and Eshkol, his successor, agreed to ad hoc American inspections, but citing the biases of the International Atomic Energy Agency (IAEA), refused to allow the imposition of safeguards by that organization. (In return, Aronson and others report that the United States agreed to supply conventional arms.)[11]

The inspections (which ended by 1969) and the debate which surrounded them not only failed to diminish the ambiguity and uncertainty surrounding Israeli intentions and capabilities, but actually enhanced uncertainty. Technically, brief inspections during the initial operating period of the reactor could not have been expected to reveal much about Israeli intentions, as these operations could have served civil and military purposes equally well. It is only a process of continuous inspection over a period of years, and testing of the end product, which can indicate with any confidence, the "purpose" of the operations. As a result, the "inspections" did not yield definitive answers which would either have declared that Israeli activities were designed to develop nuclear weapons, or, the opposite, would have "cleared" Israel of any intention to produce nuclear weapons. Instead, the exchange between Israel and the United States on inspection only reified ambiguity and drew increased international attention to this issue.[12]

The events immediately preceding the 1967 Six-Day War, and the war itself, had a major impact on the development of Israeli nuclear weapons policy and the ambiguity which surrounded it. In the first place, the crisis preceding the war reignited Israeli fears of annihilation. Before the war, when Israeli conventional capabilities had not been proved, concerns for the ultimate ability of conventional forces to guarantee the survival of the state were highlighted. Even after the Israeli victory, these fears remained, and were coupled with Arab threats of a subsequent round in which Israel would finally be crushed. The sudden loss of French support and arms at the beginning of fighting reinforced these concerns.

As a result, reports regarding Israeli nuclear activities increased. *Time's* magazine story on Israeli nuclear capabilities, published in 1976, claims that construction of a plutonium separation facility was started immediately after the war, and that tests took place in 1969. In 1969, *Der Spiegel* "revealed" that Israel possessed nuclear weapons, and in 1970, the director of the CIA told the U.S. Senate that, at least in the CIA's judgment, Israel possessed nuclear weapons.[13] This report was also leaked to the *New York Times*.

The Israeli response to these reports was carefully noncommittal. In many cases, they were ignored by Israel. When pressed by the Johnson administration, Ambassador Rabin announced that Israel would not be the first to introduce nuclear weapons in the Middle East.[14] Observers noted that such a pledge was open to many interpretations, particularly in that the United States and the Soviet Union can be considered to have "introduced" nuclear weapons in the region via their sea-based weapons in the area. At the same time, the combination of reports from the outside, sensationalist speculations in the press, and Israeli efforts to avoid making a commitment reinforced the ambiguity.

The 1973 Yom Kippur War focused further attention on Israeli nuclear capabilities, and in the process, further crystalized a policy of *deliberate* ambiguity. The war itself, with its combination of surprise, Israeli casualties, and the initial Arab successes (which, for a time, seemed to threaten national survival) led to speculation concerning a potential Israeli "bomb in the basement." By 1973, the Dimona reactor had been operational for a number of years, meaning that sufficient plutonium for ten to fifteen bombs might have been manufactured, even in the period since 1969, when U.S. inspections apparently ended. On this basis, *Time* reported deployment of Israeli Phantom aircraft during the war for "use as a last resort" to deliver nuclear weapons. Other reports of initial pessimism and panic, including the fear, allegedly attributed to Dayan that "the Third Temple was coming to an end,"[15] suggested Israeli possession of and willingness to use nuclear weapons in the context of the war. There is also speculation which attributes the failure of Egyptian forces to advance in the Sinai after the first week of fighting to the deterrent effect of the Israeli nuclear potential.[16] In addition, reports of the deployment of Soviet Scud missiles with nuclear warheads during the war were seen by some as a stimulus to Israeli nuclear deployment, and by others as a Soviet attempt to counter what it acknowledged as an Israeli nuclear capability. Similarly, massive U.S. resupply efforts have been attributed to U.S. fears that in desperation, Israel would use nuclear weapons.[17] As before, the reports and speculations, offered with little or no evidence, served to increase the deterrent effect of the Israeli nuclear threat at little or no cost to

Israel. Following the war, the number of pertinent articles, both scholarly and journalistic, increased. Furthermore, a number of Arab figures publicly addressed the issue of Israel's nuclear capability. Some, like Egypt's Haykal,[18] concluded that indeed, Israel possessed a nuclear option.

The press reports, coupled with U.S. government reports from congressional committees and the CIA (ostensibly classified, but usually "leaked"), maintained international focus on the issue. In general, these reports, which were initiated in Washington (or in a few cases, in London or the United Nations in New York), were ignored in Israel. The reports were not denied, or in most cases, even acknowledged. Indeed, the U.S. government found itself responding to the reports. Thus, in 1978, after a set of CIA reports were made public, President Carter's press secretary announced that, "The Israeli government has declared that Israel is not a nuclear power and will not be the first to introduce nuclear weapons into the area. We accept this as the official position of the government of Israel."[19] Except when forced by persistent questions during news conferences or press interviews, the Israeli government ignored these reports. While the failure to deny the rumors and speculation was often treated as a form of confirmatory evidence, the net effect was to increase ambiguity.

The impact of the studied silence which emanated from the Israeli government on this issue was illustrated in an incident which occurred in December 1974. During a meeting of American and European science writers in Jerusalem, President Katzir, a biologist by profession, was asked whether Israeli nuclear activities were a matter for concern. In reply, he asked, "Why should this worry us? Let the rest of the world worry about it."[20] This comment, although something less than the usual denial, added very little to what was already known. Any importance that might have been attached to this statement should have been tempered by the realization that in Israel, the presidency is largely an honorary post, and its occupant is essentially outside the policymaking process. Yet despite these facts, Katzir's comments were featured on the front page of the *London Times* and were widely reported around the world. This attention led to the president's office to issue a clarifying letter, which stated that Katzir was referring to the "general potential in Israel of scientists and general scientific-technological experience that objectively could be implemented if Israel so desired."[21] For good measure, the usual disclaimer about not being the first to introduce nuclear weapons to the region was added. The Israeli government, for its part, maintained its studied silence.

During this period, however, as described by Efraim Inbar elsewhere in this book, a major debate on nuclear policy was occurring within the Israeli government and political establishment. Signs regarding the nature and participants in this debate began appearing in the early 1970s, and in 1976, Moshe Dayan addressed what appeared to have been the major points of the debate. In a public statement, Dayan argued that Israel should develop its nuclear option into a usable weapon. In broaching the formerly taboo subject, he stated: "The option is no secret and I don't think these things should be covered up." The thrust of his argument was based on the increasing burden of maintaining a conventional deterrent. Thus, "should the Arabs decide one day to throw against us the thousands of tanks and missiles they are accumulating, we will be able to tell them that we can destroy you too."[22]

Public discussion and governmental response to this proposal was muted, and the government was quick to note that Dayan was speaking on his own and had not cleared his remarks in advance with Prime Minister Rabin. Indeed, shortly thereafter, Rabin stated that, "Conventional power suffices to guarantee Israel's security in the near future. Attempts to rely on mystical weapons are negative trends."[23] Foreign Minister Yigal Allon, who opposed an overt Israeli nuclear weapons capability, also responded to Dayan. Thus, he announced that Israel had no nuclear warheads, and that "Israel stands by its pledge not to introduce atomic weapons first." He added his hope that some form of agreement between Israel and the Arab states would allow the region to remain nuclear-free.[24]

In the course of the next few years, Dayan, then serving in the Begin government as foreign minister, raised the issue again. Thus, in July 1980, he declared that "Israel will not be the first country to introduce nuclear weapons into the Middle East, but it would not wait until it is too late before using them." Here again, Dayan noted the problem of maintaining an adequate conventional deterrent in the face of massive Arab arms buildups supplied by the Soviet Union and the United States.[25] Finally, in June 1981, following the Israeli destruction of the Iraqi nuclear reactor, which again focused world attention on Israeli nuclear capabilities, Dayan told an Italian television interviewer that "Israel has the capacity to produce nuclear weapons in a short time, and should be ready to do so if the Arabs produce them first."[26] These comments not only continued to raise the specter of Israeli nuclear weapons in the eyes of the Arab world (reinforcing deterrence), but also triggered a debate in Israel which has yet to end.

The Nature of the Debate

By the end of the 1970s, the question of Israel's nuclear stance had become a significant policy issue within Israel. The ambiguity which had been cultivated over the previous two decades was challenged by Dayan and later by others.

The debate revolves around a number of distinct, if interrelated, concerns. Arguments against the current posture of ambiguity focus on the perceived benefits of an overt nuclear force. Such a force would, it is argued,[27] provide a substitute for conventional forces, give Israel an advantage in the inevitable nuclear arms race with the Arabs, and provide a deterrent to direct Soviet military threats to Israeli security. In addition, advocates of an overt posture point to perceived weaknesses in the current policy of ambiguity. A clear, tested, and overtly deployed force, they argue, would strengthen the credibility of the Israeli nuclear deterrent, which, in its present state is subject to misinterpretation or misperception. An overt system would also allow Israel to develop and display a secure, survivable second strike capability which would ensure nuclear stability. The current system, in contrast, is seen as ad hoc and therefore unstable. According to this argument, nuclear weapons would also bring stability to the region and end the warfare which continuously characterizes the Arab–Israeli conflict.

In response, defenders of the current system point to the benefits of ambiguity and the costs of an overt posture. Ambiguity provides deterrence without providing an incentive for a response in kind, maintains freedom of action, delays a regional nuclear arms race, and leaves open the possibility, however remote, of establishing a nuclear-free regime in the region. (See chapter 8, by Avi Beker, in this book.) An overt posture would bring sanctions, not least from the United States, and would further stimulate Arab nuclear efforts. Furthermore, many of the benefits attributed to an overt posture will not materialize (that is, diminished conventional force requirements), and many of the defects found by critics, particularly concerning credibility, are rejected. Each issue is complex and each demands a detailed analysis.

Issues and Responses

An Overt Nuclear Force as a Substitute for Conventional Forces

In his public discussions of the subject, the late Moshe Dayan argued that the cost of the conventional arms race with the Arabs was becoming unbearable. As Soviet arms delivered to Syria, Iraq, and Libya continue to grow both in quantity and quality, and as the scope of Saudi Arabian, Kuwaiti, Egyptian, and Jordanian purchases of U.S. arms increases, Israel is finding it more and more difficult to field a credible conventional deterrent. Egypt and Syria alone now possess 6,000 tanks, and 5,000 artillery and multiple rocket launcher (MRL) units, and Saudi Arabia now has airborne warning and control system (AWACS) aircraft and F-15 fighters.[28] The 1973 Yom Kippur War, and the speed with which Syria, with Soviet assistance, recovered from the severe military defeat in 1982, gave Israel's leaders pause regarding their long-term ability to maintain a conventional force adequate for deterrence, and if deterrence fails again, for survival.

Israel's ever-present economic crisis has contributed to this concern about the cost of maintaining sufficient conventional forces in the long term. While, in theory, Israel might be able to acquire conventional forces to match those of the Arabs, in practice, the cost is already proving to be overwhelming. Israel currently spends one-third of its gross national product on defense and another third paying interest on loans used to finance arms purchases. With inflation soaring, the high cost of weapons acquisition is being reexamined, and alternatives sought.

Nuclear weapons seemed to provide an inexpensive and effective antidote. Thus, Shai Feldman argues, "As Israel moves from [conventional] defense to [nuclear] deterrence, the formal burden imposed by its current posture, as well as the need for enormous quantities of sophisticated conventional weapons, would decrease."[29] Tucker also notes that by limiting the need for conventional weapons, Israel's dependence on the United States and its vulnerability to American political pressures would be reduced.[30]

This is not the first time that such an exchange of "inexpensive" nuclear weapons for a costly and insatiable demand for conventional arms has been proposed. In the United States, the Eisenhower administration's "New Look" of the mid-1950s was based on the same principle. After the Korean War, Soviet (and Chinese) threats were to be deterred via the threat of "massive retaliation" involving nuclear weapons.

This American experience and failure demonstrated the general difficulties in relying on nuclear weapons in place of conventional forces. Theories of nuclear deterrence, beginning with Herman Kahn and Thomas Schelling, note that credibility is essential to deterrence. Nuclear threats which do not involve national survival are not generally credible, and even in such extreme cases, may still not be credible. Threats of massive retaliation did not prevent confrontations in Berlin, Vietnam, or Latin America.

Acknowledging this limitation, Feldman has suggested that as Israel's nuclear deterrent becomes explicit, the Jewish state also withdraw from the territories captured in the 1967 war. Thus, any Arab attack would, a priori, threaten the survival of the state, and in this circumstance, a nuclear threat might be credible.

On the other hand, Arab leaders might also note that even in such circumstances, Israel would be reluctant to use nuclear weapons. Because of their destructive power and the threat of escalation, nuclear weapons are, in most cases, "self-deterring." Given the vulnerability of the Jewish population, Israeli leaders would be reluctant to begin a nuclear exchange in all but the most desperate of circumstances. Relatively small border incursions, regional battles with Syria for control of the north (of Israel or of the area immediately beyond the border which has been used as a staging area for terrorist attacks), and possible future conflicts with Egypt over the Negev are unlikely to evoke credible nuclear threats. In other words, even an Israel reduced to its pre-

1967 borders would be vulnerable to "salami tactics," against which nuclear weapons are largely impotent. Large conventional forces would still be required and any significant trade-off between overt visible nuclear weapons and conventional weapons is unrealistic.

A Means of Strengthening the Credibility of Israeli Retaliatory Options in the Event of Threats to National Survival

According to Feldman, ambiguity currently surrounding the nuclear deterrent has led to a tendency to dismiss its credibility. To support his case, Feldman cites a number of Arab leaders as denying that the present Israeli nuclear capability has any deterrent value at all. Still others deny the existence of Israeli nuclear capability. In 1981, Egypt's minister of foreign affairs said, "We have no information confirming that Israel has nuclear weapons."[31]

On the other hand, many Arab leaders have explicitly acknowledged the Israeli capability, and its implications. The efforts of these states to acquire their own nuclear weapons are justified in terms of the need to counter an *existing* Israeli capability. Arab academics, such as Fuad Jabber,[32] have claimed that the Israeli nuclear arsenal is being used to maintain the status quo in the region and deter Arab efforts to "recapture" the territories lost in 1967.

In a broader context, efforts of nonnuclear nations to publicly diminish or deny the significance of a rival's nuclear force are readily understandable and common. Nuclear deterrence is based on the communication of the threat of nuclear retaliation. Deterrence cannot be successful if the target of these threats can credibly demonstrate that the threats are not taken seriously. During the period of the U.S. nuclear monopoly between 1945 and 1949, the Soviet leadership frequently announced that nuclear weapons made no difference to the international balance of power. Of course, once the Soviets could display their own weapons, the Soviet leadership suddenly acknowledged the destructive power of nuclear weapons. Similarly, Chairman Mao frequently declared that China was impervious to nuclear threats, until the Chinese had developed their own deterrent force. In other words, given the asymmetry which exists between Israel and the Arab states, one would expect the Arab political leaders to understate or publicly deny the existence of an Israeli nuclear deterrent capability. At the same time, this does not indicate that these leaders remain undeterred. Indeed, as noted previously, some analysts see the tacit Israeli nuclear threat as the basis for limited Syrian and Egyptian military objectives in the 1973 war and the fundamental point that led Anwar Sadat to renounce the goal of destroying the Jewish state. If this is true, an overt Israeli nuclear force would seem to add little.

A Deterrent to Arab Nuclear Forces

In addition to worrying about Arab conventional forces, Israel is concerned about Arab acquisition of nuclear weapons. Successive Israeli governments have used diplomatic and other means to delay this process of proliferation, most spectacularly in the case of the destruction of the Iraqi nuclear facility.

As Pakistani nuclear capabilities grow, so do fears that this country, or perhaps India, Brazil, or China will sell nuclear know-how or a nuclear arsenal to Libya, Iraq, or another of the Arab rejectionists. (Recently, Belgium was reported to be negotiating with Libya for the sale of nuclear facilities and material.)

Advocates of a change in policy see an overt and technologically dynamic Israeli nuclear posture as a means of establishing the basis for a stable deterrent relationship with the Arabs. Feldman, for example, points to the U.S./Soviet deterrent system, which has been maintained, in part, by continued U.S. development of increasingly sophisticated systems which have allowed the United States to stay ahead of the Soviet Union. Similarly, Israel's technological lead over the Arabs should provide a basis for nuclear stability in the Arab–Israeli context.

On the other hand, as other contributors to this book point out, an overt and highly visible Israeli nuclear force might also act as a stimulant and lead the Arab countries into accelerating the development of their own nuclear forces. While many Arab states have already sought such capabilities, those with perhaps the best infrastructure for such a task, such as Egypt, have given this effort a low priority. Even Iraq adopted a rather slow and indirect route to the development of nuclear weapons. A sudden change in the Israeli posture would act as a catalyst in the region, leading to demands that the Islamic world "catch up." This process is illustrated in the case of the Pakistani effort, which was stimulated by the Indian nuclear test. Once the public challenge had been offered, Pakistani leaders gained political support by declaring that they too would develop a bomb, even if the nation "had to eat grass."

Improving C³ and Crisis Stability

Critics of Israeli nuclear ambiguity also note that the current posture is inherently unstable in crises and that the efforts to maintain ambiguity prevent the development of necessary command, control, and communication (C^3) systems. The current system discourages clear lines of communication and crisis simulations involving the use of nuclear weapons. As a result, the system is prone to panic and instability in crises. Such assessments are consistent with the reports published in *Time* regarding panic in the Israeli leadership during the Yom Kippur War. In another, similar crisis, Israel might find itself immobilized and such confusion might impair the credibility of nuclear threats. On the other extreme, a "bomb in the basement" is potentially subject to accidental or unauthorized use.

An overt nuclear force, in contrast, would allegedly be subject to the type of exercises and simulations which the United States (and presumably, Soviet) forces undergo. These exercises lead to the development of a "standard operating procedure" which acts to prevent chaos in a crisis. Furthermore, an overt force would lead to the "hardening" of lines of command, control, and communication, and thus prevent accidental or unauthorized use of nuclear weapons.

This is perhaps the strongest argument against nuclear ambiguity. While it is true that uncertainty and fear of panic and irrationality can themselves contribute to deterrence (according to Schelling's concept of the "rationality of irrationality"), this does not answer the problems of command and control. Indeed, here ambiguity is seen as a potentially dangerous contributor to nuclear war.

A Deterrent to Soviet Threats to Israel's Survival

For many years, the Soviet Union has issued a number of threats, both veiled and direct, against Israel. In 1956, Khrushchev threatened to use nuclear weapons to dislodge Israel from Sinai. The 1973 confrontation between the superpowers was apparently the result of such threats, as were reports of Soviet missiles delivered to Egypt during the war. More recently, Israelis saw Soviet assertions that U.S. Pershing 2 missiles were to be based in Israel as providing a possible pretext for future Soviet involvement. Furthermore, recent actions against Soviet Jews and a resurgence of official and overt anti-Semitism have rekindled fears of "racially" inspired attacks against Israel.

Some advocates of an overt Israeli nuclear posture argue that it would be a deterrent to Soviet military threats against Israel. Echoing Gallois' justification of the *force de frappe,* Feldman argues that the high cost of absorbing even a small Israeli nuclear strike would make the Soviet Union abstain from threats against Israel.

By the same token, however, such an overt Israeli nuclear force might be seen as an intolerable threat to the Soviet Union. In recent years, the Soviet Union has repeatedly warned Israel against accepting U.S. cruise missiles and Pershing 2 missiles on Israeli territory. The various agreements for strategic cooperation which have been signed between the United States and Israel and which specify the Soviet Union as a target have drawn angry Soviet responses. Thus, far from acting as a deterrent to the Soviet Union, an overt Israeli nuclear force is more likely to increase Soviet hostility and invite preemption.

The Costs of an Overt Nuclear Posture

American and Soviet Responses

For the past two decades or more, the United States has placed great emphasis on containing the proliferation of nuclear weapons. In addition to pursuing the Non-Proliferation Treaty, the United States has sponsored the creation of the London Suppliers Group, which has attempted to place restrictions on the transfer of nuclear material to nonnuclear states. The U.S. Congress has also been active in this area, placing restrictions on U.S. aid to countries which detonate nuclear explosives and attempting to pressure other countries into accepting "full scope safeguards."

In light of this history, U.S. reaction to Israeli adoption of an overt nuclear posture could be expected to be significant. While the extent of the response and the form it would take would depend on the circumstances, nuclear tests and missile deployments would undoubtedly lead to some form of sanctions. Unless explained by an immediate Arab threat, disapproval could be expected in both the executive and in the legislative branches. This disapproval might take the form of foreign aid suspension or weapons embargoes, as called for in the Export Administration Act of 1979 and as implemented in the case of Pakistan. At the same time, as Inbar argues in chapter 5 of this book, whatever leverage Israel retains vis-à-vis the United States in maintaining an implicit threat to "go nuclear" would be lost.

The Soviet Union could also be expected to react. In addition to the possibility that the USSR might fear that the Israeli nuclear force is directed at them, the Soviet leadership would find itself under pressure from its Arab clients in the region to respond. This reaction might take the form of increased conventional arms support for these states, greater direct Soviet military involvement, or some form of nuclear guarantee for the Arab states. This might involve the construction of missile silos appropriate for nuclear systems, although given the Soviet record, it is unlikely that the USSR would directly supply the warheads themselves. Even such a limited response, however, would be costly for Israel.

The Costs of a Regional Nuclear Arms Race

In his opposition to Dayan's public advocacy of an overt Israeli nuclear force in 1976, Foreign Minister Yigal Allon stated his fear that an overt Israeli nuclear weapons capability would further diminish an already narrow hope that the region and the Arab–Israeli conflict could remain innocent of the costs of a nuclear arms race.[33] He suggested that some form of agreement between Israel and the Arab states would allow the region to remain nuclear-free. While this hope is generally acknowledged to be slim, and the probability of success in the long term very small, the benefits would be very great. Since critics of proposed changes in Israeli nuclear policy discount the benefits which have been outlined here, the hope embodied in continued ambiguity, however small, of avoiding a nuclear arms race is worth maintaining.

Furthermore, even if the dream of a regional nuclear-free zone is utopian, a nuclear arms race delayed is better than one which is accelerated. Proponents of an overt Israeli nuclear deterrent suggest that to be survivable and possess an assured second-strike capability, at least twenty missiles are required.[34] In an idealized static world, once this force were in place, it would be sufficient for some time. In reality, however, the maintenance of an adequate deterrent is generally a dynamic process. In the case of the United States and USSR, new technological developments and political pressures have led to a seemingly unstoppable and very expensive and progressively destabilizing arms race. In the case of the Arab–Israeli conflict, the adoption of civil defense measures, or the introduction of a small-scale ballistic missile defense (BMD) system would increase requirements significantly. A moderate-sized Arab nuclear force would probably lead to Israeli fears of a counterforce strike, and in response, Israel would increase the size of its own nuclear deterrent. While such a regional nuclear arms race may be, in the long term, inevitable, it can be delayed and slowed by maintaining an ambiguous nuclear posture.

Conclusions

Assessment of the costs and benefits of the Israeli policy of nuclear ambiguity is a complex process, and subject to varying interpretations and perceptions. Nevertheless, considering Israeli national interests, it would appear that on balance and in the current circumstances, the costs associated with abandonment of the policy of deliberate ambiguity would not be balanced by the benefits of an overt nuclear posture. The argument that the credibility of the Israeli nuclear deterrent is in doubt in the absence of overt deployment is certainly not conclusive, and expectations that an overt nuclear force would significantly diminish conventional force requirements are also unsupported by the full weight of the evidence. Thus, there appears to be no overriding justification for making Israel's tacit nuclear threat explicit.

Indeed, while the suggested benefits of such a policy change are highly uncertain, the costs are probably inescapable. There is little doubt that the United States and the Soviet Union would react negatively and, at least in the case of the United States, Israel would find this reaction quite costly. Furthermore, such a move would necessarily be a stimulus to Arab efforts to acquire nuclear weapons. Finally, and perhaps most importantly, an overt Israeli nuclear deployment would almost certainly end any prospects for nuclear restraint in the Arab–Israeli conflict, and would represent a major step toward a costly, dangerous, and unstable technological arms race in the region.

4

Israel's Conventional Deterrent: A Reappraisal

Avner Yaniv

The decision to disclose a nuclear option is at once ominous and irreversible. Such a momentous step can therefore be justified only if all other feasible measures of self-defense have been exhausted. To be sure, the two instances in the contemporary world where this has been tried (the United States and the Soviet Union; India and the People's Republic of China) suggest that disclosed nuclear postures enhance reason and introduce an important element of self-restraint. But these advantages have been accompanied by three colossal drawbacks: they have encouraged nuclear proliferation; they have given rise to frightful arms races; and they have increased the probability that nuclear weapons will ultimately be used again.

But even if these three drawbacks are ignored, the fact that the United States, the Soviet Union, India, and the People's Republic of China have adopted explicit nuclear strategies does not support the notion (implicit in the case for disclosure) that they were motivated by a search for stability. Indeed, it seems plausible that all of these nuclear powers have "gone nuclear" because they were trapped in an arms race and (like all actors in the prisoner's dilemma) yielded to its imperatives. The main lesson from these experiences is thus *not* that nuclear disclosure should be encouraged for the purpose of controlling conflicts. Rather, although nuclear arms races may not necessarily lead to Armageddon, they should be avoided wherever possible. It follows that as long as nuclear disclosure is not mandated by the exigencies of a conventional arms race, the temptation to cross the line that separates a "bomb-in-the-basement" posture from one of "disclosure" should be resisted.

What is generally true should also apply to the specific case of Israel. It may well be that sooner or later Israel will have exhausted its ability to survive and to defend its values on the basis of an exclusively conventional deterrent. When such a point is reached, Israel might have no alternative but to "go nuclear" overtly despite all the risks which this entails. But, it will be argued here, such a point has not yet been reached and does not even appear imminent. Israel's conventional deterrent, despite its many imperfections, has been a resounding success. It has the potential for continuing to succeed in its main purposes for the foreseeable future. There is no need to abandon it, though its efficacy has often left much to be desired.[1]

Whether or not this thesis is valid depends, of course, on one's definition of what deterrence is all about. If it is assumed, first, that deterrence only succeeds when it is absolute; if, second, it is argued that in order to succeed deterrence requires a perfect symmetry between the parties, then, logically, the argument that Israeli deterrence has failed in the past and has no future seems perfectly plausible. If, on the other hand, it is accepted that *no* form of deterrence is foolproof and that it is precisely under conditions of asymmetry that deterrence is the only available strategy, then the thesis that Israeli conventional deterrence has been successful is perfectly valid.

That no form of deterrence is absolutely reliable seems so self-evident that it hardly requires an elaborate proof. The notion of "deterrence," Raymond Aron once reminded us "is as old as humanity."[2] The attempt to deter through the accumulation of military force, through both overt and covert threats, as well as through alignment with other powers, has been the hallmark of national strategy since long before the nuclear age.

On many occasions this strategy succeeded for a while. But, judging by a rather elaborate recent survey, there have been very few cases where deterrence has worked indefinitely. Sooner or later it collapsed for a variety of reasons.[3] The only exception to this rule has been nuclear deterrence. Since 1949 the United States and the Soviet Union have never engaged in open conflict—not because they do not have their acute differences, but because of a readily admitted fear that if they do there will be no winners. A nuclear exchange between them is likely to be so devastating that nothing has so far justified the risk to either power.

But is this really sufficient proof that it will never happen? Clearly not! The *probability* that it will not happen seems high. But probabilities should not be confused with certainties. Theoretically it remains a virtual certainty that sooner or later a superpower nuclear war will be fought.

There are, however, reasons to believe that a nuclear deterrent is more likely to last for a longer time than a conventional one. Differently stated, though *all* kinds of deterrence are *in principle* tentative, nuclear deterrence is presumably less tentative than its conventional alternative. In fact, if this hypothesis is correct, one can speak of an infinite number of deterrence gradients arrayed along a spectrum. It begins with small and primitive military forces whose deterrent effect is minimal. It moves on to massive and technologically sophisticated conventional balance systems whose deterrence efficacy is far greater but still relatively low. The next range of deterrence effectiveness includes instances of primitive nuclear balances. Finally, there is the familiar situation of a highly sophisticated nuclear balance. Not one of these general types is foolproof. But a high correlation between deadliness and efficacy most probably exists.

The inherent fragility of deterrence turns it into an imperfect strategy.

Why, then, bank on deterrence and not on a more reliable alternative? Such a question cannot be fully answered without a clear perception of the differences between three generic types of national strategy: an *offensive* strategy, a *defensive* strategy, and a *deterrence* strategy, respectively.

In a broad sense the difference between them can only be clearly underlined through a distinction between means and ends. An *offensive* strategy is characterized by the combination of an anti–status quo set of national objectives with a reliance on offensive means. In this sense the national strategy of Nazi Germany was inherently offensive. It had clearly articulated offensive ends and it did not desist from relying on offensive means for the attainment of these ends.

By contrast, a defensive strategy combines a commitment to the status quo with a determination to protect it through exclusively defensive means. The overall posture of the British Empire in the period between World War I and World War II falls squarely into this category. Britain's aim was to preserve the European status quo and she would only rely on strictly, some say too strictly, defensive means for the furtherance of this end.

A defensive strategy is often referred to as deterrence by denial. By contrast the quintessential form of deterrence constitutes, in the most fundamental sense, a cross between an offensive strategy and a defensive strategy (or a strategy of deterrence by denial). Much like the latter, it is predicated on a commitment to a given status quo. But it entails a readiness to resort to offensive means in order to further this defensive end.

Such a posture is confusing to friend and foe alike. It makes one suspect of duplicity. It tends to add fuel to arms races. It generates domestic criticism and schisms which undermine its efficacy. It exacerbates relations with allies. In short, it is hardly an attractive posture. What should be emphasized, however, is that deterrence, despite its imperfections, is only chosen when the other two alternatives, which are far more coherent, do not really exist.

Two factors render a strategy of deterrence a rational choice despite its imperfections. The first is the overall correlation of forces between the country in question and its adversaries. When one's adversaries are far superior, when administering a decisive defeat to them is not a viable proposition, neither the offensive option nor, indeed, the strictly defensive option really exists. A fundamental inferiority makes an offensive strategy look entirely irrational. It may accrue certain very short-term advantages but in the final analysis it is bound to lead to virtual suicide.

But a fundamental inferiority also precludes reliance on a strictly defensive posture. It is manifested by vast disparities in territory, manpower, strategic depth, technology, and wealth; in fact, it can be reflected in all, or at least in most of the components of national power. Under such circumstances the inferior party cannot afford to rely on a defensive posture because it can easily be defeated both through a surprise attack and through protracted attrition. Owing to its inferiority it does not have the resources which are required for the purpose of a solid defensive shield. It has to assume that a perfect defense does not exist even under conditions of perfect symmetry. It has to accept the proposition that under conditions of a glaring asymmetry a perfect defense is even less likely. And it is almost certain to come to the conclusion that, given this inherent constraint, the scarce resources at its disposal cannot provide for both a defensive shield and an offensive sword. A choice between the two is imperative or else the defender might wind up having neither. The upshot is bound to be a preference for an almost exclusive reliance on an offensive posture.

The second factor which shapes the choice of a national posture is the nature of the regime. While nondemocratic societies are not necessarily bound to opt for an offensive posture, pluralistic societies are by nature more inclined to reject the offensive option. This has little to do, it should be emphasized, with their moral superiority. It merely reflects the fact that pluralistic societies tend to have a preference for an inward looking allocation of resources.

In a sense, one can almost argue that pluralistic societies are less inclined to opt for an offensive posture because of their built-in "self-centeredness." In such societies a government's legitimacy largely reflects its efficacy, whereas its efficacy is largely measured by its perceived success in allocating resources for private consumption. The essential norm on which pluralism is founded is that the government is but a means to an end. It is a necessary evil which has to be accepted only to the extent that it maximizes the well-being of the populace. Masses can be moved by jingoism only as long as foreign adventures seem to increase the individual's well-being. Protracted conflicts have a tendency to drain resources. They accrue certain benefits too. But in the long run they involve a colossal waste.

What all this implies is a simple truism. In political systems where the populace has a say in determining national priorities, an inward emphasis in the allocation of national resources is more likely than its outward looking alternative. Hence, such political systems are less likely to rally to an offensive national strategy than they would be in a political system which is based on a statist universal vocation.

The logical corollary to this assumption is that pluralistic societies would be more inclined to prefer an inherently defensive national strategy. Indeed, they are. But a defensive posture also has its drawbacks. To be effective it should strive to maintain armed forces of at least one-third of the size of the armed forces of the adversary. That is a tall order. If a clear and present danger presents itself, if the overwhelming majority of the population is convinced of this, maintaining an adequate force structure may not be so difficult even in pluralistic societies. But the more successful a defensive posture in dissuading the adversary from mischief, the greater the difficulty of maintaining it at the required level.

The upshot is a cumulative buildup of domestic pressures for major cuts in defense budgets. Under such circumstances, a government which wishes to be reelected—and governments in pluralistic societies wish to be reelected by definition—will find it impossible to resist the temptation to effect cuts in the defense budget in order to facilitate increases in outlays on social services or on other domestic benefits. At the same time, no government would ever put itself in a position in which insufficient attention to defense would result in a calamity. Unilateral disarmament is thus as unlikely as maintaining defense budgets at the required level. The golden mean between these two opposite courses is a defense budget which facilitates an offensive strategy. When this is not accompanied by a change in ultimate objectives, when the overall national purpose remains to preserve the international status quo, the result is inevitably a strategy of deterrence.

What has been argued so far, then, is that asymmetry in terms of power and/or a pluralistic domestic structure could render deterrence—a mixture of a defensive purpose with offensive means—the only possible national strategy. It follows that when both conditions exist simultaneously, namely, when the defender is both inherently inferior and has a pluralistic political system, the choice of deterrence is rendered even more inevitable. In such a case an offensive national purpose is ruled out, a defensive organization of the means (the armed forces) is an unreliable luxury, and the domestic political process forces an even greater effort to reduce costs than in a centrist or totalitarian regime. Deterrence under such circumstances remains pervasively imperfect. But it is nonetheless the only available option. Israel, it will be presently seen, is a perfect illustration of this logic.

The Calculus of Israel's Conventional Deterrence

To speak about Israel's deterrence rationale is to indulge in conjectures. No authoritative statement of this rationale has even been published. One doubts, in fact, whether such a statement has ever been written. The Israeli administrative culture shuns doctrines,[4] whereas the Israeli obsession with secrecy in all matters related to security[5] (and that, in the Israeli definition, includes a great deal[6]) has permitted very little information about plans and contingencies to reach the public.

There is, to be sure, a great deal of material in an ever-growing literature consisting of memoirs, diaries, speeches, and well-informed analyses. But none of these sources has ever included any coherent and systematic statement of official doctrine. The observer is thus left with little choice. He must draw inferences from a reconstruction, based on a random selection of what might be construed, of pertinent policy positions.

What emerges from such an exercise at identifying doctrine is roughly the following: Arab intentions are not clear, perhaps even to the Arabs themselves. The Arabs are not reconciled to the existence of a Jewish state in their midst for a variety of often conflicting reasons. But what they would do about it depends entirely on perceived opportunities. Given an opportunity, they would not hesitate to destroy the Jewish state altogether. Denied an opportunity they would grudgingly accept her existence. Given limited opportunities for limited harassment they would be unable to resist it. Hence, what Israel should do is to limit such enticing opportunities and steadily increase the cost for any hostile action.

More specifically, according to this reconstructed doctrine, the rationale as well as the main features of the Israeli conventional deterrent can be summed up under nine headings. First, the most important source of Arab hostility is the glaring inferiority of the Jewish state vis-à-vis her adversaries. It makes perfect sense, the argument runs, for one hundred million Arabs in twenty-one states controlling such vast resources, to believe that ultimately they can defeat less than four million Jews locked in a tiny piece of territory, isolated from the rest of the world and lacking in any significant natural resources. From this point of view Arab hostility will remain an unalterable "given" unless Israel succeeds in somehow altering the Arab calculus.[7]

Second, while Arab superiority renders a decisive Israeli victory leading to peace an utter impossibility, the size and complexity of the Arab world reduces the actual significance of Israel's inferiority to manageable proportions. The Arab world consists of a complex coalition of states. Almost each one of the member states is internally divided on ethnic, religious, social, economic, ideological, and personality grounds. The twenty-one members of the Arab League are similarly divided among themselves. And since a common language and a modern media make them exceedingly penetrable to one another's influence, their internal divisions and their external divisions tend to be mutually reinforcing. All this provides Israel with ample opportunities to drive formidable wedges between them as a means of weakening the cohesion of their anti-Israel war coalition.[8]

Third, these weaknesses of the Arab world are the prime reason why—despite its overwhelming superiority over Israel in terms of basic war potential—the Arab coalition has failed so abysmally in its attempts to subdue the miniscule and beleaguered Jewish state. Having gradually come to grips with these weaknesses, the Arabs have shifted (in the Israeli perception) from an emphasis on an all-out war to an emphasis on a multifaceted war of attrition. Israel's small size, long and exposed boundaries, isolation in the world, semi-integrated social makeup, short economic breathing space, and above all, high sensitivity to casualties, render it exceedingly vulnerable to a war of attrition.[9] It may be capable of concentrated military strikes. But it is not capable of competing with the Arab's overall endurance.[10] Therefore the Arabs have a vested interest in entangling Israel as intensely as possible in low-level warfare, terrorism, economic boycott, political pressure in international organizations, and, occasionally, full-scale wars. Such wars may be lost by the Arabs, but their cumulative effect on the Jewish state is bound to be devastating.[11]

Fourth, faced by such a threat Israel has no hope of deterring the Arabs from launching *any* hostilities. Indeed, even if Israel's war potential is mobilized to capacity and employed optimally, the Jewish state would still have to expect a major war at least once every eight to ten years.[12] An Israeli deterrent should therefore seek to change the Arab calculus *gradually*. If every military encounter, small or large, ends with a clear-cut Israeli victory, and does not last more than a few days, the price of maintaining the war effort against Israel would gradually become prohibitive from the Arab point of view too. When the Arabs arrive at such a conclusion—which might take decades if not, indeed, generations—peace will become a realistic possibility.[13]

Fifth, to achieve this goal Israel should concentrate her efforts, first and foremost, on the prudent construction of a war-winning conventional capability. Since its purpose is to survive Arab pressure in the long run the Jewish state should avoid total mobilization. Differently stated, the maintenance of large forces has been ruled out from the start. Instead, Israel should, and has, relied on an integrated force consisting of approximately one-third regulars and two-thirds reservists. The regular nucleus should be sufficient to take care of small-scale routine security threats, of maintenance and training duties, and, for not more than seventy-two hours, of a full-scale Arab invasion. Such a span of time should be sufficient to call up the reserves who, in turn, should be able to repel the invaders, deny them territorial gains, and force them to do battle on their side of the border.

The overall organization of these forces has been highly centralized from the very beginning. Only a very small part of them were assigned defensive duties. The bulk have been organized for a fire and movement operation emphasizing armoured "fists" for "vertical" penetration and encirclement operations as well as a tactical air force. To the extent that a defensive deployment was planned at all, the emphasis was on "spatial defense," namely a system of regional organizations along the boundaries in which kibbutzim, moshavim, and small urban communities were armed, trained, and integrated into a military structure. Their function was, as a leading Israeli strategist put it, to compensate for the lack of strategic depth by creating systems of well-defended "hedgehogs" capable of pinning down large contingents of enemy forces for the duration of the war's initial seventy-two hours.[14] This spatial defense was coordinated with a nationwide system of civil defense. However, with the mechanization of the Israel Defense Forces (IDF), the cost of maintaining offensive capabilities became so high that both the "civil" and the "spatial" defense systems were gradually downgraded in importance until they became virtually insignificant.

Sixth, aware of the shortcomings of this war-winning military capability, Israeli policymakers were constantly in search of additional deterrent devices. One of the most important of these devices to have been gradually evolved was an inventory of enunciated *casūs belli* (sometimes referred to as "red lines" or as "security margins"). The main advantage of announcing in advance what Arab actions would be regarded as acts of war was that it gave Israel additional early warning without having to occupy Arab land. Thus, the Arabs were told repeatedly that Israel would not tolerate the following: (1) concentration of Arab forces on her borders, (2) interference with sea and air routes, (3) the stationing of foreign forces on the territory of all countries which have a common border with the Jewish state, (4) an inordinate level of Arab guerilla activity, (5) an attempt to deny Israel water resources, (6) the placement of surface-to-air missiles (SAM) along Israel's borders, (7) any attempt to develop a nuclear capability.[15]

Seventh, yet another compensating device on which Israeli policymakers lay a great stress was essentially political in nature, namely the indirect tapping of the power and resources of other states through latent, and, if possible, formal alliances. The immediate and more conspicuous purpose of this effort was to obtain access to weapons, to gain political support in international organizations, and to cultivate threats to Arab adversaries on their borders with third parties, which, Israel hoped, could result in pinning down Arab armies a long distance from Israel's borders. A more general purpose of these links was, however, to reinforce Israel's ability to deter the Arabs from hostile action by adding to her own (limited) strength the weight of committed allies.[16]

In specific terms this policy had three focal points. The first was *global* and led to reliance on the Soviet Union (during 1948–1950), on France (during 1956–1969), and on the United States (ever since 1967). The second was *regional* and led to a tacit peripheral alliance with Iran and Ethiopia (an attempt to draw Turkey into the scheme failed to achieve any results). The third was *minority* oriented and led to the cultivation of military links with the Kurds in Iraq, the Christians in Lebanon, and, to a lesser extent, the southern Sudanese rebels.

The alliance facet of Israel's conventional deterrent produced a number of critical benefits for the Jewish state. These included an almost steady flow of arms, a great deal of critical political support, the effective neutralization of an incipient Soviet threat, and the pinning down of large Arab forces to theaters of operation a long way from Israel itself (Kurdistan, North Lebanon, South Sudan). But Israel has never succeeded, despite some painstaking efforts, in her attempts to gain formal alliances which commit other powers to her defense if and when she is attacked.[17]

The combination of this weakness in Israel's posture with the shortfall of her military capabilities and of her deterrent casūs belli has had one important implication. The basic inability to influence the Arab calculus sufficiently to ensure that the Arabs would not resort to war has persisted, at least until the peace with Egypt in 1979. Consequently the assumption that wars were likely every decade or so has also remained pertinent. The logical corollary to this view, namely that the use of force by Israel would remain an integral part of the nation's deterrent, constitutes the ninth aspect of Israel's tacit deterrence doctrine.

The most effective way to dissuade the Arabs from resorting to force, or at least to reduce the Arab incentive for doing so, would be a declared reliance on the fearsome (conventional) triad of first strike, massive retaliation and countercity targeting. Specifically, if Israel were to commit herself explicitly to a preemptive doctrine as well as to a deliberately escalatory doctrine of retaliation, it would gain an image, which the late Moshe Dayan once described as a "biting beast" or as a "detonator."[18] Such an image would almost certainly increase Arab insecurity and further stimulate escalation and the arms race. But, it would also increase Arab risk aversion. Differently stated, such a strategic doctrine would almost certainly improve the effectiveness of Israel's deterrent.

In practice, however, such a posture has seldom been systematically sought and might, indeed, have never been feasible. To the extent that can be judged, such an ominous posture was advocated only by Dayan (in the late 1950s) and by Sharon (in the early 1980s).[19] But their advocacy failed to convince their colleagues for at least two reasons: A declared first-strike posture would have brought upon Israel unbearable levels of international pressure, especially from the United States. It would have also generated an acrimonious and highly undesirable domestic debate. Therefore it was simply assumed. But it would have been imprudent to enunciate it explicitly.

A declared policy of massive conventional retaliation would present Israel with similar difficulties and for the same reasons. Therefore this policy could be practiced and was in fact practiced extensively both with reference to low-intensity warfare and with reference to full-scale wars. But although specific Israeli commitments to escalate disproportionately have been issued profusely (during the 1953–1956 period of border violence,[20] during the 1958–1967 conflict with Syria,[21] during the 1969–1970 canal war[22] and during the 1967–1982 conflict with the Palestine Liberation Organization)[23] an explicit doctrine of massive retaliation has been avoided.

Countercity targeting (by air power or by missiles) has not only been discarded as an explicit strategy, but, with a few notable exceptions, it has also been avoided in practice. The reasons are both ethical and practical. Ethically, countercity targeting is incompatible with the Israeli military ethos—in itself an offshoot of Israel's broader political culture. Having always attempted to present the Arabs as vicious and cruel, the Israelis have developed a concept of "purity of arms" (*tohar haneshek*) which exalts the merits of distinguishing between harmless civilians on the one hand and combatants on the other hand. The Arabs, or so runs our reconstruction of Israeli doctrine, are uncivilized and inhumane. They often treat each other barbarically and would therefore not hesitate to deal in such a way with Jews. Israel's ability to withstand the Arab pressure stems primarily, according to the doctrine, from Israel's own superior moral standards. Therefore Israel should avoid warfare against civilians to the best of its ability.[24]

Whether or not this ethical doctrine has prevented Israel from practicing countercity warfare remains, however, a moot point. For in practice, such a strategy would not be adopted without serious consequences for Israel itself. Indeed, there is no doubt that the perception of Israel as being more vulnerable to countercity warfare than its adversaries had at least as much to do with the decision to eschew countercity warfare as ethical considerations. More than half the Jewish population of Israel lives in the Haifa, Tel Aviv, Jerusalem, and Ashkelon-Ashdod-Beer Sheva urban clusters. Given budgetary constraints, this population could not be provided with adequate air raid shelter facilities. Hence it has always been in the Israeli interest to cultivate the avoidance of countercity warfare as a tacit rule in the Arab–Israeli conflict. The method of cultivating such a rule has been two-pronged. Israel has retaliated forcefully against any attempt by her adversaries to engage in countercity warfare. At the same time she has avoided doing so herself except when the price of doing so was considered unacceptable.[25]

If these nine features of Israel's strategy of conventional deterrence are seen as a whole, they provide a yardstick with which to evaluate the efficacy of this strategy. If the Arab calculus has changed, if (specifically) the Arabs have moved from an explicit commitment to destroy the Jewish state to a readiness to accept her, Israel's strategy of conventional deterrence has been successful. If, on the other hand, declared Arab goals as well as the actual conduct of the Arabs in the conflict have not changed significantly, Israel's strategy cannot but be seen as a failure. If an overview of the Israeli experience leads to the first of these possible conclusions, the conclusion that Israel has succeeded in changing the Arab calculus, the argument that the Jewish state should "go nuclear" will appear singularly unconvincing. If, on the other hand, the second alternative—that Israel has failed in her attempt to change the Arab calculus—seems more plausible, nuclearization will inevitably appear to be a rational course of action. Which of these hypotheses is more convincing is the topic of the next section.

The Efficacy of Israel's Conventional Deterrent

Broadly speaking, Israel's ability to dissuade her adversaries from resorting to force has been steadily on the rise. In 1948 seven Arab states invaded the

Jewish state as soon as it came into existence. By 1985 the number of Arab states in Israel's immediate vicinity which are still committed to an armed conflict against Israel has been reduced to one, namely Syria. Egypt, the single most important actor in the Arab coalition, has signed a peace treaty with Israel and has not rescinded it even in the wake of the Israeli bombing of Osiraq and the Israeli invasion of Lebanon.

Jordan has not signed a formal document terminating the technical state of war existing with Israel. Yet it has not only stated repeatedly its readiness to sign a peace treaty, but has also avoided any hostilities against Israel since 1967. Indeed, the Jordanian policy of avoiding confrontation with Israel withstood even the 1973 crisis when the temptation for Hussein's regime to join Egypt and Syria must have been immense.

Lebanon's war with Israel was always little more than an expression of lip service to the Arab world. Thus, among Israel's immediate neighbors, Syria remains the only one whose posture vis-à-vis Israel is still conspicuously warlike. Yet even Syria's position has been significantly altered. In 1975 Syria signed an extensive disengagement agreement with Israel which has since maintained complete tranquility in the Golan. In 1976 Syria and Israel reached a tacit understanding concerning their relations in Lebanon. Syria persistently observed the letter as well as the spirit of this understanding. The fact that Israeli and Syrian forces fought again during the 1982 war in Lebanon was the result of Israeli actions.[26]

None of those clear indications of change in Arab conduct can be attributed to a fundamental change in the Arab perception of the Jewish state. By all accounts the Arabs still view Israel as an affront to everything which they cherish. To the extent that there has been a change in Arab behavior, then, it should be attributed to a transformation of the Arab calculus. In the middle of the 1980s Israel is still as unacceptable from the Arab point of view as it was forty years earlier. At the same time, Israel's most important Arab adversaries must have reached in different ways the conclusion that, at least in the foreseeable future, the Jewish state cannot be subdued by force of arms.

This purely strategic evaluation is at least partly the consequence of Israeli policy. Israel may have paid dearly for the many years of conflict herself. But she has also exacted a high price from the Arabs for their belligerence. The latter have gradually reviewed their priorities and ultimately concluded that carrying on the conflict through political and military means has become, at least for the time being, undesirable. Such a conclusion is not irreversible. But it is not likely to change as long as the present strategic realities remain as they have been in the past decade.

To be sure, other factors which are not at all related to Israeli action have also contributed to the change in Arab priorities. Among these, three seem to be of particular importance. First, the decline of Pan Arabism as a slogan capable of mobilizing Arab masses and as a framework for the political programs of particular Arab regimes,[27] has undoubtedly reduced the importance of the Palestine question as a galvanizing issue. Arab governments have become far less concerned with proving their loyalty to this common cause and, as a byproduct, far less motivated to expend resources on wars with the Jewish state.

Second, the Iran–Iraq War has confronted the Arab world with a formidable new challenge. Iraq, a vociferous champion of militancy against Israel, has been virtually disarmed insofar as waging war against Israel is concerned. Less directly, but almost to the same extent, this war has eliminated whatever interest the oil powers might have had previously in promoting the anti-Israeli campaign. And since Syria has sided openly with Iran, the rules of the Arab balance of power system have compelled Jordan and Egypt to drift toward support for Iraq.[28]

Third, somewhat fortuitiously, the dynamics of the Arab–Israeli conflict have turned a high level of commitment to war against Israel into a virtual synonym with dependence on the Soviet Union. When the Arabs had the option of U.S. patronage (in the early 1950s) they rejected it rather brusquely. It was thus not surprising that the United States drifted toward supporting Israel. As a result, Israel's adversaries soon reached a point at which they could only abandon the Soviets if and when they became prepared to accept Israel. This process has not yet been completed. As long as Syria remains a Soviet client, one can only speak of a potentially reversible trend. But, the Egyptian about-face in 1972 must have affected the perspective of the entire Arab world on this issue quite dramatically.

It is virtually impossible to say whether Israeli actions had a greater effect on the Arab calculus than such fortuitous factors or vice versa. A balanced evaluation would probably lead to the conclusion that the effects of both factors converged. Differently stated, while it was not only due to the success of Israel's conventional deterrence that Israel's adversaries have changed their postures, it cannot be said that Israel's strategy had no impact either. At the same time, the efficacy of Israel's conventional deterrence has varied greatly over time. During certain periods since 1948 it was basically ineffective. During other periods, on the other hand, Israel's conventional deterrent was moderately and even highly efficacious. The overall trend, however, is from weakness to strength.

A brief overview employing as yardsticks for evaluation some of the notions discussed in the previous section will underline this last point. During 1949–1955 the IDF's power to deter the Arabs from an all-out attack was high. This must have been the result of Israel's impressive victory in 1948. But owing to Israel's weakness in other components of her deterrence strategy the disuasive effect of this victory was rapidly eroded. In the first place, the victory of 1948 encouraged Israel's adversaries to resort to effective forms of

indirect warfare, especially low-intensity commando-type activities and political and economic boycott. Second, Israel failed abysmally in all her attempts to obtain great power security guarantees and in obtaining a steady
flow of arms. Third, isolated as she was, Israel was too sensitive to great
power reactions to state her casūs belli as boldly as might have been needed
to deter aggression.

The upshot was an ever intensifying Israeli resort to massive forms of
retaliation. In turn, Egypt and Syria were encouraged to turn to the Soviets
for assistance. This led to the Soviet-Egyptian-Syrian arms deal which upset
the arms balance in one fell swoop. At this point Israel's deterrent virtually
collapsed. The Israeli decision to preempt Egypt was thus a form of acknowledgment that Israel had lost the ability to deter its neighbors from resorting
to force on a large scale.

The decisive Israeli victory in the 1956 war with Egypt recharged the
batteries of Israeli deterrence considerably. The lesson was not lost on either
friend or foe. France was now willing to upgrade its relations with Israel to
the level of a tacit but highly conspicuous alliance. The United States gradually became more receptive to Israeli requests for support. The terms of Israeli
withdrawal from the Sinai contained two explicit casūs belli: the reentry of
Egyptian troops into the Sinai and the resumption of the blockade on shipping to Eilat. The IDF gained in stature and at last had access to adequate
quantities of arms. Jordan tacitly agreed to refrain from introducing heavy
arms into the West Bank—in effect to the partial demilitarization of the strategic salient from which Israel's main centers could be easily threatened.

All this was sufficient to keep the Arabs unwilling to challenge Israel
again for nearly eleven years—but not for more. Nasser's challenge to Israel
in May 1967 when he ordered the Egyptian army into the Sinai, and the
United Nations out of Sharm el Sheikh and Gaza, reimposed the blockade on
Israeli shipping and openly invited Israel to a duel, clearly signaled yet another collapse of Israel's deterrent. After the dramatic Israeli victory of 1967,
the Israeli deterrent seemed to have been, once again, restored. But was it?

The answer is yes, but only six years later—following the 1973 war. The
results of the 1967 war failed to restore the Israeli deterrent for two important reasons: First, the Israeli conquest of the Sinai, Golan, and West Bank
dramatically increased the Arab grievance. In fact it created a situation to
which not only the Palestinians but also—and far more important strategically—the Egyptians and the Syrians could not possibly be resigned. Second,
contrary to the views of many Israelis at the time (and ever since), the occupation of the Sinai depreciated the deterrent halo of the IDF. It denied the
IDF the advantages of casūs belli and forced the IDF into static forward deployment. It faced it with a permanently vast Egyptian army at a range so
close that it increased the likelihood of a successful surprise attack. It length-

ened Israel's internal lines so considerably that the time lag between alert and the arrival of reserve reinforcements from Israel's rear became unacceptably long.

Thus, despite the fact that in 1973 the IDF had become far stronger than ever before, despite the forging of a virtual alliance with the United States, and despite the advantage of strategic depth, the result of the 1967 war was to weaken Israel's deterrent.

By the same yardsticks, the post-1973 agreements with Egypt and Syria greatly strengthened Israel's conventional deterrent. The alliance with the United States was, if anything, further consolidated. The return of a strictly demilitarized Sinai to Egypt provided Israel with a tremendous external strategic depth which is buttressed by explicitly stated casūs belli and by U.S.-controlled early warning systems. The Egyptian grievance has been so dramatically reduced that any Egyptian government can now afford to remain disengaged from the Arab–Israeli conflict. As a result, the entire Arab–Israeli balance of forces has been significantly tilted in Israel's favor at a time at which the IDF's numerical and technological strength has reached an unprecedented peak. Last, but not least, the fact that the IDF succeeded in militarily defeating both Egypt and Syria in a war which they began at a moment of their choosing and with the advantage of complete surprise must also weigh heavily on Arab calculations for war and peace.

Israel's wrestling with the PLO in Lebanon during the 1973–1982 period and the political failure of the 1982 invasion of Lebanon demonstrate that even with all the aforementioned advantages the Israeli conventional deterrent remains what it has always been, namely an imperfect instrument of policy. Nevertheless, the 1982 invasion has only marginally affected the efficacy of Israel's conventional deterrent. This war demonstrated again that militarily the IDF remains formidable. At the same time the war revealed that domestic and international constraints set a limit to Israel's ability to convert military power into political gains. In other words, Israel may have accumulated a significant ability to dissuade her neighbors from launching wars. But she remains unable to follow a grand strategy of compellence. Tactical compellence confined to limited operations is one thing. Strategic compellence designed to coerce other powers into undoing major political and military facts is quite another.

Implications

This chapter began with the axiom that disclosing a nuclear option amounts to an irrational decision unless and until no other alternative exists. As long as a more or less viable conventional deterrence is feasible, there is an acceptable alternative to an overt nuclear posture. Whether or not Israel should turn to nuclear weapons depends, therefore, on how successful its attempt to rely on a conventional deterrent has been. This, in turn, is largely a question of definition.

If standards which apply to the U.S.–USSR *nuclear* balance (that is, avoidance of all conflict) are employed as the sole legitimate yardsticks for evaluating the efficacy of Israel's *conventional* deterrence, Israel has failed abysmally and should, logically, turn to nuclear weapons. If, as has been argued here, Israel's conventional deterrence is presented as a *relative* and a *cumulative* concept whose real test is not in the short-term but rather in the long-term alteration of the adversary's calculus, then Israel has been very successful in her strategy of conventional deterrence.

Judged in terms of this concept, Israel should continue to avoid an explicit reliance on nuclear weapons. Such a policy, which is sometimes referred to as "the bomb in the basement"[29] or a policy of ambiguity,[30] has a number of advantages. In the first place it has already succeeded in having an effect on the Arab, or at least the Egyptian calculus.[31] Second, it will save Israel friction with the United States and (for different reasons) with the Soviet Union. Third, it might assist in slowing down a dangerous Arab–Israeli— and, as a secondary result, Middle Eastern—nuclear arms race.

Of course, a successful Israeli conventional deterrence is not guaranteed forever. As was pointed out in this analysis, Israel's success was at least partly assisted by fortuitous factors over which the Jewish state has had no control. If these factors change, and if, specifically, a united Arab coalition reemerges, the efficacy of Israel's conventional deterrent might be dangerously undermined.[32] If it should ever come to this, the question of whether or not Israel should "go nuclear" will most certainly become pertinent again. Meanwhile, however, there is no reason for Israel to rush headlong into the nuclear abyss.

5

Israel and Nuclear Weapons since October 1973

Efraim Inbar

In the period following the October 1973 war, Israel appeared politically isolated and more dependent than ever on the United States. This became a serious problem because the differences between the two countries regarding the Middle East had grown considerably.[1] Further, in spite of the fact that U.S. influence in the region seemed to be on the rise following the 1973 war, the United States was actually more susceptible to Arab demands. The United States had a stake in the Arab oil-producing states; it wished to preserve Egypt's turn toward the West and hoped to attract radical Arab states to its fold. Therefore, the United States put greater pressures on Israel to accommodate Arab desires.

In addition to the growing international isolation of Israel, the 1973 war produced considerable internal unrest. As a result of various pressures, a change of guard in the Israeli leadership took place and a new government was formed, to be headed by Yitzhak Rabin. The war and the subsequent visible dependency upon the United States shook Israeli confidence, and fundamental assumptions of national security became subject to public self-searching. The nuclear path, as we shall soon see, attracted greater support than before the war. More voices were calling for an Israeli nuclear force.

In spite of these voices within Israel calling for a nuclear deterrent as a radical solution to the problems of national security, the Rabin government opposed them. Realizing the gravity of the problems facing Israel, Rabin directed the thrust of Israel's diplomacy toward Washington in an attempt to prolong U.S. support.[2] The nuclear issue had been a growing source of tension with the United States. This chapter examines initially the approach of the Rabin government to this issue.

In the 1974–1977 period, the political forces against nuclearization were stronger than ever. As a result of the paramount need to preserve good relations with the United States, as well as the desire to delay nuclearization of the region, Rabin's government reduced some of the ambiguity surrounding Israel's nuclear program,[3] emphasizing its preference for a conventional military environment. Israel under Rabin preferred a nuclear-free Middle East, but did not want to relinquish the advantages stemming from Israel's nuclear potential. The government's effort to limit this ambiguity, without eliminating it, served its strategy toward the United States. The stress on a conventional posture was also intended to please the Americans; the tacit threat to "go nuclear" was maintained in order to retain one of the few points of leverage left to Israel in its bilateral relations with the United States. This threat also served strategic needs, as it enhanced Israel's deterrent power against its Arab neighbors.

The nuclear policy adopted by Rabin and his colleagues has been continued by successive governments, in spite of the fact that the Likud bloc, an entirely new cast of political figures, took power in 1977, and has continued to have a share in the National Unity government formed in 1984. Furthermore, Rabin and some of the political figures, whose position and actions are analyzed in detail here, are once again in power. Indeed, this chapter points out the essential *continuity* in Israel's nuclear policy. The concluding section assesses policies that are available on the nuclear issue in the 1980s and prescribes a tacit regional nuclear agreement as the only realistic solution to the Middle East nuclear impasse.

I assume that an already existing Israeli nuclear force during the period under discussion was not self-evident. In spite of widespread acceptance of the existence of an Israeli nuclear arsenal, I view the "bomb-in-the-basement" speculation with skepticism. Most studies of Israel's nuclear policy concentrate on an analysis of the country's capabilities and preferred strategy. Yet, since decisions on such a sensitive issue are necessarily of a political nature, policy analysis should focus on the decisionmakers and the particular setting of the decisionmaking process. Indeed, a review of the positions of the decisionmakers involved in Israel's defense policy shows that sufficient support for acquiring a nuclear posture has been lacking in all Israeli governments.[4]

The Call for Nuclear Weapons

Israel's nuclear program and strategy have always been secret, and public discussion of military matters has been consciously restrained. Yet, following the revelation of the Dimona reactor in 1960, an Israel Committee for a Nuclear Free Zone was established. The committee initiated a public discussion on the role of nuclear weapons for Israel's security. Its activities ceased in 1963, when it was obvious that Israel, under Levi Eshkol, had no immediate plan to produce nuclear weapons.[5]

No subsequent public discussion on the nuclear option ensued until after October 1973. The debate over an Israeli nuclear force was renewed primarily because of the Israeli situation in the aftermath of the 1973 war. The

Israeli victory was eclipsed by its costliness and by the realization of the country's great dependence upon the United States. In addition, the cumulative psychological impact of the protracted conflict and the heavy political and economic costs of an apparently endless arms competition encouraged some Israelis to consider more radical security measures (that is, nuclear weapons).

Unlike the public discussion of the 1960s, the debate in the 1970s was initiated and dominated by the supporters of an Israeli nuclear force. Initially, the call to produce nuclear weapons was not explicit; rather, the inevitability of a nuclear Middle East was stressed. It was suggested that Israel had to prepare itself to live in an era of a balance of terror.[6] Subsequently several additional articles explicitly recommending the production of nuclear weapons appeared in the Israeli press.[7]

A stimulant to the public debate in Israel was provided, interestingly enough, by a foreigner. Professor Robert W. Tucker, in an article in *Commentary,* advocated an Israeli nuclear force.[8] Although Tucker's article was widely covered in the foreign and Israeli press, its impact on the Israeli public was not entirely clear. Such views continued to be aired in the Israeli press.[9]

Similar pronuclear views were repeated by the former defense minister and later foreign minister in the first Begin government, Moshe Dayan.[10] Dayan gave two reasons for the desirability of nuclear weapons. His first argument was related to the fact that the arms competition imposes too high a price for Israel. In contrast, the Arabs have greater human and financial resources to withstand a prolonged conventional conflict. Nuclear weapons would negate this Arab advantage. Dayan's second argument maintained that a nuclear Middle East would lead to a balance of terror, stabilization of the conflict. Dayan's arguments were widely publicized.

The call for nuclear weapons at a time of perceived great dependency and isolation had considerable appeal not only as a radical solution, but also because it continued a traditional Israeli pattern of self-reliance. The nuclear advocates felt that the benefits of a nuclear force outweighed the costs of losing Israel's ambiguity. Whether they believed that Israel's basement contained several atomic bombs or deplored its emptiness, they suggested building a nuclear force of respectable size, to be *openly* incorporated in Israel's military posture. The pronuclear elements thus proposed a basic change in Israel's strategic thinking.[11]

The interesting phenomenon in the nuclear debate of the 1970s was the emergence of pronuclearization voices among "dovish" circles, which were previously adamant against nuclear weapons. The argument that by arming itself with nuclear weapons, Israel could afford to withdraw from the administered territories provided some "doves" with an easy solution to Israel's territorial dilemma. This argument was, of course, based upon the assumption that nuclear weapons could be a part of the solution to the Arab–Israeli conflict. The "hawks," on the other hand, advocated a nuclear force precisely because they could not see any Arab–Israeli accommodation in the near future.

The Forces against Nuclearization

The call for nuclear weapons received little attention from its opponents until Dayan made his statements.[12] Dayan's view could, however, hardly be ignored. Such a view aroused the wrath of many on the left of the Israeli political spectrum, who favored a nuclear-weapon-free zone (NWFZ); and it forced those who favored ambiguity to clarify their position.

What was the official position in the renewed debate? It apparently did not change. The government retained the formula that "Israel is not a nuclear country and will not be the first to introduce nuclear weapons into the region." Yet the expressions and developments during the period discussed made this position less ambiguous and seemed to confirm that Israel did not intend to adopt a nuclear strategy.

Yitzhak Rabin has been since the 1960s a highly respected and influential member of the national security establishment. He was the victorious chief of staff in 1967, to whom Prime Minister Levi Eshkol (1964–1969) lent an attentive ear. In the 1968–1973 period, Rabin served as Israel's ambassador to Washington and was one of the main architects of Israel's U.S. orientation. Though somewhat of a novice in party politicking and identified as close to the Achdut Haavodah faction in the Labor party, Rabin received the support of the majority of Mapai, the largest faction in the Labor party, in his bid for premiership after Golda Meir's resignation in 1974. Subsequently, Rabin became the central figure in the formulation of Israel's national security policies in the immediate post-October 1973 period.

Rabin had supported the emphasis on conventional power as chief of staff (1964–1968) and continued to do so as prime minister.[13] His views were not well known to the public at large until Dayan made his statements. It was reported that Rabin expressed reservations about Dayan's nuclear statements at a cabinet meeting, clarifying that Israeli nuclear policy had not changed.[14] For some reason (perhaps to prevent further discussion of the nuclear deterrent or fearing the effects of Dayan's views on internal and foreign affairs), Rabin decided to clarify his position further and to speak out to the Israeli public. In a speech to the Tzavta Club in Tel Aviv, he reiterated that the official nuclear policy had not changed. He added: "Conventional power suffices to guarantee Israel's security in the near future. *Attempts to rely on mystical weapons are negative trends.*"[15]

The views of Rabin's foreign minister, Yigal Allon, against nuclearization were well known. Allon was a leading strategist and very influential in security affairs. His efforts were crucial in convincing Ben-Gurion's cabinet in

1962 to concentrate on conventional military means rather than nuclear means to defend Israel.[16]

He responded in a party forum to Dayan's public campaign in favor of nuclear weapons. Allon refrained from mentioning Dayan but claimed that talk about Israel acquiring nuclear weapons was causing immense damage.[17] The foreign minister reiterated his position in September 1976 against Israel's introducing nuclear weapons into the Middle East, in a speech at the ceremony bestowing the prize for military literature (in the presence of the security establishment). He viewed the call for an Israeli nuclear deterrent as "a result of unfounded pessimism."[18] In the power constellation of the Rabin era, Allon enjoyed more prestige and authority than ever before and probably could have blocked any nuclear decision not in conformance with his views.

Allon also had the full support of his colleagues in the nationalist leftist Achdut Haavodah faction (formerly an independent party) in the Labor party.[19] The most influential among the Achdut Haavodah cabinet members was Israel Gallili, the gray eminence in Meir's and Rabin's governments, known for his support of Allon's views on the nuclear issue.

Rabin and Allon also received support on the nuclear issue from the hawkish Ariel Sharon, an admired general (later an influential minister in Begin's governments and still a minister in the National Unity government) who expressed reservations about Dayan's declarations. In his opinion, everything would have to be done to keep nuclear weapons out of the region. He said: "A conventional balance is preferable to us."[20]

Israel was, however, governed by a "troika." The third man was the enigmatic Defense Minister Shimon Peres (the prime minister of the National Unity government) of the Rafi faction. Due to coalition-building needs and the relative decline in the political power of Mapai, Israeli politics were characterized by a growing influence of smaller factions in the Labor party and by the smaller parties that were partners in the coalition. This was true even in security matters which, until 1967, were the exclusive domain of Mapai. Rafi, the right-wing faction within the Labor party, was particularly influential. Its support was crucial to Mapai because a coalition between it and the National Religious party and the right-wing opposition Likud bloc would have had a majority in the Knesset. Thus Peres's views even when in the minority sometimes had a veto effect. His views when defense minister on the subject of nuclear weapons were not made public, though in 1966 he had opposed Israel's being the first nation to introduce nuclear weapons into the Middle East.[21] He is usually included, however, in the pronuclear faction.

Did he share the views of Dayan (his faction colleague and predecessor in the Defense Ministry) in the renewed debate? In an interview with *Davar*, Peres refused to comment on the issue of atomic weapons; yet in the same interview, he said, "We can withstand, even though not without difficulties, a prolonged arms race."[22] This statement seemed to rebut Dayan's opinions on the impact of the arms race on Israel. Peres probably favored the continuation of the "ambiguity" to keep the Arabs guessing. He never hid his delight at Arab apprehensions about Israeli nuclear bombs.[23]

The Israeli army was not pressing for a nuclear deterrent. Chief of Staff Lieutenant General Mordechai Gur (now a minister in the National Unity government) said in June 1975 that he did not fear an erosion in Israel's military superiority over the Arabs in the next five to ten years.[24] He later also rejected Dayan's argument that Israel could not support a conventional conflict in the future: "The State of Israel and the Jewish people have enough resources—financial and manpower—to resolve the State's security problems, based on the political, economic and military conditions in which Israel may find herself in the coming years."[25] In the same interview he elaborated on why an Israeli nuclear deterrent would not resolve Israel's security problems. First, nuclear weapons cannot substitute for conventional forces. Second, they would impair the freedom of maneuverability Israel needs in political areas. Gur repeated these views on January 1977, in an interview to the Israel Defense Forces (IDF) weekly magazine.[26] The fact that he, a subordinate of Peres, was allowed to state his views publicly was indicative of an anti–nuclear-weapon mood in the government.

It seems that in the Rabin government the forces against nuclearization were stronger than in any previous government. All high policy elite members, Peres included, preferred the situation as it was. This conventional preference was reinforced by the evaluation that in spite of growing Arab military capabilities, the IDF could handle the situation if properly equipped and trained. There was no drastic change in the threat perception to lead the Israeli high policy elite into a reassessment of its nuclear stand as the pronuclear advocates demanded. Actually, the growing domestic support for a nuclear deterrent forced the government to emphasize its opposition to a nuclear Israel.

Furthermore, the Rabin government desired to play down Israel's nuclear potential, for years a sore point in the relationship with the United States, because it viewed good relations with the United States as a focal point of Israeli diplomacy. It tried, therefore, to minimize nuclear publicity and whenever possible to allay American suspicions of the Israeli nuclear program.[27] Indeed, the official U.S. position continues to this day to accept Israel's pledge not to be a nuclear country.

The Rabin government did not institute a reassessment of Israel's nuclear policy. As indicated by Avner Yaniv elsewhere in this book, Israeli policies are rarely researched and formulated in a systematic fashion. Formally, Israel's policy did not change; substantively, Israel's nuclear program was probably unaffected. In the light of continuing conflict with the Arabs, the Israeli government wished to preserve its option for nuclear weapons. Yet Rabin and Allon, because of their previously held views and the growing pressures on Israel, intuitively and on an ad hoc basis emphasized Israel's preference for a conventional environment and hoped to lower Israel's nuclear profile. Peres also shared the aversion for nuclear notoriety.

The following analysis of several events impinging on the nuclear issue does not reveal any intention to go nuclear and indicates Israel's concern to refute accusations of its becoming a nuclear power.

Contours of a New Nuclear Policy

Several events throw additional light on the Rabin government's stand on the nuclear issue. The first "nuclear event" was Nixon's offer to sell a nuclear power reactor to Egypt (June 1974), which surprised Israel. Nevertheless, the Israeli reaction was persistently low key and very cautious. Yigal Allon remarked that American supervision of such an installation was quite adequate.[28] Rabin demanded of the Knesset not to spread panic, since in the long run it is not possible to prevent the introduction of nuclear power reactors in the Arab countries.[29] Consequently, he preferred an American reactor to one of another origin.[30]

Despite the calming tone of governmental statements, there was widespread concern over the American–Egyptian nuclear deal. Menachem Begin, at the time leader of the Likud bloc opposition, even moved for a no-confidence motion over the "mild" Israeli response to the American–Egyptian nuclear reactor agreement. Aharon Yariv, at that time the minister of information, admitted publicly that the government was worried and conveyed its views to the Americans, and was even considering opposing the delivery of the reactor to Egypt. Nevertheless, the Israeli government decided to tone down the criticism of the U.S. move. First, it did not believe any opposition could be fruitful.[31] It preferred, therefore, a U.S. nuclear reactor, with its more stringent control measures, which Rabin and Allon had noted, to a reactor of another origin. Only later did the government grasp the possibility of delaying or killing the deal, without having to publicly oppose the administration. Second, the government, and particularly Peres, was reluctant to raise the matter of adequate supervision because of its objection to supervision at Dimona.[32] Third, the government was concerned that such a criticism would have an adverse effect on U.S.–Israeli relations and it was careful not to spoil Nixon's visit to the region.[33] Fourth, Israel was interested in acquiring a nuclear power reactor and welcomed the U.S. offer, despite the fact that Egypt might also get one. Fifth, the Israeli government wanted to minimize internal and international attention to the nuclear issue, which could have caused difficulties in Washington. In short, the Rabin government, which viewed the relations with the United States as of paramount importance, went along with U.S. plans when opposition was deemed useless and no vital interests were immediately at stake.

Another episode which again demonstrated Israel's desire to play down its nuclear potential took place in December 1974, when President Katzir, speaking to a group of Western writers, emphasized Israel's nuclear capability and alluded to his country's resolution to use nuclear bombs if necessary.[34] Neither idea was new. Nevertheless, he was quickly reprimanded by the government, which disapproved of brandishing the nuclear option.[35]

The nuclear issue surfaced again in unexpected fashion in August, 1975. The mutual communiqué at the end of the state visit of President Echeverria of Mexico to Israel stated that: "President Echeverria reiterated the firm support that the government of Mexico gives to the establishment of a Nuclear Weapon Free Zone (NWFZ) in the Middle East. Such a zone should be arrived at, and modeled on the Tlatelolco Treaty, at a regional Middle East Conference with the participation of all the states in the area."[36]

The language of the communiqué indicated that the NWFZ was Echeverria's idea and reflected Israel's ambivalent position on the issue. Echeverria was at that time campaigning for the U.N. secretaryship and was interested in such global issues as nuclear proliferation. The Israelis accommodated Echeverria on this point and concentrated on issues more important to them, like Mexican oil and Mexico's position on the Middle East and Zionism. They probably tolerated the just quoted section because it recommended direct negotiations among the parties. A refusal to include an antiproliferation paragraph could have drawn negative publicity to Israel's nuclear program, which was considered undesirable. The language of the communiqué might have been designed by Allon to test the reaction of the supporters of nuclear ambiguity to the idea of an NWFZ.

The disclosure in September 1975 that Israel was asking for the Pershing missile again focused attention on Israel's nuclear potential. The Israeli interest in the missile indicated to some a desire to acquire an accurate carrier for nuclear warheads. Israel applied, however, for a new model of the Pershing, designed to carry only conventional warheads and not in production yet. Peres explained the need for such a missile to counteract Russian Scud missiles in the service of Arab armies.[37] The Pershing was demanded by the Ministry of Defense because it was interested in a weapon similar to the Scud, and probably also interested in its ultramodern homing technology. In addition such a request was typical of the Israeli weapon procurement pattern; Israel often included in its requirements from the United States ultrasophisticated equipment, knowing a negative answer was forthcoming. Nevertheless, it believed that expressing an early interest in a certain item facilitated its procurement at a later date.[38]

Being sensitized to the possible linkage between the Pershing and nuclear weapons, and the potential friction with the United States resulting from the request, Rabin quickly decided on a tactical retreat. In October 1975, in a meeting with the media at a symposium in Jerusalem, Rabin said:

I do not consider the Pershing ground-to-ground missile as a critical weapon in Israel's defense. I think one has to bear in mind that whenever Israel put in a request for a certain type of weapon in the past, there was a lapse of several years till we got it. For the coming years, Israel can manage without the Pershing. Secondly, I would say there should be no temptation whatsoever to view the question of whether Israel does or does not get the Pershing missile as a test case for relations between the U.S. and Israel. By no means![39]

A most significant "nuclear event" occurred on September 30, 1975. In a speech to the U.N. General Assembly, Foreign Minister Allon proposed consultations with all states concerned with creating an NWFZ in the Middle East:

Israel supports the proposal for a Nuclear Free Zone in the Middle East and will be ready to enter into negotiations with all states concerned in order to attain this objective. By negotiations we mean a process of intergovernmental consultations similar to that which preceded the adoption of the Treaty of Tlatelolco and other international instruments of like character. We do not think that so grave a matter can be settled by correspondence through the Secretary General.[40]

In January 1976, while discussing his government's anxiety about the Arab nuclear program, Allon reiterated Israel's willingness to accept an NWFZ, to be arranged through direct negotiations, and which could be established even prior to a general peace agreement.[41]

What had happened? Only one year before, in late 1974, Israel withheld her support from the U.N. General Assembly resolution to establish an NWFZ in the Middle East when it was proposed by Iran and Egypt. At that time, the Egyptians were probably attempting to pressure Israel not to go nuclear or to derive some political and propaganda advantage. It should be noted that, in contrast to the preparations for the Tlatelolco Treaty or the declaration of the African heads of state favoring an African NWFZ, there had been no prior consultations with important states in the Middle East— especially with Israel, the most advanced nation in the region in nuclear matters. Moreover, the U.N. Resolution had urged the affected countries to accede to the NPT and asked the secretary-general to ascertain the views of the different parties rather than calling for direct negotiations between all the parties.[42]

Israel's willingness to accept an NWFZ without conventional arms control was definitely a *change in its declared policy.* Israel had previously maintained that any arms control should include both conventional and unconventional weapons.[43] It was the first time that Israel openly supported an NWFZ in the Middle East with no conventional strings attached to it. No official explanation of the change has been offered. Why did Israel change its policy? Was Israel willing to forgo the last-resort weapon just when the international situation was, from her perspective, at its worst?

Several reasons can be suggested to account for the unexpected Israeli move. First, Israel did not want to vote against the Iranian resolution, which was resubmitted to the United Nations. Allon had been interested in supporting the Iranians already in 1974. At a press conference in New York, he announced Israel's support for the Iranian resolution,[44] though for unstated reasons Israel abstained. By fall 1975 Allon succeeded in convincing Rabin to support the Iranian step and to allow him to propose an NWFZ.[45] The argument that it was desirable to please Iran, Israel's main source of oil at that time and a regional ally, appealed to Rabin. At that time, Israel was somewhat concerned about a possible change in Iran's policy toward it.[46]

Second, the low probability of Israel's offer materializing convinced the proponents of nuclear ambiguity to drop their objections. The low "risk" of the NWFZ being accepted by the Arabs could have been also considered a sophisticated application of nuclear ambiguity.

Third, the U.N. speech was part of Israel's efforts to build an image of moderation and reasonableness, particularly after being criticized for intransigence, and responded to proliferating reports of alleged Israeli nuclear bombs. It also helped to refute accusations of nuclear weapons cooperation between Israel and South Africa. Indeed, Allon's speech was well received. The Israeli foreign minister received many compliments from foreign colleagues and the media for his performance at the United Nations.

Fourth, this proposal could contribute to the efforts to minimize the tensions between Israel and the United States, which was suspicious of the Israeli nuclear program. The U.N. statement was indeed shown again and again to all suspicious inquirers to prove Israel's impeccable conduct on the nuclear issue.

Fifth, the NWFZ could have been designed to allay Arab fears of an imminent Israeli nuclear force, which could hasten Arab nuclear efforts. Many Israelis feared that the Arabs would close the nuclear gap and be able to produce nuclear weapons at some point in the late 1980s or the 1990s.

The concern was shared also by the government. Major-General Shloma Gazit, director of the Intelligence Branch, IDF, in a lecture to an international symposium, disclosed that the Arab efforts to develop a nuclear infrastructure in the two years following the October 1973 war, "although not posing an immediate threat, was a source of anxiety."[47] In response to a question about the French nuclear reactor sale to Iraq, Allon said in the Knesset: "The government of Israel follows attentively and with concern the developing cooperation between Arab countries and countries having high nuclear technology."[48] Indeed, Allon engaged in an intensive effort in Paris to change critical details in the terms of the supply of the nuclear reactor to Iraq, in order to minimize the nuclear weapon significance of the deal.[49] In his opinion *everything* should be done to eliminate the danger of a nuclear-armed Iraq.[50] Arab progress in the nuclear field could increase the probability of nuclearization of the region—a development deemed undesirable by the Rabin government. Proposing the NWFZ and lowering Israel's nuclear profile could delay such a development, since Arab activity was in part a reaction to Israel's nuclear ambiguity.

Thus the Israeli NWFZ proposal appeared to be the result of a concatenation of stimuli. The desire to please an important friendly country, Iran, and of course the United States, as well as the attempt to improve its tarnished international image, and the eventuality of reduction of tension in the area, had reduced Israel's nuclear ambiguity.

Israel, indeed, made efforts to mitigate the negative results of its nuclear ambiguity. Another example of such efforts occurred during the visit of a Senate delegation to Israel in November 1976. The delegation, headed by Senators Abraham Ribicoff and Howard Baker, showed serious interest in the Israeli nuclear program, and wanted to visit Dimona, but their request was officially denied. Yet the heads of the delegation were allowed to make a secret visit to the famous Israeli nuclear installation. Such a visit did not amount to effective inspection, but the delegation's report expressed satisfaction with Israel's assurances not to be the first to introduce nuclear weapons into the region. Israel granted permission to visit Dimona in order to build up American confidence in its public statements, in a period when it was often attacked for its nuclear ambiguity.[51]

Israel also wanted at the same time to strengthen its ability in Congress to prevent the sale of a nuclear power reactor to Egypt. Israel wanted Nixon's offer to sell nuclear power reactors to Egypt to be part of a package deal that included Israel. This could give Israel a veto on the Egyptian sale. Israel made up its mind to kill the American offer, even at the price of losing its reactors. Nevertheless, Israel continued its negotiations with the Americans over the conditions of supply of the reactors. These pro forma negotiations ended in an agreement signed by Ambassador Dinitz on August 5, 1976.[52] During and after the negotiations, Israel looked for allies within the administration and Congress that shared Israel's apprehensions at supplying nuclear reactors to Egypt.[53] Egypt actually helped Israel's tactics by insisting on overall supervision of nuclear installations in *both* countries. Israel succeeded in resisting U.S. demands for overall supervision, prevented the sale of a reactor to Egypt and also did not appear the guilty party for the failure of the administration's proposal.

Interestingly, in late 1974 Israel declined a French offer for breeder reactors of the Phoenix type because of the uncertainties of the new technology of using plutonium fuel.[54] Had Israel been interested in plutonium, this would have been the opportunity to build or justify the existence of a plutonium separation plant. A review of the Israeli energy program in the post-1973 period does not reveal any Israeli nuclear intentions.[55]

These nuclear episodes show that the Rabin government tried to minimize the reasons for nuclear suspicions against Israel. The government interest in lowering Israel's nuclear profile was motivated by the recognition that the credibility of the nuclear rumors handicapped Israel's efforts in two important areas. First, its nuclear potential could lend credibility to the repeated American claim that Israel is strong enough and does not need additional weapons. Second, Israel, with a strong conventional deterrent, possibly backed up by nuclear weapons, the argument ran, could and should be more flexible on the territorial issue. Those arguments were never formally forwarded by the administration. Yet, by using leaks and background briefings, the administration seemed to attempt to manipulate American public opinion to erode understanding for Israeli contested positions. Indeed, the timing of several reports on Israeli nuclear weapons stemming from American sources makes them of questionable veracity.[56]

The reduction of nuclear ambiguity and particularly the NWFZ proposal seemed to be part of a larger tendency to support some measure of arms control. In his U.N. address Allon said: "Israel is ready at any time, even before peace is made, to consult with its neighbors on measures to limit the arms race, with all its dangerous consequences, without materially affecting the relative defense capacity of the parties to the consultations."[57] Gur revealed that in March 1975 Israel also suggested a mutual reduction of Israel's and Egypt's standing armies.[58] Rabin disclosed that Israel was engaged through the International Red Cross in an effort to exclude attacks on populated areas from future conflicts.[59] Allon, in an interview to the American Broadcasting Corporation (ABC) network, explicitly said that Israel was ready to give up its ground-to-ground missiles if the Arab countries would do the same. Defense Minister Peres repeated the same offer a few weeks later.[60]

The Arab countries have been reluctant to make official agreements with Israel. However, where there are mutual interests or fears, tacit understandings are possible. Indeed, the Israelis and the Arabs already had some experience in this area because the agreements reached since the Yom Kippur War incorporated some measures of arms control.

Another perceived benefit from airing arms control proposals was a propaganda one.[61] Arms control was a popular slogan in the United States, and at the United Nations. Yet, in order to avoid damaging the urban centers hands-off proposal, Israel also had to downplay its nuclear countervalue potential.

In summary, Israel's policy as gathered from several episodes and public statements indicates that the Rabin government attempted to delay the hazards of a nuclear Middle East and favored a nuclear-free region. The political forces behind such a position were stronger than ever before. This enabled the government not to succumb to the temptation of a nuclear deterrent, in spite of the fact that a nuclear force was vigorously advocated as a panacea to Israel's difficult situation in the post-1973 period.

The international difficulties arising from Israel's international isolation and particularly the concern with the relations with Washington, sensitized the Israeli leadership to adopt, at least at the declaratory level, a position consistent with the prevalent international norm against nuclear proliferation. Its NWFZ proposal was staged at the United Nations to gain maximum exposure in the international community and of course in the American media. Further, Israel succeeded in allaying suspicions among influential U.S. senators, by allowing a secret visit to Dimona. Israel also managed to block the U.S. plan to provide Egypt with a nuclear power plant, delaying the introduction of advanced nuclear technology to one of its opponents. At the same time, at the regional level, Israel's new nuclear declarations left open a new avenue for reduction of tensions.

Indeed, the tension reduction process engaged in by the Rabin government, resulted in the September 1975 Sinai 2 agreement and culminated in the 1979 peace treaty with Egypt, which was concluded by the Begin government.

Why Not the NPT?

If Israel preferred a conventionally armed Middle East and wanted to prove its nuclear innocence, why didn't it sign the Non-Proliferation Treaty? After all, there were some clear advantages in doing so.

First, for the near future, the loopholes in the NPT were not dangerous to Israeli security. The Arabs would still have a long way to go before becoming a serious nuclear threat to Israel.

Second, even the signing of the NPT would not deprive Israel of her nuclear deterrent option. Taking the NPT deficiencies into consideration, a country could, within the terms of the treaty, be nearly ready with a bomb, which could be assembled in case of an emergency.[62]

Third, Israeli signature and ratification of the NPT could probably reduce the threat perceived by the Arab camp; this perception is a contributing factor to the nuclear competition.

Fourth, if not all major Middle Eastern countries sign the NPT, Israel could justifiably withdraw from the treaty without international reproach.

Fifth, a constant source of tension with the United States could have been eliminated by adhering to the NPT.

The Israeli government, however, did not sign the NPT. Israel found the NPT unsatisfactory. The Israelis feared, in a worst-case analysis, that the Arabs could surprise them with nuclear weapons. Inspection by the International Atomic Energy Agency (IAEA) was believed to be unreliable both politically and technically. Israel proposed an NWFZ partly in an attempt to direct attention to NPT's deficiencies.

In addition, Israel could expect a quid pro quo and was not about to get one. Israelis felt that Israel was more advanced in nuclear matters; it should, therefore, expect "something" from the Arabs in return for relinquishing its nuclear option. At that time the political forces favoring a nuclear deterrent could not force their position, but they probably could prevent signing the NPT, which would initially be a unilateral renunciation of the atomic weapon. They could have argued with some justification that such a unilateral concession would not necessarily reduce tension but might be viewed by the Arabs as propaganda, weakness, and irresolution, or a result of U.S. or domestic pressure.

None of the Israeli governing troika was known to favor signing the NPT. Moreover, even if Rabin or Allon had decided that signing was necessary to prevent a nuclear holocaust, Peres could have chosen to resign from the government over this issue, causing a governmental crisis. Peres was waiting for a good issue to force a showdown between himself and Rabin for the position of prime minister. Signing the NPT could have been described as "appeasement" and dangerous to Israel's security. Dayan, as well as many who opposed a nuclear deterrent, could still have backed Peres. Moreover, the Israeli public, unaware of the intricacies of nuclear strategy, would undoubtedly have viewed the "relinquishing of nuclear bombs" with no immediate reduction in Arab hostility, as a foolish step.

In short, Israel refused to join the NPT primarily for substantive considerations of security. Internal politics precluded, however, even the consideration of such an option, in light of the pronuclear campaign at that time.

Continuity and Change in the Israeli Nuclear Policy

The previous sections of this chapter focused on the 1974–1977 years, when Rabin was the most influential decisionmaker in security affairs. In 1985, Rabin is again in a focal position to design Israel's national security strategy and, inter alia, its nuclear policy. Was there any change in Israel's nuclear policy during the seven years Rabin was in the opposition?

It seems that the Likud governments, in spite of the prominent position of Moshe Dayan for some time (until September 1979), continued to hold the "no first introduction" formula, as well as to adhere to the NWFZ proposal.[63] Furthermore, since 1980 Israel has started voting in favor of the U.N. General Assembly resolution to establish a NWFZ in the Middle East, which was submitted regularly by Egypt every year since 1974. This vote was an additional Israeli signal to the Arabs of its conventional preference.

Gradually Ariel Sharon's views on security affairs became dominant in the Likud governments. As noted, he belonged to the "conventional" school of thought together with Rabin, Allon, and Gur. He preferred a conventional posture and advocated active measures to prevent the evolvement toward a nuclear environment. Indeed, he was the moving force behind the decision to strike at the Iraqi reactor in June 1981.

As mentioned earlier, the nuclear debate in Israel does not reflect the cleavage between "hawks" and "doves." Another "hawk" in the Likud government that ardently supported Sharon on the nuclear issue, was Professor Yuval Ne'eman, who served as the minister of science. He reiterated the government willingness for mutual inspection within the framework of a NWFZ, including Iraq, and avowed Israel's present disinterest in joining the atomic club.[64]

It seems that the forces against nuclearization also had the upper hand in the Likud government and Rabin's policy in this area was continued. However, a new element was added to Israel's nuclear policy—the nuclear casūs belli. It was enunciated that the presence of nuclear weapons in an enemy Arab country, or the capacity to produce nuclear devices was an intolerable situation which gives grounds for Israeli military response. Sharon, when defense minister (1981–1983) delineated a set of contingencies unacceptable to Israel—*casūs belli*—which warrant Israeli military measures. As Israel under Sharon shifted to a system of casūs belli, Arab nuclear potential became a casūs belli.[65]

It is not expected that the National Unity government formed in 1984 will introduce any changes in Israel's nuclear policy. Rabin, as defense minister, aided by Sharon and Gur, also members of the cabinet, are quite an able and authoritative coalition to prevent Israel from adopting a nuclear posture. As noted, even Peres, the prime minister in the National Unity government, is not in favor of a nuclear Israel.

As a matter of fact, the temptation to go nuclear has subsided over time. The period of shaken self-confidence following the October 1973 war ended. By the end of the 1970s the IDF was again viewed as an adequate war machine ready to meet all conventional threats. Furthermore, it seems adept in dealing also with nascent nuclear threats. Indeed, in accordance with Sharon's doctrine, conventional means were used to destroy the Iraqi reactor in June 1981. Therefore, Arab progress in the nuclear field does not necessarily evoke an Israeli nuclear response.

In the past years, the process of tension reduction started by the Rabin government evolved into a peace treaty with Egypt. This peace treaty, in spite of the great territorial concessions, delayed the possible development of an acute sense of Israeli insecurity, which may bring about a nuclear posture. To some extent, the Israelis perceived greater threats because of the loss of strategic depth and the qualitative and quantitative improvements in the arsenals of Israel's opponents. Yet, the answer to those problems was found in enhanced deterrence and a shift to a system of casūs belli.[66]

Further, the Israeli–Egyptian accord could be a step toward a general Arab–Israeli détente. The Israeli government is interested in continuing the process of reducing tensions in the region. The presence of Labor ministers in the present government indicates that Israel may be willing to pay a greater price to carry on the political process than previously. The Arabs would have great difficulty in construing the deployment of an Israeli nuclear force as a move in such a direction, even if the atomic bombs were accompanied by territorial concessions as some "doves" recommend. Israeli nuclear weapons could, therefore, heighten rather than reduce tensions.

Another disincentive to go nuclear is the U.S. position against nuclear proliferation. Leaders of Israel's Labor party, and particularly Rabin, are known to be very sensitive to the "American factor." Israel's dependency upon the United States was not reduced over time. Israel's grave economic situation actually requires even greater U.S. support than before. This dependency is considered by Rabin and others as a great constraint on Israel's freedom of action, which inevitably makes Israel more susceptible to U.S. desires, including those in the nuclear field. In addition, the United States could find an Israeli decision to go nuclear a pretext to disengage itself from an uneasy relationship. It could signal the beginning of the "Vietnamization" of Israel. The United States terminated its defense treaty with Taiwan and withdrew recognition when the price of this alliance was perceived to be too high. The Israeli case may be different, but a slow process of disengagement would be possible. Such a "cooling" period could be initiated after an Israeli nuclear deterrent were announced.

As a result of the need to preserve good relations with Washington, as well as the interest in fostering a dialogue with the Arabs and in preventing nuclearization of the Middle East, the Israeli government may even try to reduce further the ambiguity surrounding its nuclear program. As argued earlier, signing the NPT in the 1974–1977 period was not a practical option. NPT deficiencies have not been corrected in the meantime. Rabin, Sharon, and Gur of the antinuclear faction, have not become supporters of this treaty. Moreover, the Israeli public is not more educated than it was ten years ago concerning nuclear weapons. Signing the NPT without an Arab quid pro quo is still considered unwise.

Is There a Way Out?

As indicated above and by Avi Beker in chapter 8 of this book, the NPT is not a promising way to prevent nuclearization of the Middle East. Israel, as well as Egypt, has proposed a NWFZ. Unfortunately, no progress has been made in order to establish a nuclear-free region in the Middle East. Is it a realistic proposal? The Israeli vision of a foolproof NWFZ with inspections is difficult to realize even in regions where countries maintain normal and peaceful diplomatic relations with each other.

Would an NWFZ sponsored and inspected by the United States be acceptable to the Middle East countries? U.S. personnel were entrusted with the supervision of the demilitarization clauses of the September 1975 Sinai 2 agreement and those of the 1979 peace treaty. Could such a role be expanded to nuclear matters? It is not clear at all whether the United States would be willing to assume such a responsibility and under what conditions. Moreover, U.S. inspection services were used *in addition* to national Israeli and Egyptian verification means. No Middle East nation seems to be in the position to trust entirely a U.S. inspection only. It is also doubtful whether, through more stringent policies on nuclear power plants, their financing, and related nuclear technology, the United States could unilaterally limit nuclear proliferation in the Middle East. The Iraqi nuclear acquisitions are an example of Washington's limited leverage.

Moreover, such a U.S. sponsored agreement could be extended only to countries favoring a Pax Americana. Israel may fear clandestine nuclear weapons development in some countries or the transfer of such weapons to others. If all countries are to be involved, the Soviet Union cannot be excluded—again creating a situation unsatisfactory to the Israelis. The Soviet Union is not considered trustworthy. Israel also dreads solutions imposed by the superpowers.

Finally, only as a part of a general reduction in the level of hostility and of threat perception would we expect Israel to relinquish totally its ambiguous nuclear policy. Political agreements in additional areas of dispute are a precondition for a Middle East NWFZ. Indeed, Peres believed that a NWFZ based on effective inspection can be established only after a peace treaty agreement has been concluded.[67] It is, therefore, impossible to treat the nuclear issue independently of the political developments in the Arab–Israeli conflict.

A NWFZ in the Middle East is, for the reasons discussed, a commendable, but probably unrealistic goal. Nevertheless, the Israeli proposal has some merits. Most important, it allows for a reduction in the Arabs' threat perception. For example, Egypt had refused to join the NPT until Israel also became a party. However, Egypt changed its policy in 1981 and ratified the NPT without linking it to Israel's signature. No pressure was applied on Egypt to change its position. The change is possibly connected to its desire to have access to U.S. nuclear technology. A more cynical interpretation is that Egypt realized that the shortcomings of the NPT could allow considerable progress on a nuclear bomb after U.S. nuclear technology was available.

In contrast, the ratification of the NPT could plausibly be the result of

Egypt's realization that Israel has chosen to maintain a conventional posture and to refrain from producing nuclear weapons. It seems that Cairo assesses that Jerusalem has no nuclear bombs in its basement. Such a position could be the result of the Israeli efforts since 1974 to stress its preference for conventional deterrents and to reduce its nuclear ambiguity. The official position in Israel, as well as informal knowledge acquired through the intensive contacts the Egyptians had with the Israelis when negotiating the peace treaty, probably contributed to the Egyptian perception.[68] The Israeli policy of reducing its nuclear ambiguity, accompanied by political agreements, led Egypt to sign the NPT. Obviously, only if Arab countries do not perceive Israel as a nuclear power is there any chance to keep the Middle East free of nuclear weapons.

The Israeli NWFZ proposal can be used to increase the channels of communication between Israel and other Arab countries regarding the nuclear issue. An Israeli call for a regional conference to establish a NWFZ could underscore Israel's desire to prevent the nuclearization of the Middle East. Discreet diplomatic initiatives could complement the public declaration. Possibly Egypt, in addition to the United States, could be used to convey messages to the Arab countries to foster some nuclear understanding. Toning down, but not canceling, the nuclear casūs belli could also be conducive to create an image of a less threatening Israel. Such an Israel is more acceptable to the Arabs and hence constitutes less of an incentive to an Arab nuclear effort. On the other hand, the present Israeli doctrine of eliminating any potential nuclear threat, though not without problems,[69] complements the diplomatic efforts to prevent proliferation in the Middle East. The Israeli threat constitutes a serious disincentive in the way of proliferation. Possibly a toned down Israeli nuclear casūs belli, reinforced by Israeli, U.S., and Egyptian diplomatic activity could bring about a de facto NWFZ. Involving U.S. help in such an endeavor could be quite appealing to Rabin and even Peres, whatever the chances of success such a plan may have. Rabin's government, as well as those of the Likud, looked for ways to increase U.S. involvement, particularly if they involved commitments to Israel's security. An Egyptian contribution to such a design could be welcomed, as it would open an additional avenue in the fragile Egyptian–Israeli dialogue. An informal regional nuclear understanding might be strengthened by an exchange of secret pledges and superpower guarantees. The main disadvantage of such a tacit solution would be the inevitable ambiguity surrounding its conditions. Risk would be high, and the emotionally charged Arab–Israeli conflict would not necessarily provide an atmosphere conducive to make such an understanding viable. Nevertheless, in the absence of a general political arrangement in the region, the only feasible option seems to be a tacit agreement not to develop nuclear weapons. If the peace process can be continued and negotiations, formal or informal, between the parties can take place, such an agreement deserves greater consideration.

6
A Nuclear or Conventional Defense Posture?

Zeev Eytan

Since the nuclear issue first began to concern Israel in the late 1950s, Israel has had seven prime ministers: David Ben-Gurion, Levi Eshkol, Golda Meir, Yitzhak Rabin, Menachem Begin, Itzhak Shamir, and now Shimon Peres. It is virtually impossible that all these heads of government and their cabinets shared one common perception of what is best for Israel.

This analysis will not discuss the changing official Israeli posture on nuclear weapons. My position represents a purely personal assessment. Whether this position agrees with or contradicts the official Israeli posture is entirely coincidental.

The Threats Facing Israel

I wish to concentrate on the most serious threats[1] to the security of Israel.[2] Contingencies that are possible with a nonnegligible probability[3] will also be included in the analysis.[4] First among those threats with a relatively high likelihood are events which have happened in the past. There are also significant threats which have not yet materialized, but whose probability of occurrence is high enough to warrant discussion.

Nuclear Threats

The nuclear threat has three parameters. (1) Who is manufacturing nuclear weapons? (2) Who is acquiring them? (3) For what purpose are they being acquired?

The manufacturing state could be any one of the following: the Soviet Union, the United States, the United Kingdom, France, India, and the People's Republic of China (PRC). Since I intend to make projections of up to five

I wish to thank Candace Salem for editorial assistance. Any errors are mine.

years, I shall add as sources all countries that may soon have the capability to manufacture and transfer nuclear weapons to Arab hands (such as the Federal Republic of Germany, Italy, Spain, Sweden, South Africa, Brazil, and Argentina[5]) as well as some Arab or Muslim countries (Iraq, Libya, Pakistan, Egypt, Syria, and Iran[6]).

Acquirers could include all major Arab countries, the Palestine Liberation Organization, splinter organizations of Palestinian terrorists (such as Abu-Nidal's), and non-Arab terrorist organizations (Iranian extremists, the Japanese Red Army, or the Italian Red Brigades). Cases such as Iraq may concern the production of nuclear weapons for her own use, as opposed to producing a bomb (e.g., Iran) and passing it to Syria or the PLO.

The purposes of acquisition could include bargaining or blackmail; deterrence of Israel, assuming (rightly or wrongly) that Israel has, or will soon have, nuclear bombs; or actual explosion on Israeli targets. These aims, of course, may be connected. Once a bomb has been acquired, there may be further developments leading the owner to change purpose from political to military functions or vice versa.

Conventional Threats

A large range of possible conventional threats faces Israel. Any such threat has several parameters. (1) Who creates or initiates the threat? (2) Who is to implement it? (3) What is to be done about it? (4) For what purpose is it made?

The threat might be initiated by the Arab confrontation states (Jordan, Syria), Egypt, Iraq, Libya, and Saudi Arabia; the Palestinian organizations or groups which have seceded from the PLO; splinter groups outside the PLO; international radical terrorist organizations sympathetic with the Arab cause; or, in theory, each superpower. In 1967 (and perhaps in 1973), the Soviet Union encouraged its Arab allies to cause crises which led to war.

A list of potential implementers could be identical to the list of initiators, though there may be important differences. One can envision a situation in which Syria encourages the PLO to take hostile measures or wherein the Soviet Union encourages Syria to initiate violence against Israel. It is, therefore, expedient to maintain a separate list of implementers and one of initiators.

Possible threats might include (1) terrorist or guerrilla activity against Israel or Israeli targets abroad; (2) border shelling against Israel; (3) maritime blockade of shipping to or from Israel, or interference with Israeli flag-carrying ships worldwide; (4) hijacking of aircraft to and from Israel; (5) aerial blockade of flights to and from Israel, or of Israeli flag-carrying aircraft; (6) limited war by regular armies or PLO forces; (7) full-scale war by regular and irregular forces.

Each threat could have one or more purposes, including (1) to keep one's own ranks (PLO or Arab states) satisfied about stated commitments and proclaimed ideology (to "liberate Palestine" or to "regain the Arab lands," say); (2) to attract political sympathy to one's cause; (3) to set "political momentum" into action; (4) to score "points" with other actors (such as increasing the Soviet Union's influence in the Middle East, or hurting U.S. interests there); (5) to weaken Israel by harassment, causing a waste of the nation's economic resources, hurting her morale, and possibly leading to the emigration of Israel's Jews; (6) to regain part of the territories lost in 1967; (7) to regain territories as part of a scheme to achieve total step-by-step victory; (8) to destroy the State of Israel altogether.

Other Threats

Other threats are those involving chemical or biological warfare. In terms of probable casualties and damage, this category more closely resembles the conventional than the nuclear threat. It can, therefore, be included reasonably in the conventional category.

Capabilities and Probabilities of Implementing the Threats

I have not mentioned any threat to Israel in the previous section unless a capability to implement the threat exists and there is a positive nonnegligible probability that such implementation will occur.[7] All dangers and threats listed have a positive, nonnegligible probability of happening, either presently or within five years. The probability of any one of the threats is not equal to that of any other threat.[8] All depend significantly on the capability of implementation. Such capability, in turn, depends at least in part on what Israel and other actors (the United States, the Soviet Union, Egypt, Syria) may do.

For example, there is a danger that a combination of Arab states will choose the option of total war against Israel. This threat is "possible," but only if Israel were to make serious errors in strategic judgment.

In estimating the real danger to Israel, it must be understood that no single actor "has" or "has not" the capability to implement each of the threats. This capability is contingent upon certain conditions.

Do the Arab countries possess the capability to manufacture nuclear weapons on their own within five years? We know that Iraq, Libya, Egypt, and Syria are making efforts which might lead to the possession of indigenous nuclear weapons. We do not know whether or not these countries will get the necessary foreign aid or overcome various foreseen and unforeseen difficulties. And we can say that there is a nonnegligible positive probability that one or more of them will have a locally made nuclear bomb within five years.

The Nuclear Threats

The United States, the Soviet Union, the United Kingdom, France, the PRC, and India possess nuclear devices. The probability of their using these devices against Israel is so low that it can be ignored. The likelihood of the United States, the Soviet Union, or the United Kingdom transferring nuclear bombs to an Arab actor is negligible and can be ignored except for one case: if Israel were to go openly nuclear, the probability of the Soviets passing nuclear weapons to a pro-Soviet Arab actor such as Syria or Iraq would increase. Such an eventuality might be connected with controls over what the recipient may do with the weapons.

The probability of France, India, or the PRC passing a nuclear weapon to a friendly Arab state is low, but not negligible, especially were Israel to decide, for one reason or another, to go openly nuclear. Of these countries, France, prior to June 1981, transferred a nuclear reactor and 70 kilograms of weapon grade material (uranium enriched to over 92 percent) to Iraq.[9]

The probability that Pakistan will develop a nuclear weapon within the next five years is intermediate, which means it may have the required capability. The Arab countries, including Libya, have been financing the Pakistani nuclear effort and may have asked for the bomb once it is available.[10] I would estimate the probability that Pakistan will have the bomb and transfer it to an Arab country as being low, but not negligible.

The probability of an Arab country managing to develop an indigenous nuclear bomb within five years (not excluding some technical assistance from "advanced" countries) is between low and intermediate. The next step, if and when such a capability has been achieved, is tilted in favor of using the nuclear capability for purposes of bargaining, deterrence of Israel or possibly blackmail. If and when such a capability exists in one or more of the Arab states, the probability of constructing bombs for actual strikes against Israel is low though not negligible.

The probability of an Arab country, the PLO, or another Arab or radical non-Arab terrorist group acquiring a finished nuclear weapon from an outside source within five years cannot be disregarded. The source might be any of the countries not yet openly nuclear. The capability to manufacture a bomb might also be available in nongovernmental enterprises in the technologically advanced countries. This contingency has a doubly low probability of occurrence—as there is uncertainty as to which if any of the aforementioned actors will have nuclear weapons within five years, and whether this actor would be willing to transfer them to an Arab state or organization. If one of the prospective source countries will have a nuclear weapon, and seek desperately needed funds or be sympathetic to an Arab actor (as Iran might be), the weapon might be transferred to one of the Arab states, to the PLO or to other terrorist groups. This scenario has a low, yet nonnegligible probability of occurrence.

While the delivery systems available to the Arab states would be either aircraft or missiles, subnational organizations might prefer a boat or a suitcaselike device.

Conventional Threats

Terrorist or Guerrilla Actions against Israel or Israeli Targets Worldwide. Such actions, of course, have occurred on and off since the 1950s. They have occasionally focused attention on the Palestinian cause, and on most occasions have positively affected the morale of the Palestinians or other Arabs. The Israeli response to terrorist or guerrilla activities has been only partly successful. Therefore I estimate that continued use of this kind of threat has a high probability of occurrence.

Border Shelling of Israel. This has occurred, as mentioned previously, with some Arab success. Examples include the Syrian shellings in the 1950s and 1960s on the Israeli Galilee, from the Syrian-held Golan Heights; Jordanian shelling along the Jordan Valley, specifically at the Beit She'an region from 1969 to 1970; Egypt's shelling in 1969–70 of the Israeli positions along the Suez; Syria's shelling the Israeli settlements in the Golan between 1967 and the 1973 War, and immediately after the 1973 War; and finally, shelling by the PLO forces stationed in Lebanon since 1973, and, with high intensity, in the summer of 1981.

In June 1982 the PLO's repetition of the shelling gave Israel the pretext to invade southern Lebanon and strike against the PLO forces there. The probability of such a threat materializing again in the next five years hinges on a *common border* (applicable only with regard to Jordan, Syria, Lebanon, and Egypt); *capability* (which exists, as all the above countries possess artillery); and *willingness to act*. The PLO, at the moment, does not have artillery pieces or rockets near the Israeli borders, though they may within five years regain such a capability, either by returning to southern Lebanon or by acquiring facilities in Jordan or Syria. The probability of such a threat being implemented is intermediate.

A Successful Maritime Blockade against Israel. This was undertaken by Egypt, in collaboration with Saudi Arabia, in the 1950s (it held until the Israeli Sinai Operation in 1956). In 1967 the blockade pushed Israel to launch the Six-Day War. The probability of repetition of such a threat by Egypt is not high; however, there are other Arab actors who might try it. Libya, possessing a strong navy, and being located quite distant from Israel, might be tempted to blockade shipping to and from Israel in the relatively narrow waters of the central Mediterranean. The probability of this threat may be judged as intermediate.

Hijacking of Aircraft Flying to and from Israel. This was attempted by PLO member organizations from 1968 to 1977. There were, from the Israeli perspective, several cases of success in foiling hijacking attempts, yet there were also failures. The same has been true for the PLO: they had several successes, mixed with failures. Aircraft flying to Israel have been successfully blown up twice. From the Israeli perspective, the security measures undertaken since 1968 are a nuisance and require money and personnel which could be (otherwise) employed in a more productive manner. The threat of hijacking aircraft to and from Israel, or blowing them up in midair, has an intermediate probability of occurrence in the future.

An Aerial Blockade of Israel. This was undertaken by Egypt before 1956, and in May and June of 1967. An aerial blockade of Israel along the Mediterranean routes has not been undertaken, though it is not beyond the capabilities of Syrian, Libyan, or Egyptian aircraft. It would very likely invite an Israeli response, either in kind or of even greater severity. Therefore I estimate the probability of such an occurrence as being rather low, though not negligible.

A Limited War, by Regular Armies or the PLO. This occurred in 1973. The goals of such a future war might be (1) to regain some territories, (2) to cause Israel many human casualties (judged to be intolerable for Israel), (3) to cause a renewal of political negotiations under conditions more favorable for the Arabs, or (4) to beat Israel step by step rather than in one war. These goals were achieved in part by the Syrians and Egyptians in 1973. War may be launched by a single Arab state (Syria being the most likely candidate), several states (Syria plus Jordan) or all of them. In a war started by one state, others might be dragged in later, either to share the spoils or to rescue the "beaten" ally. At the moment Syria is isolated from most Arab states (though not from Libya); Iraq is preoccupied with Iran; Egypt maintains peace, though a chilly one, with Israel; and most of the PLO forces are scattered far from Israel's borders.

But all these facts are temporary; alliances and rivalries in the Arab world change quite frequently. In 1967, it took Nasser three weeks to overcome Arab rivalries and form an anti-Israel coalition. Within five years Syria might be friendly with Iraq, or Egypt, and so on.

The probability of a limited war happening next month is low. The probability of such a war happening within five years is intermediate, especially if we take into account the low opinion of Israel's economic and political stability held in the Arab world. Also, the Arab initiator of such a threat might attempt to achieve surprise, to catch Israel napping and attack before Israel manages to mobilize its reserves.

A Full-Scale War by a Coalition of Arab Actors Intended to Destroy Israel.
This could hinge on an assumption that Israel can be surprised. The Arab
states, possessing more than 500 high-quality aircraft within striking distance
of Israel, plus surface-to-surface rockets, are perceived as capable, to some
extent, of penetrating Israeli defenses. As Israel has no more than ten military
airfields, and may have no more than twelve within five years, a surprise
attack maiming the Israeli air force might seem tempting. It is also possible
that a war might start as a "limited" war and, if successful at the beginning,
cause a change of goals on the Arab side. Therefore the probability of such a
war within five years is intermediate.

Evaluation of Danger of the Threats

There is no method by which to scale exactly the degree of danger of a given
threat to Israel, or to any other country. Therefore we must use a rather crude
judgment, dividing the possible threats into "highly dangerous," "intermedi-
ately dangerous," or of "little danger." We may disregard those threats which
would cause little harm to Israel.

The danger a threat poses is tied closely to the probability of its occurrence, and hinges on its capability of implementation.

The nuclear threat against population centers (countervalue threat), if
materialized, could destroy a significant part of the population of Israel, and
leave Israel unable to resist any full-scale attack by enemy forces. Although
the probability here is low, such a threat is highly dangerous, whoever the
aggressor might be.

It is possible that a small terrorist organization might get hold of a nuclear device, succeed in getting it into Israel (into the center of Tel Aviv, say)
and explode it. In such a case, Israel might easily suffer over 100,000 fatalities. If the opportunity were maximized, the control centers of Israel, such as
the Defense Ministry, might also be destroyed. The terrorist group responsible
for the explosion would be incapable of independently implementing the required "follow-up"; that is, occupying and destroying the remnants of the
State of Israel. However, once such an explosion took place, the temptation
for other Arab actors (such as Syria) with a conventional military capability
to exploit the "new" circumstances would be high, as would be their chances
of success. Therefore all nuclear threats belong to the "high" danger class,
even though the probability of their occurrence is low.

Nonnuclear terror, hijacking, and maritime and aerial blockades may be
grouped together. All these have an intermediate probability of happening,
though Israel has withstood similar threats in the past with some success.
This group is not highly dangerous for Israel.

The probability of shelling Israel's border is intermediate. The associated
danger, however, is not high. Israel would not fall to pieces if this threat were

implemented, nor would the casualties suffered be extremely high.[11] Still, such a threat could lead to the evacuation of villages or towns, as happened in Kiryat Shmona in 1981. This, in turn, might lead Israel to opt for escalation, which might cause a larger war.

What about a conventional attack against Israel, intended to achieve total destruction of the state? The probability of success is low and positive only under a specific set of circumstances. The probability of occurrence is intermediate. If successful, such a threat falls into the "high" danger class. Even if undertaken without success, such an attack would cause Israel human and material losses. As for the political consequences, an unsuccessful Arab attack might result in calamity in the Arab states, although Israel might not reap any political profits from her success on the battlefield. The qualification should be that such a threat is confined only to certain actors: a coalition of all Arab states, or most of them (the confrontation states), with the military forces of the PLO. It might include participation of Soviet forces of one kind or another. The PLO, or other terror organizations, are not at present capable of implementing this threat on their own, though they may be able to start a chain of events which would affect Israel, trigger Israeli reprisal, drag other Arab states into a response, and ultimately lead to an all-out Arab war.

An Arab victory could conceivably result in the destruction of the State of Israel. Israeli casualties, in such an eventuality, would be very high, though certainly not as high as the casualties suffered from a successful anti-Israel nuclear strike. For these reasons, a conventional attack against Israel, aimed at total destruction of the state, carries a "high" danger to Israel. This is so, even though the probability of success within the coming five years is low, and depends on very specific conditions.

Participation of Non-Arab Forces in a Future War

What about the danger of participation of non-Arab forces in a conventional Arab–Israeli war? In 1948 several British officers, seconded to the Jordanian army, fought against Israel. In 1970 the Soviet Union, in response to a request by Egypt, sent regular Soviet units to Egypt, in addition to the Soviet instructors and advisors already there. The forces sent included a Soviet Air Defense Division, with Soviet manned surface-to-air missiles (SAMs), control centers, radars, and allegedly 150 Soviet-flown fighter aircraft.

The total number of Soviet personnel in Egypt in 1970 is estimated to have been at up to 20,000, with about 15,000 belonging to Soviet units proper. These units were stationed at a specific sector of the Egyptian defense, including Port Sa'id, and normally not along the first line of defense, but rather to the rear of it, thus enabling Egypt to send more of its own men and material to the front. As Israel attacked not only the first line of Egyptian defense but also struck at "the depth" of Egypt, Soviet personnel were involved directly in activity against Israel.

It has also been confirmed by both the Israelis and the Egyptians that a dogfight between Israeli and Soviet aircraft occurred, in which the Soviets lost four, and according to one source five, aircraft, while Israel lost none. Soviet forces have manned SAM batteries (SA-5s plus other SAMs to defend the SA-5s) in Syria since the 1982 war in Lebanon. Soviet threats to fire rockets against Israel were made in Prime Minister Bulganin's letter to Israel following the 1956 Sinai Campaign. Soviet threats to intervene in the 1973 War and relieve the Egyptian Third Army were made October 24, 1973, and led to a U.S. worldwide alert on October 25. So far no nation other than the Soviet Union has sent troops to assist the Arabs in their struggle against Israel.

How dangerous is this to Israel? At the tactical level, if the Soviet Union were to send one, two, or five divisions, or air defense units, or squadrons of fighter aircraft—Israel could cope with the new menace, though it would cost many Israeli lives. At both the political and psychological levels, this would be especially dangerous. As the capability of the Soviet Union to send additional units is almost unlimited, Israel could not win in such an engagement. The United States might neutralize the Soviets, but this is uncertain, and even if it were to happen, may not be to Israel's long-term benefit. Therefore Soviet participation in an Arab–Israeli war, even if not large scale, would pose an intermediate danger to Israel, though it would not likely cause Israel's total destruction.

Conclusions on Dangers and Probabilities

In view of the dangers, capabilities and probabilities of the threats against Israel, the most dangerous threat is the nuclear one, which has a low probability of occurrence. The threats of a conventional war with limited goals and of a total conventional war are both very dangerous to Israel and have an intermediate probability of occurrence. The danger of shelling Israel's border is intermediate, with a similar probability of occurrence. The danger of participation of Soviet forces in a conventional war is intermediate. The danger of terror attacks, hijackings, and maritime or aerial blockade is low; the probability of most of them is intermediate or high.

A Nuclear or Conventional Defense Posture?

There are basically two defense postures available to Israel: (1) an openly nuclear defense posture or (2) a conventional defense posture.

A third defense stance may be available, namely one that attempts to reap the benefits of both of the other two postures without incurring the costs. However, this is quite problematic and could have the opposite result. I will discuss this posture which is not openly nuclear, nor strictly conventional. It might include a "bomb in the basement," though it does not include open testing of nuclear devices or actual demonstration of capability to produce a bomb.

Irreversibility

As can be seen from the other chapters in this book, there are various opinions as to where Israel stands at present. Those who claim that Israel has "bombs in the basement" have surely not proved it.[12] I accept what Professor Yuval Ne'eman has said: "Israel, fifteen or twenty years ago, saw to it that she would not be helpless. We have created a nuclear potential, we have skilled personnel, we have the infrastructure, but we have not crossed the nuclear threshold. We have no bombs."[13]

Whatever the situation, it is irreversible. If Israel passes from a conventional posture to a bomb-in-the-basement posture, or to an openly nuclear posture, such a change can not be reversed. Thus far no country in the world has destroyed its own nuclear arsenal.

An Open Nuclear Defense Posture

An openly nuclear defense posture would require that Israel demonstrate an ability to acquire nuclear weapons, and devote a significant portion of her defense efforts, including a significant part of her budget, to nuclear development. It would not require that Israel totally neglect her conventional capabilities. It can be assumed that the United States, fearful of nuclear proliferation, would cut aid to Israel if Israel were to go openly nuclear on its own before any of her Arab adversaries had done so.

The United States might prefer to offer Israel nuclear protection rather than encourage Israel to go openly nuclear. It is also possible that, if an Arab country goes openly nuclear, the United States may permit Israel to use U.S. aid funds in order to catch up. An Israeli decision to go nuclear first might also antagonize the Soviet Union, which shares U.S. fears of proliferation. In such an eventuality, the Soviet Union could respond in one of four ways: (1) issuing threats against Israel, (2) offering a nuclear umbrella to pro-Soviet Arab states such as Syria and Iraq, (3) offering a certain number of nuclear weapons to pro-Soviet Arab states, (4) negotiating with the United States in order to bring U.S. pressure on Israel to stop her nuclear efforts. One can safely assume that if Israel adopts an openly nuclear posture, the Arab states will accelerate their indigenous efforts to produce nuclear bombs.

A Conventional Defense Posture

When considering a conventional defense posture, we use the same constraints regarding human capital, industrial capabilities, budgets, and financial aid from the United States. The United States has passed bills giving Israel $1.4 billion in military aid in 1985, as a grant, all of it devoted to conventional defense. When referring to a conventional defense posture, there must be no open Israeli demonstration of nuclear arms possession, or any bomb explosions.

If a certain portion of the budget goes to nuclear research and development, it cannot be a major share, as the conventional posture itself requires these same funds and industrial capabilities. Such a posture limits the nuclear effort to research and to steps taken "in case" there will have to be a change of policy in the future. Side by side with the conventional defense posture, some effort may be made to keep Israel in a state of know-how regarding nuclear physics and nuclear industry. Moreover, there is no guarantee that an Israeli conventional defense posture will assure that the Arab states will not accelerate their efforts to go openly nuclear, or at least to achieve a nuclear option.

The Bomb in the Basement

The bomb-in-the-basement defense posture must include "deliberate ambiguity" on the part of Israel. There must be no open testing of bombs, nor any openly pronuclear statements. Neither can all of Israel's resources appear to be devoted to conventional arms and a conventional posture. If successful, such a "bomb in the basement" might keep Israel's enemies fearful that Israel has nuclear weapons, yet not fearful enough to accelerate nuclear development in the Arab countries.

It is possible that the nuclear efforts of several Arab states will proceed, regardless of what Israel will or will not do in this field. It is also possible that the Arab states' nuclear effort is already well under way, influenced by what Israel has accomplished in the nuclear field since the 1950s. The bomb-in-the-basement posture must also be sufficiently subtle so as not to antagonize the United States or the Soviet Union. If Israel were to exceed a certain threshold, the "basement" posture could lead to those outcomes associated with the openly nuclear posture; that is, it would antagonize the United States, antagonize the Soviet Union, and accelerate further the Arab efforts to go nuclear.

Summary of the Possible Postures

Each of the defense postures is in itself a composite of subpostures. The nuclear posture could be divided into a counterforce or countervalue posture; into one relying on delivery by aircraft, or by missiles. The conventional posture could be further divided into one relying on regular forces, or on reserves; relying predominantly on an air force or on ground forces. The list of specific subdivisions of each posture is virtually endless, and by generalizing I do not ignore them.

The "Other Things Being Equal" Assumption. When analyzing policy options, it is convenient to assume an "everything else equal" assumption. In this case, the chosen defense posture has to share one defense budget (with a slight qualification to be explained soon), one population, one set of human experts, and one industrial base. It is impossible to expand conventional forces and the nuclear capability at the same time. It is an "either–or" choice, or a trade-off between the two. One must decide how to share a pie (national resources) of a given size.

The one qualification regarding the size of the defense budget is as follows: Israel currently spends about $4.25 billion per year on defense. This sum comes from two separate sources: Israeli gross national product, and U.S. military aid (in 1985 a grant of $1.4 billion per year). The available resources from both appear to have reached the maximum possible level. Some claim that expenditure is higher than the maximum desirable and should be reduced.[14] It is certainly not feasible that either source will become considerably larger in the near future.

If one of the major defense postures, the nuclear posture or possibly even the bomb-in-the-basement posture, antagonizes the United States, the U.S. aid component of Israel's defense expenditure could be cut. A cut in U.S. aid could also affect U.S. economic aid to Israel ($1.2 billion in 1985), and a reduction in technological cooperation. This would harm the Israeli high-technology industries,[15] which in turn would affect Israel's domestic defense production.

A deterioration in Israel's relations with the United States or the European Economic Community (EEC) would lead to a reduction in purchases by the United States and the EEC countries from Israel—that is, a decline in both Israel's exports and her GNP. This would force Israel to reduce its defense expenditure. The Israeli military industry, very proud of its achievements, is highly dependent on strategic raw materials, such as steel, acquired from the pro-Western world; and on a considerable technical exchange of information, including access of Israeli scientists and engineers to facilities and know-how abroad. These could be cut off if Israel adopts the openly nuclear defense posture (assuming Israel does so first, and in contradiction of U.S. policy). If Israel goes openly nuclear after one or more Arab countries have done so, or following thorough policy coordination with the United States, the U.S. response would probably be different.

The Defense Postures and the Threats

I will now examine the extent to which each of Israel's defense postures can cope with each of the threats.

Nuclear Threats

Israel has no effective way of responding to the transfer of nuclear bombs by the Soviet Union to an Arab country. Such an action could be balanced by a U.S. move, be it a counterthreat against the Soviet Union or a transfer of similar weapons to Israel. Such a response by the United States is possible so long as Israel has done nothing to antagonize the United States, a criterion best met by the conventional posture.

There is a limit to what Israel could do if France, India, or the People's Republic of China were to pass nuclear bombs to an Arab state. The conventional posture would be an inappropriate response to such a French–Arab, Indian–Arab, or Chinese–Arab move. The probability that the United States would effectively neutralize such a move is low, and, from Israel's perspective, cannot be relied upon. Yet, even an Israeli nuclear posture might have limited effectiveness. France, India, or China, if they decide to supply bombs to an Arab state, might be able to supply more than a "nuclear Israel" possesses.

The conventional response would be inappropriate to a successful openly nuclear posture in an Arab country with indigenous production of bombs. A bomb-in-the-basement posture might encourage the Arab states or some of them to "go nuclear." An Israeli response of going openly nuclear second might be best, though, if too late, it might provoke the Arab actor to utilize the initial success of having bombs by striking first.

The response to the acquisition of a bomb by an Arab or non-Arab terrorist organization is problematic for Israel, and it is my opinion that none of the preceding postures is appropriate, as terrorists attempting to smuggle a bomb into Israel would have few inhibitions about Israel's response.

Conventional Threats

A terrorist or guerrilla operation by the PLO or a radical Arab state, motivated by ideology ("Keep the struggle going") or the search for political sympathy, would not be deterred by an Israeli nuclear posture. A nuclear posture, by convincing the Arabs that a nonnuclear all-out war has no prospects of success, might only accelerate terrorist or guerrilla acts of the PLO or other Arab actors. The only possible response to small-scale armed actions against Israel is a conventional one. Even if they were to possess an openly acknowledged nuclear arsenal, the people and government of Israel would not possibly approve the employment of a nuclear reprisal against perpetrators of "small" aggressions. Furthermore, as a nuclear posture would come at the expense of modernizing and upgrading Israel's conventional capability, the only appropriate Israeli response to terrorist and guerrilla activity would be a conventional defense posture.

Israel could respond to a conventional Arab war with a conventional defense posture, as long as the aggression remained on a scale not immediately endangering its existence. Even if Israel had openly acknowledged nuclear bombs, the Israeli people and government would not approve their use in such a contingency. Furthermore, as such a threat might actually succeed in triggering political momentum toward negotiations (as happened after the War of Attrition in 1970, and after the 1973 Yom Kippur War) the Israeli response to the events would have to be not only military, but also political.

An Arab war or renewal of hostilities in order to "score points" with the Soviet Union, or hurt the U.S. interests in the Middle East, or try to induce the United States to limit its support of Israel resemble the last threats cited. A conventional Israeli defense posture has good chance of coping with such a threat, provided that the capability to escalate and damage the Arab actors by a successful all-out war exists as it did in 1967, and to some extent in the second part of the 1973 war.

A war of attrition aimed at causing Israeli waste of economic resources, casualties, and so on is similar to a limited Arab war in its implications. The best Israeli response would be a conventional one, including a threat to escalate to an all-out war.

A war to regain part or all of the territories lost by the Arabs in 1967 is, from Israel's perspective, similar to a war aimed at beating Israel step by step, first cutting off some of the territories, and later proceeding to the next phase: total destruction of Israel. If such an Arab threat were successful there would be a great temptation on the Arab side to "go for it."

There is an undefined threshold between an Arab war to regain territories lost in 1967, a war to do the same as a "step" toward destruction of the remainder of Israel, and a war setting in advance the maximal Arab goal of destroying Israel. In all three cases, Israel would be required to respond with its conventional armed forces. It is reasonable to expect that the Arab side would be vague about its goal (be it a limited "regaining of territories" or destruction of Israel).

As this Arab threat is a conventional threat, the Arab actors may or may not be deterred from launching conventional all-out war against Israel if Israel were to adopt an openly nuclear posture. It is more likely to persuade them to proclaim their goals as limited, and not justify Israeli use of nuclear weapons. As the Israeli deterrent would thus fail to prevent the Arabs from launching a conventional war, Israel (assuming she had adopted an openly nuclear defense posture) would have to decide if and when to use it. As long as the conventional Israeli forces managed to cope with the threat, there would be no justification for using nuclear weapons.

Under what conditions, if and when Israel had nuclear bombs, would their actual use be accepted by the government and people of Israel? A precondition is that the Israeli situation be desperate, that is, a large segment of her armed forces defeated, a large portion of her efficient air force, her command and control facilities destroyed, and part of the territories held by Israel (both territories taken in 1967 and territories belonging to pre-1967 Israel) lost. Under such conditions, however, it is not certain that Israel would still be capable of launching an effective nuclear strike.

If Israel adopts the openly nuclear defense posture, it implies that her conventional forces would be weaker (assuming the "everything else assumption" as discussed above). Therefore, when facing the threat of an Arab all-out conventional war, the Israeli optimal posture is not clear. There are benefits to be attributed to an openly nuclear posture, as part of an effort to convince the Arab actors to drop altogether the threat to launch an all-out conventional war against Israel. There are also incentives to repel such a threat by an efficient conventional armed force, which implies devoting all or almost all resources available to improving Israel's conventional capabilities. But the conventional Israeli defense posture is not foolproof. A conventional defense posture combined with Israeli errors could lead to a successful Arab surprise attack.

Perhaps no absolutely successful Israeli defense posture exists, and Israel has to make its choice between two or three options, without knowing for sure that she "is safe" once and for all.

To What Extent Can Israel Rely on Foreign Aid in an Extreme Emergency?

Since 1948, Israel has had a unit from a friendly foreign armed force on her soil to help her only once. This was one squadron of French fighter aircraft during the 1956 Sinai Campaign. Even this single occasion of a foreign unit aiding Israel in an emergency was unnecessary, and Israel would have been better off if this step had not been taken. She was, even then, quite capable of handling the situation on her own. In 1948, 1967, 1969–70, 1973, and 1982 Israel fought her enemies without the aid of friendly troops. Friendly foreign troops are unlikely to participate in any future Israeli–Arab war, and Israel would do better without them.

Moshe Dayan, Israel's chief of general staff (1953–1958) and defense minister (1967–1974) publicly told the United States that Israel does not ask them to shed the blood of a single American soldier for Israel's defense. This approach prevails today, and conversely the United States, the country friendliest to Israel, is very hesitant, after Vietnam and after Lebanon, to send troops to allies abroad if there is no specific commitment to do so. Currently there is no such commitment, though Nasser before 1967 said that it is not only Israel he has to fight, but the "imperialists" who would come to her aid.

What kind of aid can Israel expect from the United States or other friendly countries if a war breaks out? Israel has received several forms of aid in the past, and by and large, these could be given in the future.

Financial Aid for Defense. This type of aid has been received especially since the 1969–70 War of Attrition peaking with the 1973 War and the Egyptian–Israeli agreement, plus Israel's withdrawal from Sinai. Financial aid has been suspended or reduced on all occasions of strong political disagreement between Israel and the United States. I expect that financial aid will be cut if Israel goes openly nuclear in a manner that antagonizes the United States.

Sale or Grant of Arms and Ammunition. In all past wars Israel has obtained, for free or under convenient terms of payment, arms, ammunition, and spare parts from friendly countries, specifically the Soviet bloc in 1948, France in 1956, and the United States in 1970 and 1973. One outstanding illustration of Israel's vulnerability to the policy preferences of the arms supplier was given in 1967, when France objected to Israel's decision to launch the 1967 Six-Day War and embargoed the supply of arms, ammunition, and spare parts to Israel. Fifty Mirage fighters (already paid for) and some French-built missile boats were held back for a long time. The United States suspended the supply of arms to Israel on several occasions (in 1976, when Israel did not go along with the U.S. request to accept the intermediate agreement with Egypt, and in 1982 when, as a result of disagreement regarding Israel's conduct of the Lebanon War, the United States temporarily suspended supply of F-15s and F-16s). Israel has thus far managed to get the arms needed to defend herself, yet supply has depended on "no major political disagreement" between the supplier and Israel.

Political Support. This form of aid to Israel has included U.N. votes for Israel, veto of U.N. Security Council resolutions against Israel, and negotiations with the Soviet Union regarding the latter's intervention (or lack of it) in the Arab–Israeli conflict. As in the case of financial aid and arms transfers, political support for Israel has come from the United States or other countries (the Soviet Union in 1948, France in 1956, the Federal Republic of Germany on various occasions) when there was political understanding between Israel and the specific country. Israel's conventional defense posture is better suited to the maintenance of political understanding with the United States and Europe than would be a nuclear one.

There is no mutual defense treaty between Israel and the United States, nor is such a treaty likely to be signed. The three kinds of U.S. support to Israel weigh heavily in favor of Israel. The support permits Israel to be well armed with conventional weapon systems and deters the Arab actors from waging a war they calculate they are not (yet) prepared to win. The Arabs assume that in the event of another war, the United States will continue to provide Israel with money, arms, spare parts, and political support. The availability of foreign aid weighs heavily in favor of Israel opting for a conventional defense posture.

The Appropriate Israeli Response to Threats

There is no single Israeli defense posture which would cover adequately all possible threats. There are even some threats, though not highly probable, to which no one of the three major defense postures discussed is an appropriate response. It follows that a foolproof defense posture is not at hand, and Israel has to make her choice by a criterion other than one which covers all possible contingencies.

The openly nuclear defense posture has the advantage of being a relatively efficient response if one or more Arab states go openly nuclear (as there are signs several such states may do). It has the advantage of being unequivocal, with a better chance to deter the Arab states, if they have the bomb. This is the argument that leads Shai Feldman to advocate an openly nuclear posture.[16] It does not cover the gamut of conventional threats, guerrilla activities, terror, maritime or aerial blockade, hijacking of aircraft. It is likely to draw U.S. response in the form of cutting aid and support, as well as cutting Israeli access to high technology. It is certain to encourage Arab states to go nuclear, though they may do so even if Israel maintains a conventional defense posture.

The conventional Israeli defense posture has the advantage of coping well with all conventional threats, though with no absolute certainty that deterrence will work, and with no guarantee that in case of a war in which Israel makes unforeseen errors, the end result would be favorable for Israel. It would contribute to continued U.S. aid to Israel, political support, and cooperation. It has the disadvantage, however, of not coping with a nuclear threat from an openly nuclear Arab state, nor is it certain that the conventional Israeli defense posture would deter the Arabs from trying to implement the conventional threat of all-out war.

The bomb-in-the-basement defense posture tries to minimize some of the deficiencies of both the open nuclear and the conventional defense postures. It may reap the benefit of keeping the enemy uncertain as to Israel's actual nuclear capability, thus acting as a deterrent. It runs the risk of wasting too many resources on a "limited" (and not open) nuclear effort at the expense of the conventional forces while the most probable threat is that of full-scale conventional war. It could be highly provocative, and might prove inadequate to deter any or all the Arab states from going openly nuclear. It might also fail to deter an attempt at full-scale conventional war. Last, it suggests cheating and may antagonize the United States, resulting in a deterioration of Israeli–U.S. relations, with a corresponding decline in aid and cooperation.

There are threats which cannot be covered by any of these defense postures, such as the threat of terrorist activity, especially if terrorists manage to obtain nuclear weapons. Also, no Israeli defense posture is, on its own, capable of coping with a threat in which the Soviet Union participates massively. In this respect, the cooperation of the United States is among the best things Israel can hope for. Therefore Israel should choose the best defense posture available and most suited to the assumed threats, while making every effort to find solutions to those threats not covered by that defense posture.

Because of the intermediate probability of a full-scale conventional war (possibly starting with limited objectives and later accelerating into a war to destroy Israel), a conventional defense posture would be most appropriate. Nonetheless, Israel has to be prepared in case one or more of the Arab states reach the stage at which they will "almost" have a bomb available. At such a point, Israel would have to rethink, and might then change her posture to a "basement" or nuclear one. To enable Israel to make such a change when required, she must maintain scientific and technological know-how in the nuclear field. I therefore recommend a conventional defense posture; that is, an allocation of most of Israel's resources to the effort to maintain and improve conventional capabilities, yet without impairing Israel's ability, within a short time span, to produce nuclear weapons if required. Although Israel, as a small state, cannot anticipate every conceivable threat, a proper choice means that Israel will have done the best possible to defend itself.

7
The Imperative to Survive

Robert Harkavy

I n contrast to other selections in this book and to the bulk of the extant
academic literature on this subject, I will argue that Israel probably requires a nuclear arsenal (or other equivalent mass destruction deterrent)
to survive. For Israel, survival under the best of foreseeable circumstances is
highly precarious, but possession of nuclear weapons will likely improve the
odds. How much so, and under what circumstances, is of course highly
conjectural.

By long habit and inclination I am more at home with a technical, de-
scriptive, or straightforward historical style of writing on such subjects than
with policy advocacy or normative analysis. But I have been requested to
argue from a prescriptive position in this chapter. Hence, the cards will immediately be placed face-up on the table. My values and predictions will,
partly because of space limitations, appear raw and unvarnished, somewhat
lacking in the nuance which might be allowed for in a longer effort. So be it!
The prospect of post-Holocaust Jewry's need to resort to mass nuclear destruction is by its nature an emotion-laden, raw subject. And, the subject is
one for which examination of worst-case scenarios is fully justified.

Assumption 1

A "permanent" peace in the Middle East, or even a semipermanent one involving a lengthy peaceful truce following a "comprehensive peace agreement," is highly unlikely, in the near or distant future. This is assumed to be
the case even if a formal comprehensive Arab–Israeli peace agreement were
signed, one which involved all of the relevant regional nations, the Soviet
Union, and the United States; one which resulted in a fully independent Palestinian state led by the Palestine Liberation Organization, with its capital in
East Jerusalem, and a *complete* Israeli withdrawal to the borders of June 5,
1967 (that is, the return of "every inch" of pre-1967 Arab territory). The
same goes for a solution involving the internationalization of Jerusalem! The

same goes, indeed, for an Israeli return to the pre-1948 borders defined by the partition which preceded the War of Independence.

While one or another such "final" peace agreement would be greeted with even more widespread euphoria than Camp David, the peace would be temporary, a mere interlude preceding a "final" assault on a truncated and weakened Israel (either with or without the "demilitarization" of the West Bank). The only relevant questions would be the length of the interlude, and the length to which Arab leaders might or might not bother to go to mask their ultimate intentions.

The reason for this pessimism—sited at one extreme of the spectrum of such perspectives—involves a belief that at its essence, the Middle East conflict is not fundamentally one of territorial irredentism or self-determination, nor is it simply a zero-sum clash of rival nationalisms over control of Palestine. Those are, of course, contributing factors. But a more fundamental reason that a "permanent" peace assumes the nature of a virtual "impossibility" is the overwhelming, deep-seated humiliation felt by all Arabs over having been defeated some six times in wars by Israel. This humiliation has caused the Arabs, most importantly in their own eyes, to become virtually a laughing stock of the world. The following quotation drawn from a *New York Times* interview after Anwar Sadat's assassination captures some of the flavor of what is involved:

> Tallal's depression and subsequent turn toward a more fundamental belief in Islam after the 1967 war is, by all accounts, not uncommon. Many people feel that the resurgence of Islamic militancy in Egypt dates to that overwhelming defeat . . . everyone was questioning themselves after the war . . . they kept asking what it was about our society, our culture, our political system that could pave the way for such a defeat.[1]

Hence, the near-overwhelming craving for vengeance to remove the stain of humiliation and disgrace (and it should not be forgotten that analyses of Arab political culture, even in other contexts involving domestic politics, stress the crucial importance of "face" and shame). Witness, indeed, the young men in Beirut careening about on the backs of jeeps, with their mounted machine guns; the truck bombings; the biting off of heads of snakes and stabbing of puppies on Syrian television; the seemingly desperate irrationality of Arab politics; even the occasional confession to Westerners that Arab perspectives on Israel are something simply not understood, not to be talked about.

Such humiliation and its various symptoms can, of course, have been observed elsewhere in the wake of defeat in war, for instance, in post-Falklands Argentina. But there is something unique, something much deeper about Arab humiliation.[3] The Arabs have long maintained a self-image of themselves as a warrior people with a proud history best exemplified by Saladin's ultimate defeat of the Crusaders. And, like many Westerners, they have long thought of the Jews as an altogether contemptible, despicable bunch of over-intellectualized sissies, a people well suited for law, finance, or sociology, but never war.[4] To be defeated six times by such sissies—and vastly outnumbered sissies at that—has resulted, for the Arabs, in what without exaggeration might be described as history's most stunning case of collective national, "testicular" devastation. On such a basis, peace cannot easily be grounded; the Arabs desperately require vengeance. Israel is riding the proverbial tiger! And, as has so often been pointed out, the Arabs can lose many wars; Israel's first defeat will be its last. These matters are both obvious and banal, yet their ultimate meaning is often submerged or obscured by the day-to-day barrage of minutiae detailing the latest Talmudic interpretations of PLO–Jordanian communications or the modalities of Israeli withdrawal from Lebanon. Trees and forests, indeed!

Assumption 2

A shift in the conventional military balance in favor of the Arabs is, ultimately, inevitable. Whether that will occur in two, five, ten, or twenty years is hard to say, but only the timing would appear at issue.

Projection of this balance is, of course, not only conjectural but also subject to vastly fluctuating interpretations in the light of the most recent wars or developments in weapons and major power arms transfers. The 1967 war gave rise to euphoria in Israel about a long-term military preponderance; the war in 1973 seemed to suggest a far more precarious outlook, all the more so as the assumed demise of "King Tank" and tactical airpower seemed to suggest an historical shift in advantage to defensive, attrition warfare which would be highly disadvantageous to Israel.[5] But then in 1982, with Egypt on the sidelines, Jordan neutralized, and Iraq otherwise occupied, Israel's astounding success with its newer weapons and tactics (air-to-surface missiles, drones, remotely piloted vehicles (RPVs), battle management, new tank ammunition and armor, etc.) seemed to suggest a still newer phase of preponderance, maybe a widening gap, with some pundits heralding a new electronic age of warfare deemed highly advantageous for Israel.[6] But then, more recently, studies at Tel Aviv University's Jaffee Center for Strategic Studies waxed pessimistic about the emerging Middle Eastern military balance. They and others saw the advent of pushbutton warfare as perhaps transcending qualitative manpower distinctions.[7] "Fire and forget" weapons could be operated and maintained by peasants! And, some military analysts, Trevor DuPuy and Michael Handel among them, warned, citing Clausewitz, that *mass* counts, that there is a point at which quantity overwhelms quality, a "law" to which even the exalted IDF must submit.[8] All in all, the jury seemed out, but among the critical variables to be watched were the following:

The extent to which Arab oil revenues (here dependent on the future of the Organization of Petroleum Exporting Countries) can be translated into further increases in crucial, fieldable combat manpower in the Arab confrontation states, particularly Egypt and Syria (I assume that Egypt will again become a confrontation state, perhaps sooner than later)

The extent to which the Arabs can coordinate offensive strategies among all or most possible participants in conflicts and hence conduct simultaneous warfare on several fronts (including, at maximum strength, full participation by Egypt, Syria, Jordan, Iraq, Saudi Arabia, and Lebanon, and at least token participation by Kuwait, Sudan, Libya, Algeria, and Morocco)

The extent to which U.S. arms shipments to Israel continue to match (or maintain present ratios) quantitatively and qualitatively those to the various Arab states from the Soviet Union and Western Europe, as well as from the United States

The extent to which emerging weapons technology and associated doctrines and tactics will allow Israel to pursue its traditional, preemptive-offensive short-war strategy emphasizing armor and tactical airpower shock assault tactics[9]

The extent to which Israel can successfully assume a new, essentially defensive warfare strategy (or a defensive/offensive counterattack strategy) based on the realities of new weapons technologies, without suffering unduly from the potential human and economic losses entailed

The extent to which Israel's continuing imperative to preempt under certain circumstances would be restrained by U.S. diplomatic pressure, with its underlying threat of arms cut-off

The willingness and capability of the various major powers to resupply arms to both sides in extended conflicts

The extent to which a physical Soviet intervention on behalf of the Arabs would be likely to become a factor and under what circumstances

Future Israeli morale, in turn related to a host of gradual, ongoing internal societal changes

The future ability of the Israeli economy to sustain its war machine: "de-bureaucratization," monetary reform, U.S. aid, "high-tech" export industries, etc.

Overall, the keys would appear to be two: the role of Egypt's now increasingly huge army, and the extent to which Israel's qualitative gap in manpower and weapons is narrowed so as to tip the overall balance. In my judgment, ten years is about the maximum period Israel can count on maintaining its edge.

Assumption 3

If Israel should one day suffer a decisive conventional battlefield defeat, a terrible full-scale massacre would ensue, even in the face of last-minute American entreaties (later I shall note the relationship of Israeli nuclear weapons to a possible "Exodus-withdrawal" scenario). This follows almost automatically from the previous comments regarding the depth of Arab shame over previous defeats. Further (and this point would appear a bit more speculative) levels of anti-Semitism throughout most of the world would rise rather than fall if Israel were destroyed and its population massacred. Contrary to common yet idle speculations about widespread guilt reflexes in response to the Holocaust, there has been an historical psychological connection between Jewish defeat and pathos, and sadistic anti-Semitism; this predicts a still more nightmarish Jewish existence in a post-Israel world. In the United States and elsewhere, anti-Semitism was (as I have experienced it) at a high level right after 1945, declined significantly after 1956 and much more so after 1967, then rose again after 1973. In this sense too, Israel (and world Jewry) has a tiger by the tail.

Value Premise

Other selections in this book have treated the subject from the perspectives of international law, and of Jewish morality. One can respect the motives of such arguments, but they appear irrelevant, weak, or trivial in relation to the magnitude of what is here involved. In a perhaps more cynical and pessimistic vein, the resort in this case to legalistic and moralistic arguments must be interpreted, variously, as a curiously stubborn masochism which runs like a red thread through Jewish life (no better illustrated than by the recent attempts at reestablishing a "black–Jewish alliance" in the face of persistent anti-Semitism on the part of the bulk of America's black political leadership), a peculiar arrogance or condescension which refuses to take others' emotions and "irrational" drives seriously, or simply a pronounced tendency, borne of centuries of terror and victimization, to avoid reality.

Quite simply stated, my view is that the relentlessly hysterical level of opprobrium and anti-Semitic hatred directed at Israel by most of the world's nations (best exemplified by the interminable verbal onslaught within the United Nations and other international forums) over the past decades completely erases or negates any possible moral obligation that Israel might otherwise hold toward the remainder of mankind. As applied to the possession or use of nuclear weapons, this means that the criterion of Israeli survival must vastly outweigh other putatively moral or legal concerns. Israel owes the so-called international community nothing. The latter deserves nothing. And, indeed, the bizarre and one-sidedly vicious behavior of the representatives of this "international community" render fatuous any discussion of international law in connection with Israeli security. As for moral tradition, I would prefer the norms of the Bronx or Yonkers, familiar to many American Jews, rules which hold that a people, or gang, or individual outnumbered, outweighed, or whatever by bullies holding a preponderance of 20 to 1 or 50 to 1 has the "moral" right to use an "equalizer." For Israel, nuclear weapons are the moral and practical equivalent to a knife or pistol wielded by a scrawny man in a menacing neighborhood, particularly when threatened by a mob.

If there is any external audience or body of opinion to which Israel owes a "moral debt" or to which it ought to feel obliged to listen, it is the American people and their political leadership. That and that alone! That people and their government—not without a few ups and downs—have treated Israel with an astounding decency and generosity over many years, through thick and thin, and often in the very face of the seeming imperatives of national interest. That decency has further been maintained even despite the often inexplicable antics of the U.S. Jewish left, seemingly ever-bent on self-destruction, and frozen in a pattern of policy preferences so obviously damaging to retention of the crucial U.S.–Israeli tie.[10]

If the conventional military balance should shift against Israel, only one of two things could then maintain its survival: deterrence with weapons of mass destruction, or, an ironclad U.S. security guarantee (either in the form of a formal alliance or a widely understood intention to use force to ensure Israel's survival).[11] The latter is the sole alternative to the former if, in the long run, Israel's own conventional deterrence cannot remain viable and credible. And despite the foregoing comments, if the United States in the future is unwilling to underwrite Israel's security, or if in a particular crisis it is unwilling to act (perhaps because of then current vicissitudes of domestic American politics), then the one reasonable *moral* argument against Israel's use of nuclear weapons will have vanished. If the United States lets Israel down in the clutch, it cannot expect Israel to listen to moral arguments which amount to passive acceptance of its own destruction.

Some As Yet Unanswered Questions

A number of earlier open-source analyses, including my own, have been devoted to speculative histories of the Israeli nuclear weapons program, such as it is and has been.[12] Those analyses have traced the lengthy skein of published overt developments beginning with the Franco–Israeli collaboration of the mid to late 1950s; the origins of the Dimona reactor and of alleged U.S. inspections thereof; *l'affaire* Apollo, PA/NUMEC Corporation (Nuclear Material and Equipment Corporation) in its various versions and the associated perspectives thereon of U.S. governmental agencies; the significance of the Jericho missile program which came to light around 1966; and the various "exposés" of the alleged Israeli program in *Der Spiegel, Penthouse, Ramparts,* and *Time* magazines and others, each of which raised interesting questions about who was leaking what and for what purpose.[13] Afterward followed the rumors of Israeli nuclear deployments and threats in October 1973, the mysterious flash over the Indian Ocean in 1979 (variously speculated upon as an Israeli, South African, joint Israeli–South African, Indian, or even French nuclear bomb test, along with a plethora of more benign explanations involving space debris, faulty satellite monitoring, natural atmospheric phenomena, and so on), the Israeli preemption of Iraq's nuclear facility, and even a bewildering, contradictory, and somewhat inexplicable series of official and semiofficial Israeli statements broaching the possibility of a Middle Eastern nuclear weapons free zone.

By 1985 the jury still seemed out regarding an outside assessment of the size, scope, or mere existence of an Israeli nuclear weapons program. Some preferred to see it as a mere bluff and continued to treat Israel's very decision to go nuclear as still contingent and up for grabs. At the other end of the spectrum there were wild, hushed rumors in Washington corridors of an Israeli nuclear arsenal of up to 200 deployed weapons—thermonuclear weapons, neutron bombs, and tactical as well as strategic weapons were whispered about, albeit on the basis of no more than prurient scuttlebutt. Generally, the speculations covered two related, fundamental sets of questions.

1. *The historical course or route of Israel's nuclear development*—how and when nuclear weapons-grade material was obtained, when and why go-ahead decisions were made, what internal divisions there have been among Israel's national security elites

2. *The current state of Israel's nuclear weapons program*—number and types of weapons systems, designated delivery systems, deployment, or use of storage sites, related command, control, communication, and intelligence (C^3I) capabilities, alert and dispersion procedures and capabilities, nuclear doctrines and contingent decisionmaking (is there an Israeli SIOP [Single Integrated Operational Plan]?)

I don't pretend to know the answers; indeed, I do not know whether truly accurate answers are held within relevant U.S., Soviet, or other intelligence agencies. That being said, the literature appears to reveal a central, convergent core of "received wisdom" on this subject (whether accurate or not, who can tell?), which in admitting to some variations on a central theme, goes something like this:

The basic decisions to go nuclear, or to provide for that option on a relatively short-term basis, appear to have been made in the late 1950s and early 1960s. The actual first deployment of weapons—or, short of that, a short-term capability realizable by a "turn of the screw"—seems to have been achieved somewhere between about 1966 and 1970–71 (one great conundrum involves the point at which Israel first began to reprocess plutonium, either on a large scale or perhaps in a so-called hot lab on a very limited basis). Most analyses have Israel deploying nuclear weapons between the 1967 and 1973 wars, in response variously to events surrounding the former (U.S. reluctance with diplomatic support in connection with the Straits of Tiran closure, overall diplomatic isolation, alleged Egyptian nerve gas stockpiles in Sinai); to events surrounding the 1969–70 "War of Attrition" (particularly the more active role taken by Soviet pilots and air defense cadres); or to the sheer technological momentum of a program coming to fruition during this period. Occasional rumors have Israel nuclear-armed at the time of the 1967 war; if so, that would appear to point to transfer of either weapons-grade nuclear materials or bombs by France, or to the development of weapons in 1966–67 based on U-235 spirited out of NUMEC/Apollo. If a later date is preferred, say 1970–1973, that would appear to point to initiation of reprocessing somewhere during that period, though to this day, little if any public information to that end has surfaced.

By now, of course, Dimona has been in operation for some twenty-four years, presumably providing the basis for a nuclear force of at least forty warheads.[14] Whether a supplementary centrifuge or laser-isotope-separation facility can produce U-235, or whether a step toward thermonuclear weapons has been made is not known here. Noteworthy too is the fact that the Jericho program has received little notice (with one exception[15]) during the past decade (though in a related vein, one hears the rumors about the Ze'ev surface-to-surface missile claimed to have been used against Syrian surface-to-air missile (SAM) sites in 1982,[16] albeit of a reported range well below Jericho's earlier estimated range of some 280 miles). Israel has, however, now had a lot of time to resolve the earlier rumored problems with Jericho's guidance; for that matter, time as well to move ahead with a new generation of missiles.[17] And, the startling performance of numerous Israeli, indigenous weapons systems in 1982—avionics, remotely piloted vehicles (RPVs), antiradiation missiles, command and control, artillery, tanks, and so forth—bespeak a variety of capabilities germane to nuclear precociousness. The public silence seems both deafening and telling.

Earlier post-1973 reports had Israel planning to configure its F-4s, Kfir's, and Mirages for nuclear use, perhaps to be supplemented by Jericho. In combination (and keeping in mind Israel's control over Sinai for some seven years after 1973), that appeared to provide deterrence vis-à-vis Damascus, Beirut, Amman, Cairo, Alexandria, and Aswan.[18] The effective use of Arab air defenses in 1973 then seemed to point toward increased difficulty for Israel regarding penetration by aircraft in a crisis, further focusing attention on Jericho (assumed movable if not mobile) as the ultimate deterrent delivery system). Hiding, hardening, airborne alert, and positioning of delivery systems amid hostage Arab populations within the West Bank or Gaza all appeared vital to coping with the threat of a Soviet preemptive strike in a crisis.

Israel's raid on Baghdad's nuclear reactor in 1981 provided a glimpse of the potentially longer nuclear reach provided by newly acquired F-15 and F-16 fighters abetted by tanker refueling. That reach would now presumably extend to Tripoli and the Persian Gulf oilfields as well as to Baghdad, the matters of intrawar alerts (hence, difficulties in achieving surprise) and of Saudi airborne warning and control systems (AWACS) momentarily aside. Israel's navy (perhaps capable of shipborne nuclear delivery) now also had a much longer reach. Lance missiles, perhaps even despite U.S. restrictions on nuclear use, might supplement Jericho for short-range delivery. Meanwhile, the startling electronic warfare (ECM) capability displayed by Israeli aircraft in 1981 seemed to promise an extended period in which its nuclear-armed aircraft might penetrate Arab air spaces for missions of desperation. All in all, the trends regarding Israel's capability to deliver nuclear weapons in a crisis do not appear unfavorable, at least in the short run.

But, for Israel, there is one ominous specter on the horizon in the form of the possible rival U.S. and Soviet deployments of space missile defense systems—in the U.S. case, the strategic defense initiative (SDI), or "Star Wars."[19] Those developments are, of course, now embryonic, and are subject to possible arms control restrictions as well as to technical infeasibilities. But increasingly, there are reports of forward movement on a number of system types—ground- and space-based lasers, kinetic energy weapons, particle beams, and related sensors—some of which could later provide the big powers the easy capability to destroy Nth power nuclear-armed missiles in their boost phases. Whether such capability could be extended to that of negating endoatmospheric, short-range missiles or cruise missiles remains yet to be seen. It is worth noting, however, that Israel's presumed present assumptions about assured delivery capability via missiles could later be called into question, perhaps even in circumstances where there would be a convergent U.S.–Soviet interest in suppressing a desperate last-resort nuclear attack. That in turn focuses attention, however hazily, on a possible later Israeli requirement for circumventing SDI, perhaps by atomic demolition munitions (ADMs—"suitcase" bombs), or other exotic methods or one or another manner of dispersal.

Nothing here is known about Israeli nuclear storage policy (centralization versus dispersion), or about C³I capabilities related to contingent nuclear decisionmaking. Those subjects are both vitally important in connection with deterrence, war-fighting, probabilities of accidental war or unauthorized launch, vulnerability to preemptive attack, and other issues—and utterly obscured by secrecy. It can probably be assumed that they receive very extensive attention from top Israeli military planners. The nation's very small size (and the probability that even that limited space would be reduced in a crisis requiring consideration of use of nuclear weapons) and vulnerability either to a "bolt from the blue" or intrawar nuclear preemption render these very critical and sensitive problems. If Iraq or other Arab states acquire their own nuclear weapons anytime soon, those problems will be compounded, quite probably in the direction of increased overall nuclear crisis instability.

Whether or not internal Israeli security decisionmaking now involves a nuclear doctrinal dimension is not known. There is nothing in the public domain to indicate whether there have been fluctuating doctrinal debates—familiar to U.S. policymakers—involving massive retaliation versus flexible response, counterforce versus countervalue strategies, differential targeting of elites (decapitation), preemptive first strike versus deterrence via escalation dominance, tactical versus strategic use. (Such questions in the United States have often contained ideological divisions, also interservice rivalries.) These matters will, however, subsequently be incorporated into a discussion of nuclear rationales, involving a host of issues which impinge upon or cut across those involved with doctrines and strategies.

The Rationales for Israeli Nuclear Weapons

A number of years ago, in discussing the possible utility of Israeli nuclear weapons, I presented the following list of rationales, in no particular order of priority or significance. The reader is referred to the accompanying discussion, not repeatable here in full because of space limitations. It may be worthwhile, however, now almost a decade later, to ask what may have changed in *relative* assessments of these rationales. What remains valid, what has changed? How may some perceptions have been altered? Preceding a scenario for the last-resort contingency which is at the core of the problem, some brief updates of the remaining rationales follow.[20]

A "last resort" countercities deterrent in the face of conventional warfare defeat and of the overrunning and possible wholesale massacre of the Israeli homeland and population

A deterrent to massacre of the Israeli population in circumstances where its evacuation outside the Middle East might be possible if time permitted—the withdrawal scenario

Use of tactical, battlefield nuclear weapons in situations either of last resort or various crises short of that

A hedge against Arab acquisition of nuclear weapons and sudden use in a preemptive or disarming first strike, and against terrorist or other use of weapons of mass destruction within Israel

Deterrence of massive Arab use of conventional city-busting weapons (aircraft or missiles) or of chemical, biological, or radiological warfare weapons

A psychological weapon against the Arabs, intended to discourage their goal of final annihilation of Israel and to make them more amenable to a final peace agreement entailing acceptance of Israel's existence

A latent, if weak, threat against the prospect of a series of wars of attrition which could bleed Israel white or destroy its economy, or against significant escalation of boycotts and other forms of economic warfare which could cripple Israel

A weak deterrent against Soviet involvement in a conventional war, even if that were only intended to forestall an Israeli march on Damascus or Cairo

Deterrence of other nations not now involved in the Arab–Israeli confrontation (particularly Iran and Turkey) entering the fray on the Arab side

Posing a triangular second-strike capability against Arab cities and the Soviet Union to deter possible Soviet intentions to destroy Israel, either for political-strategic reasons or in further escalation of anti-Semitism in the Soviet Union to the level earlier exhibited by Nazi Germany[21]

A weapon of leverage against the United States and possibly other Western states to ensure a continued supply of conventional arms and a modicum of diplomatic support, banking on big power fears that Israel might be forced to adopt a massive retaliation doctrine, and on anxiety about catalytic nuclear war escalating to the superpower level

Achievement of a psychological sense of independence for Israel to offset uncomfortable though necessary dependence on the United States (explicable in the light of centuries of Jewish dependence on gentile assistance or forbearance for survival)

Assurance of ultimate survival for Israel which would allow the government to divest conquered territory in response to pressure and in the face of resistance at home

Use of nuclear technology transfer as a bargaining chip in dealing with other nations, perhaps in exchange for cash, trade outlets, diplomatic support, raw materials supply, or conventional arms acquisition

There is little to reveal whether Israel has moved, over the past decade, toward contemplation of use of tactical nuclear weapons. With the passage of time, the presumed growth of Israel's inventory of nuclear-grade material would appear to allow for stockpiling of weapons *both* for countercities and battlefield use (in a technical sense, there is not much distinction, save for the issue of relative sizing). Stated another way, Israel could deploy and use some battlefield weapons, and still retain an ultimate countercities threat needed for escalation dominance relative to the Arabs, the major problems of a Soviet response momentarily left aside.

The small size of the military theaters Israel must defend, and the seemingly favorable possibilities for "channeling" and then destroying numerically larger Arab armies appears obvious. But, there are also problems here for Israel. Nuclear use in Sinai in particular might pose a reverse downwind radiation threat to Israeli cities, in turn focusing at least hypothetical attention on low-radiation weapons or neutron bombs. And, of course, if the Arabs too were to acquire tactical nuclear weapons, a battlefield nuclear exchange which heavily attrited both sides might work to the advantage of the numerically superior side. But, if the alternative were complete conventional collapse, and defeat, then that might be perceived as a lesser of evils. First use by Israel might bring a dramatic Soviet response, raising in turn the question of Israel's countercities deterrence vis-à-vis either Arab or perhaps Soviet cities. But then, such use might also scare the superpowers into arranging a ceasefire lest the conflict escalate out of control. Much depends on Israel's back-up nuclear deterrent threat *after* tactical battlefield use, and how that is perceived elsewhere.

In recent years, the well-publicized moves both by Iraq and Pakistan toward nuclear weapons status have raised the threat to Israel of an Arab preemptive nuclear strike to serious levels. This point retains its salience even if it is the case that Arab or Islamic nuclear acquisitions may be perceived as reactive and primarily intended to diminish the efficacy of Israel's nuclear deterrent, and even if it is further the case that the Arabs would most likely be happier with a nuclear-free Middle East which would promise them an ultimate military preponderance based on numbers. Israel must, in the future, fear the possibility of a preemptive first strike, even a "bolt from the blue" not connected to an escalating crisis. And given the mystery of the Pakistani program, Israel may never again trust—on verification grounds alone—the assertion of a nuclear-free region. Beyond that, Israel, particularly given its small size and concentrated populations, must now worry about hiding or dispersing its nuclear deterrent, and about maintaining the effectiveness of its nuclear command and control even in the wake of an intended disarming first strike which, by its very nature, would also obliterate most of Israel. Quite probably, this is now a more or less permanent condition, notwithstanding the temporary respite provided by the Baghdad raid. Further, whatever hope might once have existed of a permanently nuclear-free Middle East has quite probably faded, perhaps forever.

Deterrence of Arab use of chemical or biological weapons may also now be considered a matter even more serious than during the period subsequent to the 1967 war, when Israeli troops were claimed to have captured Egyptian nerve gas reserves in the Sinai (the latter may well have been an important impetus to Israel's subsequent deployment of nuclear arms). The use of such weapons by Iraq, rumors of impending Iranian retaliation, and Soviet use of poison gas and toxins in Afghanistan and Laos in combination appear to have lowered the threshold which has been, with a few exceptions, maintained since World War I. Whether Israel banks on its own chemical warfare or biological warfare capabilities to deter Arab use of same, or rather—similar to apparent U.S. planning for Central Europe—banks on nuclear arms for that purpose is not at all clear.[22] Deterrence of terrorist use of weapons of mass destruction might appear, simultaneously, less ultimately vital in connection with Israel's sheer survival, but also more problematic in light of the nearly irrational elements involved.

Whether or not the late President Sadat's visit to Jerusalem and the subsequent Camp David accords—assuming the latter were sincerely entered into by the Egyptians—were at least in part impelled by the assumption that Israel's nuclear weapons assured the survival of the Jewish state, is not at all clear.[23] Suffice it to say that speculation has been advanced. Whether the same "facts" have moved other Arab states (such as Jordan, Saudi Arabia, and Iraq) closer to resignation to Israel's existence, is equally unclear. The answer, of course, is embedded in broader uncertainties about Arab intentions and perceptions, short and long run, subject to the usual vicissitudes. The view here, generally, as previously stated, is that Arab intentions to destroy Israel have not much abated, nuclear weapons to the contrary.

The economic rationale for Israeli nuclear weapons (that they would allow for leveling off of overall military expenditure) has, of course, been advanced by Moshe Dayan and others.[24] Those arguments have usually stopped well short of advocacy of full abandonment of conventional deterrence and of resort to what would then be, if only implicitly, a massive retaliation doctrine à la John Foster Dulles, circa 1954 (noteworthy, in the U.S. case, based upon the assumption of clear nuclear superiority). By 1985, however, the awful disarray of the Israeli economy, seemingly kept afloat only by increasing but precarious U.S. aid, seemed to give added credence to arguments that Israel's overwhelming conventional defense requirements were gradually destroying its economy. Hence, the arguments for a shift to reliance on nuclear deterrence (with all that entails regarding credibility and escalation, not to mention the political costs in Washington) were likely to grow, perhaps not in politically predictable ways. But, the advent of Arab nuclear capabilities may subsequently weaken those arguments.

Whether the Soviets' relatively passive response to Syria's debacle in 1982 can in any way be attributed to the Israeli nuclear threat is difficult to say. There is no solid evidence to that end. It is noteworthy, however, that the Soviets have since become more vocal about extending a nuclear umbrella over Syria—that is, a threat to respond to any Israeli nuclear use in kind. Just how strong a deterrent that would pose if Israel's conventional forces should collapse is problematical and will be addressed more fully below.

Likewise unclear are the trends regarding Israel's possible nuclear threat against the Soviet Union itself. Heretofore, that has been discussed primarily in the context of the outside chance that Israeli fighter bombers could somehow, amid a crisis, penetrate Soviet air defenses, and reach Baku or Odessa or Sevastopol—in all cases, no easy task.[25] Recent years have seen rumors of Israel's development of cruise missiles which might range into the Soviet Union. But the latter is upgrading its defenses against U.S. cruise missiles (fighters with "look-down, shoot-down" capability), and a version of SDI may later be in the cards. The net trend is unclear. Still, the Soviets must take into account Israel's long-vaunted and astounding capacity for innovative and daring special missions; that tradition does presumably carry nuclear deterrent value. Also not fully to be discounted is Israel's capability to emplace atomic demolition munitions (ADMs) within the Soviet Union before or even during a crisis.

As part of its (never merely hypothetical) "worst-case" planning, Israel must take into account the possible formation of a "grand coalition" of Islamic states, the hitherto chronic fragmentation of the Arab and Islamic "world" notwithstanding. In past wars, nations such as Morocco, the Sudan, and Saudi Arabia have made token contributions of ground troops. In the future, however, Israel must at least take into account possible large-scale contributions from Iran and (if a shift either toward Islamic fundamentalism or Marxism should occur) perhaps Turkey. Addition of the latter's large and formidable army on the Arab side in conjunction (relative to the Iranian case) with relatively short logistical lines via Syria could by itself totally upset the Middle Eastern conventional military balance. That eventuality could one day require deterring by Israeli nuclear weapons, and Israel's now longer delivery reach could be important to that end.

In 1973 it was widely rumored that the U.S. decision to resupply Israel after some ten days of war was impelled, at least to some degree, by fear that the latter's nuclear option was about to be invoked.[26] Since then, there have been periods of U.S.–Israeli tension (for instance, after Israel's raid on the Iraqi nuclear facility and during the 1982 war) when Israel's primary source of arms has been curtailed or made relatively more uncertain, though at no time with even the hint of a full embargo. Still, Israel must worry and its now burgeoning indigenous arms industry, though truly amazing for a nation of 3–4 million persons, can never supplant Washington for the "big ticket" items such as sophisticated aircraft, missiles, and helicopters. Washington is aware, moreover, of the "doves' dilemma" as applied not only to Israel, but to other pariah states (Taiwan, South Korea, South Africa) and to Pakistan, among others.[27] It is a quiet factor in keeping the arms pipeline open, a rarely mentioned but tacitly recognized rationale, though the grounds for it are not shared by all U.S. decisionmakers. The doves' dilemma could, however, one day be posed much more starkly in the event of a U.S. administration only lukewarm in support of Israel or a revival of OPEC oil and financial leverage. The same factors do not normally affect European decisions on arms sales to Israel (most European nations either embargo Israel, de facto, or engage in very limited and nonvisible transfers), for the simple reason that they bank on Uncle Sam to keep Israel armed.

It remains to be seen whether there will be yet another major conventional war between Israel and the Arabs (Egypt's participation is not necessarily excluded, Camp David to the contrary) in which Israel's survival will again hinge on the requirement for massive arms resupply. Not precluded is the possibility that such a crisis could again cause Israel to invoke its nuclear threat, perhaps in a more open and explicit fashion. The current U.S. role as primary arms supplier to Egypt as well as Israel, also to Jordan and Saudi Arabia, may make more likely an all-around "evenhanded" U.S. embargo in another crisis, with the bipolar U.S.–Soviet aspects of previous wars somewhat diminished even if Syria and Iraq remain Soviet arms clients.

The role played by nuclear weapons in Israel's past and present decisionmaking regarding peace arrangements is both obscure and vital. Though many other criteria were involved (not least of which were U.S. pressures) in the decision to return the Sinai as part of the Camp David accords, the nuclear factor was possibly more prominent than generally realized. The possession of nuclear weapons may have rendered an always insecure Israel just a bit more secure about return of Sinai, particularly as Egyptian leaders are thought fully aware of the implications of those weapons. On the other hand, loss of Sinai entailed for Israel a vast reduction in the space available to hide and disperse nuclear delivery systems; loss of a buffer in which tactical nuclear weapons might have been particularly effective and also further removed from Israeli urban centers; and apparent removal of the Aswan Dam from Jericho missiles' targeting range. A possible later decision by Israel to give up all or part of the West Bank as part of a "settlement" with Jordan or the PLO might also have profound implications in connection with Israeli nuclear weapons: further reduction in space for maneuvers of Jericho and the like, increased vulnerability to overrunning of the Dimona complex; a more sensitive nuclear preemptive condition because of Israel's overall greater military vulnerability; the increased vulnerability to conventional missile strikes of Israel's airfields and missile sites; and decrease for Israel of the utility of West Bank Arabs as nuclear hostages within whose bailiwick Israeli nuclear weapons might be deployed.

Israel's use—potential or actual—of its nuclear precocity as an instrument of diplomacy remains unclear. There has, of course, been much speculation about a "pariah international" nexus stretching across Israel, Taiwan, South Africa, and perhaps one or more states of the South American "southern cone."[28] Just what is rumor and what is fact I don't know. The seemingly natural complementarity of nuclear capabilities between Israel and South Africa is apparent: Israel has bomb design capability, delivery systems, and Dimona; South Africa has raw uranium, the nozzle process, a steel industry, and vast spaces for testing. U.S. and other sensibilities aside, the objective conditions for collaboration are obvious. Taiwan's steel and electronics industries and its apparent interest in inertial navigations systems provide for still another possible venue of interpariah collaboration, notwithstanding the rival Saudi–Taiwan tie involving both ideology and the realities of oil, construction contracts, and other matters.[29] All in all, one can merely say there are strong hints of a pariah nuclear nexus, according to some rumors even extending to joint development of cruise missiles.[30] There is also a seeming link to Israel's arms sales to other pariahs, providing a salient parallel to the Franco–Iraqi tie, perhaps too those involving West Germany, Brazil, and Iraq.

Last-Resort Deterrence—The Dominant Scenario

It is generally agreed that the most useful, credible, and compelling rationale for an Israeli nuclear capability is its potential as a "last-resort" countercities threat, with the implied threat of total retaliation for vengeance sake if the deterrent should fail. As some Israelis themselves are wont to state, the overarching imagery is of Samson, not Masada. With the complex problems of penetration and survival capability in mind, one possible scenario will serve to illustrate how the "last resort" scenario might be applicable.

Let us imagine that at some point in the 1990s the Arabs launch an assault similar to that of 1973. This time, however, emboldened by the fact of an obviously shifting balance of power and no longer as cowed by the Israeli blitzkrieg mystique as in the years preceding 1973, Jordan and Saudi Arabia enter the fray at the outset, as does a now engaged Lebanon, so that Israel is immediately confronted by a war on several fronts, further complicated by serious uprisings of Arabs in Israel and the West Bank which preoccupy a portion of the Israeli army. Iraqi, Kuwaiti, Moroccan, Iranian, Sudanese, and

Libyan forces are also in evidence, mobilizing and moving into advanced positions at the war's outset.

Israel, having failed to preempt, but not wishing to be caught flat-footed as in 1973, reacts hastily, after rancorous discussions with a now only moderately friendly U.S. government which makes, on the basis of telltale intelligence indicators, the usual last-minute attempts to dissuade the Arabs from war while leashing the Israelis. Under the circumstances, the Israeli action succeeds only in the sense of getting its army mobilized and into defensive positions. The Arabs' acquisition of truly huge arsenals of conventional arms (increasingly a *qualitative* match for Israel's) simply precludes an even approximate repetition of 1967. The combined Arab forces number over two million troops against Israel's full mobilization of some 500,000. Israel's strategy is that of a mobile defense, hoping to take advantage of an asymmetric attrition war in which its losses can be minimized and its lines of defense maintained.

At the war's outset, however, it becomes apparent that the asymmetric resupply policies of the major powers will again, as in 1973, work in favor of the Arabs. A massive Soviet sea and airlift is mounted in Syria, Iraq, and Egypt (which has by now mended its relations with the Soviet Union and is already equipped with huge quantities of U.S., British, and French arms, acquired gradually to supplement its earlier Soviet-supplied force). The United States, meanwhile, withholds resupply to Israel, hoping for another in situ, limited Arab victory. Further, the loss of the Azores base has made resupply of Israel very difficult and costly, and the Pentagon has grown much more chary of giving up large numbers of weapons on its "critical items" list or of again denuding its pre-positioned military material (POMCUS) stocks in Europe. As in 1973, and despite very extensive stockpiling of weapons since then, Israel soon runs low on ammunition and spare parts in a war of far greater scope and intensity than the earlier one.

After weeks, or perhaps months, of furious attrition warfare, Israel's army begins to crack. Outnumbered and fearfully under-armed, its morale is further sapped by continuous air attacks on Israeli cities by large numbers of bombers directed by AWACS, as well as a relentless bombardment by conventional warhead missiles. Combined Israeli civilian and military casualties mount rapidly into tens of thousands. Like many other cases in history, most recently in Vietnam, when the Israeli army begins to lose heart and crack, it goes to pieces with surprising suddenness. Egyptian armor rolls across Sinai, captures the Abu Agheila redoubt, and begins to invade Beersheba and Nitzana. Jordanian and Saudi troops complete the siege of Eilat after vicious hand-to-hand street fighting. Syrian troops enter the Galilee valleys; Jordanian units overrun the West Bank; and even Lebanon's small Muslim army crosses the Israeli border and threatens Haifa.

In the space of a few disastrous days, it becomes apparent to the Israeli leadership that the war is lost and Arab momentum irreversible. All that remains is the hopeless prospect of last-ditch, house-to-house fighting in the cities and kibbutz settlements by disorganized units using commando techniques and Molotov cocktails against tanks. In contemplating this bitter end of national existence, the Israelis see even more ominous signs: fleeing refugees from the Golan area report grisly massacres of civilians overrun by Syrian troops. The specter of genocide looms. The distraught government faces not only total defeat and yet another Diaspora, but the massacre of most of the Israeli people as well.

At this desperate point, Israel has nowhere to turn. There is no hope of succor from the United Nations, where many representatives barely conceal their glee over the imminent demise of the hated "imperialist" and "racist" state and stage an hysterical condemnation of an Israeli air raid on Amman earlier in the war in which several Third World diplomats were wounded. A final U.S. resolution in the General Assembly calling for a ceasefire is seconded only by Australia and the Netherlands, and attempts to get action in the Security Council are blocked by Soviet vetoes. In desperation (and despite earlier assurances that it would never ask for the direct intervention of U.S. combat forces), the Israelis appeal to Washington, but the president, while sympathetic, feels unable to act against strong public opposition to sending U.S. troops into the Middle East. For many years, sentiment in the United States has been turning against Israel, whose alleged "intransigence" about border withdrawals has long been an accepted dogma in public discourse, and its support in Congress has dwindled. As Israel's army collapses, there is a desultory debate in the U.S. Senate about the possibility of mounting an airlift to rescue a token 100,000 Israelis who could be brought to the United States, engendering a public outcry reminiscent of the final days of Vietnam. Diplomatic activity is reduced to quiet approaches to the Arabs, begging that Israeli civilians be spared a final massacre. Otherwise, one might also have noted the effort mounted by a group of liberal U.S. psychiatrists and social psychologists who had convened a large-scale group therapy session involving Jews and Arab "moderates" with the hope of achieving a "comprehensive" postwar peace.

Finally, there is little assurance that the United States could effectively intervene at this time, even if it wished, to rescue Israel. Earlier hints of U.S. intervention brought ominous and brutal counterthreats from the Soviets and ten Soviet airborne divisions have been mobilized. The United States, prior to the deployment of its Strategic Defense Initiative, is no longer confident either of strategic balance with the Soviet Union or of local air, ground, or naval equivalency in the Mediterranean. Indeed, in the Middle East the Soviets now hold what U.S. decisionmakers recognize as a psychological and military edge all the way up the ladder of escalation. The "overkill" myth notwithstanding, there is a gray area between superiority and sufficiency where certain kinds of crises are resolved, and the Soviets have learned that lesson well since the days of the Cuban crisis. And after a lengthy period of "oil glut," OPEC has regained much of its previous strength—American external dependence for oil climbs back up near 60 percent. There is another Arab oil embargo reminiscent of 1973, which the Saudi king has announced will be permanent pending Israel's final destruction. The United States bows to *force majeure*. The final blow, then, in this scenario, despite some lingering visceral and sentimental concern for Israel's survival, is the impotence and inaction of the U.S. government. At the moment of its impending final agony, Israel finds itself, not to its own surprise, finally and completely alone.

At this point, after acrimonious internal debate, the Israeli government concludes that the only remaining option is to invoke the nuclear threat, particularly as room for maneuver grows smaller with each passing day. Some Jericho missiles have already been destroyed by the conventional Frog, Scud, and Kitchen missiles raining upon Israel, while the Israeli Kfir, F-15, and F-16 force has been whittled down almost to its nuclear-armed component, which means there can be little aircover for nuclear missions. Immediate action is clearly imperative.

A number of alternative courses of action are now presented. First, a mere announcement of the intention to use nuclear weapons may be made, possibly coupled with an explosion (in the part of the Negev still held by Israel) to lend credibility to the threat. One disadvantage for the Israelis here is that on receipt of the threat, the Arabs will quickly evacuate their major population centers, vitiating some of its antipopulation potential. Most critical, however, at this point, would be the reaction of the Soviet Union, which quite probably would issue immediate threats of total annihilation of Israel and might, in fact, launch a massive preemptive strike in response to Israel's mere threat, counting on the approval or benign indifference of a significant number of the world's governments. Here again, of course, the viability of Israel's triangular second-strike threat—and the Soviet evaluation of that capability—would be crucial, assuming the Soviets would be reluctant to risk large numbers of Arab deaths.

As an alternative to a mere threat or demonstration test, Israel could launch one missile against one Arab population center, accompanied by the threat to unleash more if demands for the withdrawal of Arab forces and an in situ ceasefire were not immediately met. The Aswan or Euphrates dams might also be targets for a single nuclear strike. This option would be a much stronger demonstration of intent than threats, but would certainly make an overpowering Soviet response (again with the question of Israeli second-strike capability interposing) very likely. It may be assumed that Israel would not, initially, launch more than one or two missiles, since maintaining most of the Arab population centers as hostages for further strikes would be the heart of Israeli strategy for survival at this juncture, and also assuming, of course, that the situation where this alternative might be used had not deteriorated to the point where nothing remained but a nihilistic desire to wreak vengeance in the certainty of final destruction, in the manner of Samson.

Central to the bargaining which might take place at this point are the questions of triangular second-strike capability and "acceptable losses." More specifically, there is, first, the technical question of whether the Soviets could target, by satellite reconnaissance, most or all the fifty-odd mobile missile ramps mounting the Jericho, and further distinguish between decoys and real warheads. The Soviet task of targeting all the warheads might well be seriously complicated if Israel had developed delivery systems other than Jerichos; on patrol boats, submarines, or aircraft. If this scenario were to take place after Soviet deployment of SDI, then the latter's capability to interdict Israeli missiles in their boost phase would be crucial. At this point, the use of airborne alert or even launch-on-warning might come into play. If the Soviets were not certain of the ability to simultaneously target all Israel's delivery systems, the question of "acceptable losses" would arise. Given the fairly dense concentration of the Arab populations and the historical and symbolic importance of such cities as Cairo, Damascus, Amman, Beirut, and Baghdad, it is quite possible that the Arabs would have a low threshold of "acceptable" losses, even if only a small percentage of their total populations were under the threat of destruction. This would have to be balanced, however, against the prospect of victory, however pyrrhic, and Arab rhetoric has long claimed willingness to drench the Middle East in blood to attain the final objective.

Finally, Soviet calculations in this scenario would have to take into account the unlikely but possible Israeli threat to the Soviet Union itself. The Soviets would presumably have anticipated threats against their fleet concentrations in the Mediterranean and dispersed them accordingly, and they would certainly have the capability of deploying enough area weapons—even 25-megaton bombs—to obliterate Israel in one massive attack. It may be assumed that no mobile missile ramps, even with light hardening (as in caves dug into the hills of Negev or Sinai, for example) could survive such an attack. It is precisely this point which some analysts believe denies the potential for deterrence of the Israeli nuclear force and even its usefulness as a last-ditch terror threat. However, one major factor working in the Israelis' favor—and one which might preclude the Soviets taking the simple option of obliterating Israel altogether—is the existence of large Palestinian Arab hostage populations within Israel and here, again, the question of acceptable losses plays an important part. Of course, tactical nuclear weapons might provide for a considerably altered scenario.

In a crisis, the credibility of threats and perceived determination are of utmost importance. Clearly, the fact of Israel's imminent destruction would give its threats a considerable degree of credibility. Indeed, Israel would depend very heavily in a crisis on its adversaries' firm belief that it would, as a final gesture of despair and vengeance, unleash a "Parthian shot" to bring destruction down upon a significant portion of the Middle East. The credibility of this threat is further enhanced by the Israelis' long-held reputation for seeking "an eye for an eye and a tooth for a tooth," psychologically understandable in the light of their compulsion to compensate for the centuries' long experience of European Jews in absorbing punishment without ever having the means or the will to retaliate. This is, indeed, the self-perception at the core of the Israeli spirit. In short, the iron determination shown by the Israelis in many crises and their firm refusal never to allow themselves to be hit without hitting back harder would greatly enhance the credibility of the threat they would issue in this scenario, though the pullback under diplomatic pressure after the 1973 war and the pathetic Lebanon withdrawal in 1985 might diminish what would once have been the even greater force of this "final" threat. On the other hand, it might even be speculated that the Israeli government has long been aware, in handling diplomatic crises and in responding to border provocations and guerrilla actions, that it needed beforehand to set up the credibility that might one day be essential to its ultimate nuclear threat, in resolutely and continuously demonstrating its unshakeable resolve.

The Disclosure Issue: Addendum

Shai Feldman and others have in recent years advocated that Israel "come out of the closet" with its nuclear weapons, going overt in exchange for a territorial settlement, perhaps even one involving full abandonment of the West Bank and Gaza. That is, territorial withdrawal would be traded off for what would be hoped to be a more credible, near "automatic" nuclear deterrence posture, paradoxically hinged on what would then be a much greater Israeli vulnerability to conventional assault. The Arabs would be told: you have your territories back, even a Palestinian state, but one more step over the line and . . . .

In part I agree with the thrust of the strategy (among other things, it would allow for testing). But, effectively, it is precluded by U.S. legislation which requires that military and economic aid be cut off from a state that acquires nuclear arms. That is quite simply too high a price for now. And, given the usual state of U.S. arms control "idealism" when it comes to such things, not to mention the impact on other nuclear aspirants (effectively it would amount to full abandonment of U.S. nonproliferation policy), it is not likely the United States could make an exception in Israel's case, even in exchange for full territorial withdrawal and a "comprehensive peace." A quiet threat by Israel to disclose if pressured into an unwanted "peace" arrangement might, however, be another story.

Overall, Israel would probably do best to maintain its current posture and strategy. That strategy is one of coming very close to admitting to nuclear status (while denying it in formal declaratory statements), hence allowing the United States to look the other way while Israel achieves most, but not all, of the deterrent value of an open, overt, deployed program. Just how much deterrence is lost thereby is, indeed, a serious question, but the benefits of ambiguity outweigh the costs.

8

A Regional Non-Proliferation Treaty for the Middle East

Avi Beker

Immediately after the Israeli raid on the Iraqi nuclear reactor at Osiraq on June 7, 1981, some critics of Israel—assuming that nuclearization of the Middle East is inevitable—asserted that though Israel might have won some time, its air strike might encourage other countries in the area to develop nuclear programs.[1] These assessments revived a behind-the-scenes debate on the viability of nuclear deterrence in the Middle East. As for a major public debate in Israel and elsewhere about nuclear policies in the region, none materialized.

Shortly after the Osiraq military operation, as the exchange of views for and against open nuclear deterrence faded into the background, Israel continued, with virtually no public reservation, with its long-standing policy of "deliberate ambiguity." This policy stipulates that Israel will not be the first country to introduce nuclear weapons into the Middle East. Despite widespread speculation and endless attempts in the international media to "count" Israeli nuclear warheads, there is no official statement or irrefutable evidence that Israel has really crossed the nuclear threshold.[2]

Interestingly enough, the Likud government, with its more hawkish stand on foreign policy, did not provide any clue on possible modifications in the country's nuclear posture. The pronuclearization strategists in Israel and abroad,[3] who suggest open Israeli nuclear deterrence, remained a very tiny minority. And except for a few periodic items in the news, they did not inspire the kind of debate which surrounds issues related to nuclear doctrines and deployments in the West.

It seems that, among people who deal with nuclear matters in Israel, there is a virtual consensus which crosses normal ideological divisions and unites "hawks" and "doves," who usually differ strongly on national security matters. Prominent figures from the left (such as Professor Yehosafat Harkabi, a former head of Israeli military intelligence) and from the right (such as the minister of science in the Likud government, Professor Yuval Ne'eman) both reject forcefully as irresponsible the idea of "going nuclear."[4] As indicated by Efraim Inbar in chapter 5 of this book, there has never been sufficient support in Israel's governments for an open nuclear posture.

No Nuclear Deterrence

This prevailing view in Israel seems to reject any analogy between the super-powers' global balance of terror and regional rivalries. This rejection is entirely reasonable. It is a fallacy to extrapolate from U.S.–Soviet nuclear relations that nuclear deterrence could operate successfully in different regions.

In a regional context, and particularly in the Middle East, where volatile religious and territorial disputes are at issue, it may be impossible to provide the technical means to sustain the superpower balance. These technical means include sophisticated early warning, command and control, and accident-proofing systems which require advanced technology and highly trained manpower. Moreover, unlike the Soviet–American relationship, the Arab–Israeli conflict is not a simple, one-against-one adversarial situation. Israel faces many Arab opponents, most of which still oppose its very existence, and which are often engaged in their own internal rivalries. It is easy, under these circumstances, to envisage a scenario where one Arab party might serve as a catalyst to embroil Israel and another Arab state in a nuclear conflict.

Shai Feldman's idea that Israel should concentrate on developing a nuclear second-strike capability in a nuclearized Middle East is very dangerous. It is even more dangerous when those who propose to launch a "socialization process" among Middle East elites (to teach them to live with the bomb) base their expectations on Iraqi President Saddam Hussein's assurances: that an Arab nuclear capability will "secure and safeguard the peace" in the Middle East by the same logic that nuclear deterrence is maintained between the superpowers.[5] Consistent with their particular sense of stakes and goals, leaders of several countries in the Middle East have proved willing to sacrifice their people in wars against various regional opponents.

The Iran–Iraq war may well be a bellwether of a new type of war among Third World countries that are armed with modern and sophisticated weapons. Both countries are led by strong leaders, too vengeful to consider compromise, who are not reluctant to employ unconventional methods and excessively corrosive means of warfare. Disproving many conventional expectations on the Middle East and highlighting the fragility of international arrangements and rules in that region, the Gulf War points to the special meaning of rationality in regional conflicts. The Iraqi use of chemical weapons against Iran during 1983 and 1984 in violation of the 1925 Geneva Protocol, to which Iraq is a party, casts serious doubts upon those who draw comfort from Saddam Hussein's assurances or from Iraq's promised adherence to arms control agreements.

The Israeli operation against Osiraq was not just a "time-buying measure," as some have suggested,[6] but rather an important reminder of the folly of Western transfer of arms and nuclear technology to unstable and irresponsible regimes in a conflict-prone region. Yet, the element of time is itself an important factor in the Arab–Israeli conflict which should not be dismissed lightly. Today it is evident that the operation dealt a severe blow to the development of an Iraqi nuclear bomb.

A former senior official in the State Department has admitted to a general agreement within the U.S. government that Iraq's probable goal in pursuing its atomic program was to acquire a nuclear weapons capability.[7] Similarly, a *Wall Street Journal* editorial on December 30, 1981 argued that the world attitude to Iraq's nuclear program was reminiscent of the conspiracy of silence surrounding the initial campaign of genocide against the Jews during World War II. It was another instance, the editors said, of what psychologists term *denial*. Although the State Department could not bring itself to say that Iraq's nuclear reactor was intended for building bombs, the Osiraq facility had had no other conceivable purpose.

Exposing NPT Deficiencies

In addition to underscoring the cavalier and irresponsible policies of Western nuclear suppliers, the raid on Osiraq served another useful purpose: it exposed serious deficiencies and loopholes in the safeguards of the Non-Proliferation Treaty (NPT) and the International Atomic Energy Agency (IAEA) over nuclear reactors and facilities. From his own narrowly bureaucratic point of view, the director general of the IAEA was right in concluding that the operation was also an attack on the credibility of the agency's safeguards regime.[8] Long before this event, doubts were raised about the effectiveness of IAEA safeguards, but the criticism was in most cases low key and beyond public knowledge. Only after the raid on Osiraq did the criticism reach the level of official statements and receive the scrutiny of major editorials. For example, an editorial by the *Washington Post* entitled "Nuclear Safeguards or Sham?" concluded: "If the Israeli raid provokes a serious reexamination of the IAEA safeguards system and the overreliance of nuclear suppliers on NPT membership as a substitute for hard-headed and, yes, even discriminatory policies based on the most reasonable estimate of nations' nuclear intentions, the raid may turn out, paradoxically, to have advanced the cause of non-proliferation."[9]

By the end of the 1970s and the beginning of the 1980s, a growing concern was notable among experts over the operation of the existing international nonproliferation regime. On the one hand, the international consensus on preventing the spread of nuclear weapons became dangerously strained. On the other hand, technological progress in the nuclear field made it more and more difficult to rely upon IAEA safeguards to detect diversions for military purposes.

On September 7, 1980, the Second Review Conference of the NPT ended on a note of disappointment when the participants failed to agree upon a document outlining measures to strengthen the future operation of the treaty. The Third World countries, which had committed themselves under the platform of a New International Economic Order to eliminate the sources of discrimination and inequality in the international system, persistently criticized the discriminatory regime of the NPT. The NPT is indeed an attempt to freeze the number of nuclear weapons to the extant five powers and as such it divides the international community into two classes of states: Nuclear-weapon states and non–nuclear-weapon states. For the Third World and its organs such as the nonaligned movement, the NPT became a focal point in the North–South debate and the economic cleavages over development, food, commodities, natural resources, and exploration of the sea were extended to world security in the confrontation between the "military-nuclear haves" and the "military-nuclear have-nots."[10]

The North–South debate on nonproliferation merely added a new dimension, ideological in nature, to the technical problems which were already recognized as the NPT entered into force. The system of safeguards provided by the NPT consists of three main elements: material accountancy, containment, and surveillance. All are aimed to enable "timely" detection of diversion of "significant" quantities of nuclear material from peaceful activities to the manufacture of nuclear explosive devices. Experts agree, and the IAEA itself admits, that there are limits to the extent to which the agency is able to detect diversions and to guarantee an effective international response to a nonproliferation violation, even when it is detected.[11] As a study by the Stockholm International Peace Research Institute (SIPRI) indicated in 1980, the advanced technologies in the nuclear field would make it impossible to rely on IAEA safeguards to detect such diversions.[12]

It took the Israeli action at Osiraq, however, to provoke a serious reexamination of the international safeguards machinery. Only after that event did the public learn (through reports which had been prepared for the U.S. Nuclear Regulatory Commission) that IAEA safeguards have gross deficiencies.[13] One American safety expert working for the commission wrote that, since the IAEA is also engaged in promoting nuclear power, its role as a regulatory and supervising agency is compromised, a situation that allows "a large potential for cheating and unauthorized diversion."[14] The growing disillusionment with the safeguards system culminated on November 27, 1981 when, in the first such government assertion ever, a document from the chairman of the U.S. Nuclear Regulatory Commission (Nunzio J. Palladino) approved unanimously by the five members of the commission, warned of the ineffectiveness of IAEA safeguards. The letter, which was sent to chairmen of several congressional committees, determined that the IAEA is unable to detect diversions of nuclear material in some types of facilities and added that there can be no real confidence that member states of the U.N. agency "would be notified of a diversion in a timely fashion."[15]

The NPT and Middle East Security

Being in a permanent state of war with most of the Arab world, Israel cannot afford to rely upon NPT safeguards for its national security. In the Middle East it is hard to see how the detection system of the NPT might be applied. The problem is that the NPT does not provide for the possibility of carrying out special inspections on the basis of accusations or suspicion, and the whole system (including the choice of the inspectors) is dependent on the consent of the state involved. Such provisions damage the credibility of the inspectors and the system as a whole and obstruct the very notion of early detection.[16]

These deficiencies are particularly alarming because of the risk of abrogation which is inherent in the NPT system. According to article X of the NPT, each party might at any time, if it chooses to do so, openly declare its withdrawal from the treaty on three months' notice in what it considers as "exercising national sovereignty." In other words, the IAEA system, and particularly its promotional role, allows a state to proceed under the guise of the NPT as far as possible with plans for making nuclear weapons. When ready, this state may merely notify the IAEA and the U.N. Security Council that it is withdrawing from the treaty.

For Israel, the abrogation risk has particular and mostly ominous implications. As has already been noted, most Arab states still consider themselves in a state of war with Israel and refuse to recognize or negotiate with it. They argue that because the very existence of Israel is an "act of aggression," this justifies, on their part, the "exercising of national sovereignty" on what article X of the NPT terms as "extraordinary events . . . that have jeopardized the supreme interests" of the country or countries concerned. Israeli concerns are reinforced when one reads the reservation which the Syrian Arab Republic added on the occasion of its ratification of the NPT on September 24, 1969: "The acceptance of this Treaty by the Syrian Arab Republic shall in no way signify recognition of Israel or entail entry into relations with Israel thereunder."[17] Similarly Israel must take into account the fact that ten Arab countries have either not signed (among them, Algeria, Saudi Arabia, and Bahrain) or not ratified (Kuwait) the NPT and four more which did ratify have not yet complied with the Safeguards Agreement provided by the Treaty (Syria).[18]

A careful reading of the text of the NPT reveals that a central assumption of the treaty is the existence of conditions of peace, conditions which do not exist in the Middle East. The Arab–Israeli dispute is only one of several long-standing conflicts in the region bearing directly upon international peace and security. This inherent instability is in sharp contrast to the peaceful and normal relations between states envisaged by the drafters of the NPT, who wrote in the preamble that "in accordance with the Charter of the United Nations, States must refrain in their international relations from the threat or use of force against the territorial integrity or politial independence of any state, or in any other manner inconsistent with the Purposes of the United Nations."

During the hearings on the NPT in the U.S. Senate in 1968, Secretary of State Dean Rusk and Army Chief of Staff General Earl G. Wheeler made it clear that the treaty "does not apply to a situation of war" and in a war situation it "immediately becomes inoperative."[19] In the harsh realities of the Middle East, this logic renders the withdrawal clause in the treaty an absurdity. It is pointless and dangerous to expect a government in the Middle East to alert its declared enemies by giving them three months' notice. It would be more realistic to expect an immediate renunciation of NPT obligations in a condition of war or crisis. Indeed, in November 1980, Iraq blocked IAEA inspection for several months on the grounds that it was in a war situation with Iran.[20]

Before the Israeli operation at Osiraq, IAEA officials were not ready to discuss the limitations of their safeguards machinery. In this reticence they enjoyed the political backing of the major nuclear suppliers from the West. As Fred Iklé pointed out in 1980, U.S. nuclear policy has long been bedeviled by "an insouciant lack of realism about the functioning and the capabilities of the International Atomic Energy Agency." The Agency, Iklé said, was treated by U.S. officials like some closed magic box into which they can dump proliferation problems by pretending that the safeguards are safe.[21]

It was only after the raid on the Iraqi reactor that a serious debate on the viability of international nuclear safeguards was revived.[22] In his statement at hearings before the Senate Subcommittee on Energy, Nuclear Proliferation, and Government Processes on June 24, 1981, Senator John Glenn treated the event as a turning point for nonproliferation policies. For years, Glenn testified, the American and world public had been lulled to sleep by the notion that the IAEA inspections provide effective assurances against nuclear proliferation. In fact, Glenn argued, the word "safeguards" itself was a misnomer, since it connotes more "safety" and "guarding" than is warranted. The promotional provisions in the NPT mean literally "that any nation can obtain assistance in building a weapons program under the guise of a peaceful nuclear development program without violating any of the provisions of the NPT." "The message of the raid on the Osiraq reactor," Glenn said, "is that we need to construct a sturdier safeguards structure than we now have," which must include additional "bilateral and multilateral security arrangements" to strengthen the existing system of safeguards.[23]

Some change in the attitude of the IAEA can also be identified, although because of vested organizational interests, its expression was more moderate. A few days after the operation, the director general of the IAEA, Sigvard Eklund, still insisted that "there was nothing wrong with the safeguards being applied on the Tamuz [Osiraq] reactors nor any deficiencies in the inspection schedule or procedures."[24] Eklund was on the defensive because of testimony by a former inspector for the IAEA who told the Senate Foreign Relations Committee: "The IAEA safeguards are totally incapable of detecting the production of plutonium in large-size material test reactors under the presently constituted safeguard arrangements."[25]

A few months after the incident, the IAEA launched an information campaign and issued a new introductory guide on international inspections which was aimed at correcting public misapprehension and providing balanced information about the agency.[25] When Hans Blix assumed the office of the director general of the IAEA early in 1982, he was more candid and sober than his predecessor in his assessment of the limited role the agency can play to curb the spread of nuclear weapons. Blix explained that since security considerations are the most decisive factor in the search for nuclear weapons "you cannot stop proliferation by safeguards."[27]

By the end of 1984, 120 states were parties to the NPT, but for more than one-third of them a safeguards agreement was not yet in force.[28] Yet the fact that a majority of the world's states have accepted the NPT may create a false sense of security. The NPT was helpful in enlisting those countries which had already accepted the political realities of international and regional order. The treaty cannot provide security in regions wherein certain countries are determined to change the political order by threatening the very existence of others. In such regions, a country's signature on the NPT cannot be regarded as conclusive proof of its nuclear innocence but, on the contrary, can be exploited as a strategy for the acquisition of nuclear arms. A system that is inadequate for controlling international transfers of nuclear equipment, materials, and technology generally is especially impotent in dealing with the Arab–Israeli conflict.

The Tlatelolco Model

While the NPT enjoys the status of being the cornerstone of international efforts to prevent nuclear proliferation, it was preceded by a major regional treaty whose provisions go beyond the NPT: the Treaty for the Prohibition of Nuclear Weapons in Latin America. This treaty, commonly referred to as the Treaty of Tlatelolco (after the borough of Mexico City where it was signed on February 14, 1967), created the only nuclear-free zone in an inhabited area, covering some 7.5 million square miles with a population of 200 million people. There are other treaties which have established nuclear-weapon-free zones, such at the Antarctic Treaty of 1959, the Outer Space Treaty of 1967, and the Seabed Treaty of 1971, but these do not cover populated areas, did not require the consent of any local governments and were not negotiated as specific frameworks for nuclear-free zones.

The major impetus for the Tlatelolco Treaty was the Cuban missile crisis of October 1962, when the transfer of Soviet missiles to Cuba dramatized the perils of a region involved in superpower competition. After a summit meeting of five Latin American republics (April 1963), a Preparatory Commission was established in November 1964 in Mexico City and began two and a half years of intensive multilateral negotiations leading to the signing of the treaty by twenty-three states.[29]

Some provisions and principles of the Tlatelolco Treaty were copied in the NPT, and upon request of the Latin American countries article VII of the NPT provides that "Nothing in this treaty affects the right of any group of States to conclude regional treaties in order to assure the total absence of nuclear weapons in their respective territories." One can interpret this provision as implying that in some circumstances it would be safer for states to rely upon regional arrangements "to assure the total absence of nuclear weapons" than to rely upon the NPT.

The nuclear-weapon-free zone (NWFZ) in Latin America falls short of perfection because of such ambiguities as the question of peaceful nuclear explosions, the geopolitical extent of the treaty and the fact that several countries are not bound by its provisions.[30] The treaty itself, however, with its verification provisions, is considerably superior to the NPT. Unlike the Partial Test Ban Treaty (PTBT)[31] and NPT, the Treaty of Tlatelolco defines nuclear weapons (article 5) and it enumerates more specifically the obligations of the parties. Protocol II of the treaty obligates the nuclear weapon states not to threaten or use nuclear weapons against states in the zone—a so-called *negative security assurance,* which is absent from the NPT. But most significant is the comprehensive system of verification provided by the Treaty of Tlatelolco, which—in addition to IAEA safeguards—established a permanent organ of its own to assure compliance and to perform inspection. This body, the Organization for the Prohibition of Nuclear Weapons in Latin America (OPANAL), provides for challenge inspection when requested by its secretary general or when any member may suspect a violation. Such a system strengthens confidence concerning diversions of weapons-grade materials and makes it easier to detect a violation after a diversion has taken place.

As we can see, regionalism may be advanced as a practical alternative to a global approach to nuclear nonproliferation. But in the Middle East the idea of NWFZ cannot be based upon conventional premises of regionalism, namely the existence of common cultural foundations, common loyalties, and the similarity of national problems.[32] Despite the complex problems of regional differences and conflicts, states in the Middle East do have a common interest in ensuring their own survival by concentrating on the specific and limited undertaking of preventing a nuclear arms race in their region.

The idea of a regional approach to nonproliferation of nuclear weapons was already endorsed by the U.N. General Assembly in 1974 consensus resolution 3661-F(XXIX). This resolution launched a comprehensive study of the question of nuclear-weapon-free zones in all of its aspects. The study was carried out by a group of governmental experts under the auspices of the Conference of the Committee on Disarmament (CCD) in Geneva. The experts reached a consensus on certain principles governing the creation of nuclear-weapon-free zones, among them the principle that the initiative for the creation of a zone should come from states within the region and participation should be voluntary.[33]

In 1978, the final document adopted by the U.N. Special Session of Disarmament (SSD) reaffirmed the same principle: "The establishment of nuclear-weapon-free zones on the basis of arrangements freely arrived at among the States of the region concerned constitutes an important disarmament measure. . . . In the process of establishing such zones the characteristics of each region should be taken into account."[34]

The UN's Double Standard

Contrary to the claims of its political opponents, Israel has always supported in principle the establishment of a NWFZ in the Middle East.[35] Ever since the introduction of this item in the General Assembly in 1974, Israel consistently supported the Tlatelolco model in the Middle East by convening a conference of all states in the region with a view to drafting a treaty.[36] The resolution on the subject, which was introduced to the General Assembly by Iran and subsequently co-sponsored by Egypt (which later would be the dominant sponsor) and adopted every year thereafter, is misleadingly entitled a proposal on the establishment of a "NWFZ in the region of the Middle-East."

Its provisions are a far cry from the Tlatelolco Treaty and although it bears a meretricious title, which purports to promote a NWFZ, there is nothing in it pointing toward a "voluntary" or "freely arrived" initiative coming "from states within the region." The text which has been adopted annually by the General Assembly since 1974 under the title "NWFZ in the Middle East" is, rather, a call for unilateral adherence to the NPT by states in the region without any additional negotiations or specific arrangements for regional verification and safeguards. The U.N. resolution just reiterates, in one way or another, the basic provisions of the NPT, adding only the prohibition of a third-party stationing of nuclear weapons on the territories of the states entering the NWFZ. (Under the NPT it is possible for nuclear weapon states to position, under their own control, nuclear weapons in the territories of non–nuclear-weapon states, as in the case of U.S. nuclear weapons stationed in its NATO allies' territories.) In sum, the text of the NWFZ resolution adopted by the General Assembly is nothing more than an attempt to impose unilateral adherence to the NPT without any regard for the deficiencies of the treaty and its safeguards system in the Middle East.

The attempt to dictate an "ideal model" for a NWFZ by the General Assembly does not accord well with the "pragmatic and flexible" approach recommended by the ad hoc governmental experts in their report to the CCD on the subject.[37] More recently, another group of distinguished statesmen and experts chaired by Olaf Palme (who was later reelected as prime minister of Sweden) gave further endorsement to the Tlatelolco model for NWFZ. The Independent Commission on Disarmament and Security issues included eighteen members from East and West and the Third World, and reiterated the language of the SSD I Final Document on the importance of NWFZ based on arrangements "freely arrived at" by the states in the region. The commission regarded the Treaty of Tlatelolco as a "path-breaking regional arrangement in this field" promoting nonproliferation, common security, disarmament and "mutual reassurance to states preferring not to acquire or allow deployment of nuclear weapons as long as neighbouring states exercise similar restraint."[38]

The Egyptian formula for NWFZ in the Middle East (since the 1979 revolution in Iran, Egypt sponsors it alone) cannot be regarded as a regional approach to nuclear nonproliferation since it lacks the ingredients necessary for voluntary and consensual participation by states within the region. It is, rather, another ploy by the anti-Israel majority of the General Assembly. This majority tries to impose a solution on Israel that disregards the characteristics of a region which makes the NPT safeguards system especially fragile.

There is a great measure of hypocrisy in the Third World nonaligned states' attitude on this issue. Although they are usually hostile to the NPT and treat it as a taboo in their common declarations and documents,[39] they find the treaty the only existing method for nonproliferation in the Middle East. India, for instance, the chairman of the nonaligned movement since 1983, always refers to the NPT as the "unworkable" and "discriminatory" document and specifically argues that in the age of nuclear weapons NWFZ has become both impractical and unrealistic and would give only the illusion of security to the participants in such a zone.[40]

Yet the same India that rejects the Pakistani proposal for NWFZs in Asia, stating that there must be first a consensus on the matter among the states in the region, lends support to Arab demands for Israel's unilateral adherence to the "unworkable" and "discriminatory" NPT for the purpose of establishing an "illusory" NWFZ without regional consensus and mutual assurances.

A Regional Nonproliferation Regime

In 1980 Israel decided to change its policy (since 1974) of abstaining alone on the Egyptian proposal for a NWFZ and thus cleared the way for the first General Assembly consensus on the matter and for the adoption of the resolution without a vote. Various explanations and speculations were given concerning the Israeli shift, and some critics termed it opportunistic.[41] The fact of the matter is that the change in the vote was just one component in a two-pronged initiative.

Its other part was the introduction of a draft resolution calling on the nations of the Middle East to negotiate a multilateral treaty establishing a NWFZ in the region. The draft resolution as introduced by Israel's representative to the First Committee on Disarmament, Ambassador-at-Large Arieh Eilan, reaffirmed a long-standing position of Israel that "nuclear nonproliferation would best be achieved by a regional approach."[42] As indicated by Ambassador Eilan, Israel's position on the NPT remained unchanged and Israel simply followed many other nonparties to the treaty which usually join the consensus and sometimes express their reservations in an explanation of vote. The Israeli resolution called upon all states of the Middle East to convene a conference which would negotiate a multilateral treaty establishing a NWFZ in the Middle East. The preamble to the resolution explained that the treaty should provide "a contractual assurance of others' compliance with the commitment to abstain from introducing nuclear weapons into the region."

A U.N. report on "Israeli Nuclear Armament" prepared for the secretary-general by a group of academic experts stated that "Israel has tended to approach the question of both the NPT and a nuclear-weapon free zone on the basis of prior achievement of peace with the Arab states."[43] Regarding the Israeli proposal on the NWFZ this statement is inaccurate. In introducing the proposal Ambassador Eilan called upon all states in the Middle East to come together and negotiate the NWFZ in good faith "regardless of their political differences and without prejudice to any political and legal claim."

Nonetheless all Arab states rejected the Israeli initiative and criticized it strongly for setting up an unacceptable precondition to the creation of a NWFZ, namely "negotiated regional arrangements." This is an unfortunate reality of the Middle East. Arab states refuse to participate in a multinational, treaty-writing conference which would require the acceptance of Israel as a legitimate Mideast entity and might imply the beginning of formal interstate diplomacy. The Iraqi statement went even further by referring to the "Zionist entity" (a usual Iraqi practice) and in fact denying Israel's right to even be at the committee.[44] As a result, and in awareness of the prevailing Arab power in the United Nations, Israel had to withdraw its draft resolution. The Israeli representative expressed deep regrets for the fact that the Arabs were not ready to set aside, at least temporarily, their differences with Israel for the sake of saving the region from a nuclear calamity.[45]

The verbatim records of the First Committee reveal that Israel's two-pronged initiative inspired unusual support at the United Nations. Several delegates praised the "constructive approach" of Israel in joining the consensus and a few even paid tribute to the Israeli proposal. The ambassador from the United States welcomed the Israeli draft and said, "One aspect of the Israeli formulation that drew our attention was the recognition that a nuclear-weapon-free zone could come into being only with the full and free cooperation of the States in the region."[46] More conspicuous for the U.N. setting was the special intervention made by Ambassador Garcia Robles of Mexico to express his support for the Israeli initiative. Ambassador Robles, a former foreign minister, is a highly respected figure in the disarmament community and the Treaty of Tlatelolco is considered his brainchild. Robles could not disregard the statement delivered by the then foreign minister of Israel, Itzhak Shamir, when he reiterated that Israeli support for the establishment of a NWFZ in the Middle East was based upon the Tlatelolco model.[47] In his intervention Ambassador Robles expressed his appreciation that though Israel "was compelled" to withdraw its proposal it did not, nevertheless, change its position on the NWFZ idea. Robles explained that despite his country's traditional support of general Arab positions on the Palestinian question, as far as disarmament is concerned, the Israeli attitude on the NWFZ in the Middle East was a step in the right direction.[48]

Mutual Inspections

The various provisions of the NWFZ in the Middle East should be left to the give-and-take of diplomacy. The degree of cooperation between the parties will determine their ability to address the special characteristics of the Middle East. From the Israeli position, one can infer that a NWFZ in the Middle East must go beyond the NPT and IAEA safeguards. As indicated by Yuval Ne'eman, international safeguards cannot satisfy Israeli security requirements: "We would have international inspectors crawling all over us, while the Arab countries would be free to do what they want, as Iraq did."[49]

The Iraqi case highlighted the extent to which a country can take advantage of the lenient terms of the safeguards agreement with the IAEA. Besides the serious deficiencies in the detection procedures, the country to be inspected has the power to reject designated inspectors and to postpone or change the inspection date. Since 1976 only Soviet and Hungarian inspectors have been reported to have visited Iraq.

In 1980 the Iraqis blocked IAEA inspection of their nuclear installations because of "war conditions" with Iran. Finally, when an inspection was carried out in January 1981, it was conducted in darkness with the inspectors using flashlights, which limited their visual inspection of the fuel. Several fuel elements could not be verified because they were said to be locked in a vault and the key could not reportedly be located at the time.[50] A NWFZ in the Middle East will require a reliable and workable challenge system such as the Latin American OPANAL with greater inspection powers based on mutuality. As indicated by Yuval Ne'eman, a treaty establishing a NWFZ in the Middle East will require "mutual inspection by the signatories."[51]

The permanent inspection organ of the NWFZ will have to address the problematic overlap between peaceful and explosive uses of nuclear materials. One possible option for mutual security which is discussed in the professional literature is the *permissive action link* (PAL), a lock without which the reactor, enrichment plant, or plutonium separation plant cannot operate.[52] The locks will have different numeric combinations held by the parties and any attempt to tamper with the locks would be forestalled by automatic shutdown of the facility.

The prospects for a NWFZ in the Middle East do not look favorable, and the idea might easily be dismissed as impractical and naive. The paradox is that the conflictual nature of the Middle East makes the NPT and IAEA safeguards unreliable while at the same time it compels the adoption of unique methods of cooperation among hostile parties. However, a dramatic development can always occur and make the NWFZ idea more feasible. It took thirteen fearful days of the Cuban missile crisis in October 1962 before the superpowers started to negotiate on arms control. The sudden compulsion to look into the nuclear abyss taught both the United States and the Soviet Union to realize the likelihood of a nuclear war. The governments of the Middle East will have to realize that the irradiated particles that comprise nuclear fallout cannot distinguish between Jew and Arab, between Moslem and Christian.

In the real world of geopolitical competition, particularly in the Middle East, General Assembly deliberations carry very little weight. With its current anti-Israel majority, the U.N. General Assembly cannot play a positive role in nonproliferation efforts in that troubled region. The U.N. majority, which voted against the Israeli–Egyptian Peace Treaty and sought to obstruct the peacemaking process of the Camp David agreements can hardly be expected to bring together the potential members of a NWFZ in the Middle East.

I began this chapter by considering why nuclear deterrence is the wrong idea for the Middle East. I continued by explaining why the existing regime of nuclear nonproliferation based upon the NPT and IAEA safeguards is insufficient and fragile for the Middle East. What this region needs is a NWFZ based upon an improved model of the Tlatelolco Treaty—a kind of a *regional NPT* which will take into account the unique characteristics of the region.

Very few people, including Israeli diplomats, entertain the illusion that the Arab nations will soon join a treaty-writing conference with Israel. In 1980 the Egyptians even regarded such a conference as wildly improbable. However, the optimistic Israelis thought that in five years the Arabs would find out that they share a mutual interest with Israel in the field of nuclear nonproliferation.[53] In any case, it is difficult to see how a binding regional treaty could be drafted without negotiation among the relevant parties. The Arab refusal to deal with Jerusalem cannot serve as an excuse for ignoring the potential contribution of a negotiated NWFZ in the Middle East.

9

An Israeli Nuclear Deterrent: Implications for U.S.–Soviet Strategic Policies

Stephen J. Cimbala

This chapter considers the implications of a potential Israeli nuclear deterrent for the U.S.–Soviet strategic relationship. It also considers the "feedback" effects from those U.S.–Soviet relations, given the superpowers' probable reactions to Israeli options. Two of those options, the possible "bomb in the basement" and nuclear disclosure, will be emphasized in this discussion. In choosing between "deliberate ambiguity" and an openly acknowledged nuclear retaliatory capability, Israel will make a decision of importance to both regional and worldwide security.

Crisis Stability

Crisis stability is that condition in which neither the United States nor the Soviet Union is tempted to attack the other with nuclear weapons because of the "reciprocal fear of surprise attack."[1] Stability of the balance of terror depends, inter alia, upon the survivability of U.S. and Soviet strategic forces against any first strike by the opponent, and the retaliatory capability to inflict unacceptable damage against the attacker. In this relationship, the attacker and defender may share accurate or misleading estimates of what levels of damage are "acceptable" to each other.

U.S.–Soviet relations have been marked by a remarkable stability in crisis confrontations. Crises in the Middle East in 1967 and 1973 involved threats of intervention and counterthreats of reprisal, but neither side expected nuclear war. U.S. forces in 1973 were placed on "Defense Condition 3" alert but this had more serious implications for command and control than it had for U.S. intercontinental ballistic missile (ICBM) and force survivability.[2] The Cuban missile crisis is even more interesting here, since the United States had a probable first-strike capability against the Soviet Union which was not reciprocal. Even so, the undoubted potential of Soviet medium-range ballistic missiles against U.S. cities deterred U.S. leaders from excessively provocative actions and led them to emphasize a "way out" for Khrushchev.[3]

American analysts are correctly concerned about the possible vulnerability of U.S. ICBMs to a Soviet first strike, or the appearance of same, reducing
the willingness of U.S. leaders to respond to Soviet or proxy attacks on U.S.
allies.[4] The question of extended deterrence as it applies to U.S.–Israeli and
Soviet–Arab relations will be taken up later, but the ICBM vulnerability
problem requires immediate discussion. Were the U.S. strategic *triad* (land-
based ICBMs, sea-based submarine-launched ballistic missiles (SLBMs), and
strategic bombers with cruise missiles) vulnerable to a Soviet first strike, the
implications for U.S. allies, including Israel, would be serious. Such vulnerability of the entire triad is not imminent, however, according to the Scowcroft
Commission and a variety of other studies.[5]

The scenario wherein the Soviet Union might attack U.S. ICBMs while
withholding attacks against other U.S. strategic forces or command, control,
and communications (C^3) seems implausible.[6] The Soviets could not assume
that we would agree to terminate the war because U.S. postattack counterforce capabilities were now inferior to those of the Soviet Union. The countersilo duel is a useful model for illustrating the comparative capabilities of
forces, but it lacks realism for the analysis of actual conflict.[7]

Barring unprecedented and improbable technological breakthroughs,
U.S. and Soviet strategic forces should remain invulnerable to preemptive
destruction. Less certain is the survivability of the command and control for
these strategic forces. The possibility of political "decapitation" is taken seriously by expert analysts and government policy planners.[8] The forces required for Soviet blows which could cripple U.S. retaliatory strikes by dis-
rupting our strategic "connectivity" would be less imposing than those
required for a completely successful counterforce first strike.[9] The possibility
of "countercommand" attacks by either superpower against the other may
become more attractive in the near future, and it has been discussed explicitly
at the highest levels in the Carter and Reagan administrations.[10]

But the vulnerability of command structures must not be overstated. A
simple knockout blow against the "head of the scorpion" would be difficult
for either superpower to execute without also attacking the opponent's strategic forces. Those counterforce attacks could generate the very retaliation
which the countercommand attacks were designed to preclude.[11] Survivable
forces will find some survivable commanders, and vice versa, to provide retaliatory options, given the size, diversity, and complexity of the superpowers'
arsenals.[12]

Although total decapitation of the United States by preemptive or "bolt
from the blue" attack seems improbable, this improbability applies to the
deterrence of direct attacks against the U.S. homeland. Whether the deterrence of counterforce and countercommand attacks on one another's core
values can be extended to the deterrence of attacks against allies, clients, or
proxies is another matter. As I shall argue, the relevant paradox may be that

more stable superpower deterrence creates more leeway for regional nuclear-ization, which then rebounds when periods of less stable deterrence compli-cate superpower relations. Stable superpower deterrence in the short run may make the superpowers acquiesce to nonsurvivable and provocative deterrents in the hands of their allies; those deterrents may then undermine superpower deterrence stability in the long run.

To see this, consider the two alternatives noted in my introduction. The first is that Israel has nuclear weapons but does not acknowledge this capa-bility—the so-called bomb-in-the-basement posture. The second is that Israel openly declares its capability to use nuclear weapons against what is per-ceived as a threat to its vital interests.

In the first case, unacknowledged but de facto capabilities would prob-ably be assumed by worst-case analysts in both superpowers. But they could never be certain. During periods of superpower détente, worst-case analysts might not be convincing. De facto Israeli nuclear capabilities within a U.S.–Soviet détente provide the most permissive medium for Israeli freedom of action with regard to the employment of nuclear weapons. De facto capabil-ities do not require the United States to react with alarm in the way that declared capabilities almost certainly would (see below). Soviet leaders would not have to provide rhetorical guarantees of countermeasures to defend Is-rael's potential opponents.

The least restrictive environment for any nuclearization of the Israeli de-terrent would be one of good U.S.–Soviet relations. The most restrictive re-gime would follow from superpower discord accompanied by a declared Is-raeli nuclear capability. Both superpowers would have to react. And their reactions would have to take into account the reciprocal effects of the new Israeli policy on the balance of power in the Middle East, and on one another. The two balances would thus become intertwined.

If disclosed Israeli nuclear capabilities were perceived to tilt the balance of power in the Middle East dramatically in favor of Israel, then, in times of U.S.–Soviet friction, the Soviet Union could not accept the status quo without serious loss of face. She would have to promise to the Arab states opposed to Israel some support to offset enhanced Israeli capabilities. The possibilities here would include deliveries of more sophisticated Soviet military equip-ment, accompanied by Soviet technicians who can train the recipients in its use. Improved surface-to-air missiles (SAMs) supplied by the Soviet Union to its clients and allies are one obvious possibility, especially if, as seems likely, the Israeli nuclear delivery system were airborne.

More visible and tangible Soviet commitments in the region create seri-ous risks for crisis instability between Israel and its neighbors, and conse-quently for crisis instability between the superpowers. The more crisis-prone the regional atmosphere, based upon increased Arab dependency on Soviet high-technology weapons and the possible use of Soviet advisors, the more suspicious the superpowers must be of one another's motives during a crisis. This U.S.–Soviet crisis instability will be aggravated by regional expectations of crisis instability among Arabs and Israelis. Two overlapping conflict spirals are conceivable; one regional and one global, each reinforcing the other. Thus a "positive feedback loop" could be established in which U.S. and Soviet suspicions about regional motives, and about each other, lead to higher levels of regional and superpower alert, tension and crisis instability.

The construction of pertinent scenarios is not difficult. Consider the problem of U.S. command survivability as that survivability becomes more dependent upon vulnerable satellites (vulnerable to antisatellite preemption). With acknowledged Israeli nuclear capabilities on the regional chessboard and possible unacknowledged Arab capabilities to match them, a regional crisis would raise U.S.–Soviet alert levels and sensitivities. Not only are superpower decision processes sensitive to one another's crisis moves, they are also vulnerable to mutually shared pessimistic expectations about the consequences of preemption. Should either superpower assume that Israel would use nuclear weapons preemptively against its probable opponents (following the pattern applied by its conventional forces in 1967), its direct intervention to forestall such an eventuality seems very probable. The Soviet intervention would more probably take the path of threats; the United States, of blandishments. But standing aside would be unlikely, even during periods of superpower détente. In periods of superpower anxiety, fears of Israeli nuclear preemption would *require* the superpowers to act, lest either lose control of the crisis to the other.

From the crisis stability perspective, the unacknowledged Israeli nuclear deterrent is more favorable than the acknowledged capability. The "bomb in the basement" provides more leeway for the Israelis diplomatically and militarily, even during periods of superpower detente. During periods of general U.S.–Soviet tension, an acknowledged Israeli nuclear deterrent would restrict Israel's options and impel both superpowers to attempt to preempt diplomatically (in the case of the United States) or militarily (in the case of the Soviet Union) Israel's regional preemption. The worst-case scenario for Israel would be a U.S.–Soviet decision to cooperate in preventing Israeli nuclear first use. Of course, there is also the reciprocal possibility that the Arab states which feel threatened by Israel might acquire nuclear weapons and might acknowledge their intention to use them. This does not alter the basic conclusions about crisis stability, but only reinforces them. If crisis stability in regional or global terms will be more difficult to maintain when Israel is the only acknowledged regional nuclear power, difficulties will be compounded when Israel's regional antagonists also have this capability.

This suggests one difference, between the classical balance-of-power process (which might be expected if multilateral nuclearization of the Middle East followed Israel's nuclear deterrent) and a less stable "balance-of-terror" process. The classical balance of power in Europe involved flexibility of alignment and less than total objectives once war had begun. Both of these conditions would be missing in a Middle East balance of terror. Not all Arab–Israeli conflicts have involved total objectives in the past. But multipolar regional nuclear power systems would presume that ultimate values were at stake on both sides; the use of nuclear weapons for lesser objectives would be politically, economically, and militarily wasteful. Thus crisis instability based on expectations of ultimate losses would motivate both Arabs and Israelis, and their superpower benefactors, to predicate policy on worst-case analyses. During a crisis involving values of interest to the United States and the Soviet Union, this could drive both giants into the expectation of at least regional, if not global, preemption. Stated affirmatively, the likelihood of regional and global preemption varies directly with the number of regional nuclear deterrents, and grows exponentially in response to the degree of their antagonism. From the perspective of crisis stability, an Israeli disclosure of nuclear deterrence might begin or accelerate regional nuclear proliferation.

Extended Deterrence

Extended deterrence is that additional increment of deterrence provided by a guarantor to another state, whose security is presumed threatened and who requests prewar security commitments from allies to supplement its own capabilities. Extended deterrence can be conceived as a barbell with weights at both ends, although the weights may be unequal. The costs of lifting those weights, in terms of each state's domestic economic and political capabilities, may be light or considerable.

U.S. extended deterrence cannot be relied upon to prevent all conflict in the Middle East. Some events are beyond U.S. control, and others carry risks beyond the potential benefits of any involvement. Geographic and policy constraints create overlapping communities of interest and responsibility, linking U.S. policy dilemmas in the Middle East and Southwest Asia. For example, the Iran–Iraq war spills over into U.S. relations with Israel and Saudi Arabia; Israel's incursions into Lebanon draw the United States into diplomatic collisions with Syria and complicate the Reagan plan for a Middle East peace.

Thus U.S. extended deterrence of direct Soviet aggression or other overwhelming force against Israel is not unconditional. The conditions include Israel's willingness to conform to general U.S. expectations about its conduct: to minimize regional strategic surprises, to alert U.S. policymakers to significant adjustments in strategic thinking in Tel Aviv, and to maintain at least notional commitment to the Camp David peace process or its successors. Not all Israeli regimes can fulfill these expectations consistently, and some U.S. exasperation with Israeli conduct is obviously for the sake of form rather than substance. Yet real surprises are possible and create awkward moments for the U.S. State Department Mideast desk, as exemplified in the 1982 war in Lebanon and in Israel's attack against Iraqi nuclear facilities.

U.S. extended deterrence to Israel is not only conditional on Israel's behavior, but also on that of its Arab antagonists. A Saudi return to the confrontational policies of the early embargo years would find U.S. interests telescoped more clearly in the direction of Israel. Any repetition of the embargo on the scale of 1973 would not find the Western democracies as vulnerable in the 1980s or 1990s, but the potential nuisance value is not negligible. More probable as a source of U.S.–Arab antagonism and related U.S.–Israeli condominium is an escalation of Middle East terrorism directed against explicitly American targets with the declared purpose of driving the United States from the region, such as the bombing of the U.S. embassy annex in East Beirut in September 1984 and the TWA hijacking in the summer of 1985. Capture of the leadership of the Palestine Liberation Organization (PLO) and a policy initiative by the more radical and Syrian-controlled factions could provoke direct U.S. retaliation against terrorism in the region, with or without Israeli support. Although some Israelis may favor diminished influence for Yasser Arafat and Fatah and increased influence for the Syrians within the PLO, on the grounds that antiterrorism would then "have an address" at which to strike, U.S. policy has favored Arafat against presumably more radical leaders.

U.S. capabilities also limit the reach of extended deterrence for Israel. American strategic nuclear power might deter Soviet nuclear or massive conventional attack designed to destroy the state of Israel, but it cannot deter lesser provocations by Soviet clients or proxies. Soviet-supplied Syrian forces will continue to assume counter-Israeli political and military postures in Lebanon. PLO and other irregulars will be provided with Soviet and Soviet proxy weapons and training, without which their harassment of Israel would be much less persistent or successful. Even the Jordanians and Egyptians are not perpetually immune from Soviet blandishments. Escalation of Mideast arms races offers the Soviet Union opportunities to improve its relations with Egypt and other "moderate" Arab states, especially if those states perceive imminent increases in Israeli capabilities.

Thus the credibility of Soviet threats to influence the direction of war and peace in the region is enhanced to the degree that their involvement produces a pattern of "successful deniability." Soviet proxies can start wars which Soviet policy would rather not see provoked, but a continuing climate of hostility toward Israel on the part of Syria, Jordan, and other potential adversaries results in many net advantages to Moscow. Not the least of these is the opportunity to sell Soviet weapons abroad for hard currency. Another residual benefit for the Soviet Union of Arab–Israeli hostility is the continued perception that Israel is the United States's client in a developing culture. This perception has a durability among Third World political leaders despite historical conditions in which the process has worked the other way around, and the United States has found itself committed to support Israel despite consequences and repercussions in other areas.

If U.S. nuclear deterrence can be extended to Israel only to deter Soviet nuclear or massive conventional attack, then it cannot be extended into the deterrence of those threats most immediate to Israeli security. A major concerted attack by Israel's Arab neighbors, designed to eliminate it from the map entirely or to shrink its borders significantly, might be unresponsive to any threatened U.S. nuclear riposte on behalf of Tel Aviv. U.S. nuclear diplomacy is reserved with any credibility for the prevention of direct Soviet intervention into the region, and that credibility is tenuous even in this event. One can argue with some logic that U.S.–Soviet allies in the wars of 1967 and 1973 almost dragged both superpowers over the abyss, although the case seems more compelling for 1973.[13] But it is more likely that the omnipresence of U.S. and Soviet arsenals helped to bring both conflicts to a conclusion, which was more tolerable to both Arab and Israeli antagonists than any solution imposed by either, or both.[14] Sadat's willingness to risk war in 1973 was for limited objectives and his strategy would have had no long-term benefits had the war expanded into direct superpower involvement.[15]

Thus, their nuclear arsenals keep the superpowers removed from direct involvement in the Middle East more than they dissuade allies and clients from going to war. The evidence is slender that the Israelis or the Arabs have been deterred from launching surprise attacks by the potential nuclear or massive conventional commitments of the superpowers, even when those attacks were already risky without superpower involvement. It may be that a precondition for the Arab attack in 1973 was the acquiescence of Soviet patrons to the assault, but acquiescence is a very different matter from instigation. Nor has the Soviet nuclear deterrent prevented Israeli surprise or retaliatory strikes against Egypt, Syria, and Jordan when Israel's vital interests are perceived threatened. For the moment the nuclear diplomacy of the superpowers affects their dyadic interactions more than it does the initiation of Arab–Israeli conflict.

That this might change in the future in the presence of a disclosed Israeli nuclear deterrent is clear. Shai Feldman has usefully distinguished an Israeli "nuclear option" policy, in which Israel has the capacity to make nuclear weapons but has not actually done so, from the "bomb-in-the-basement" and "overt deterrence" policies. The latter two options would involve the actual manufacture of nuclear weapons or components (and, presumably, their delivery systems) but would differ on the acknowledgment of their status. The "overt deterrence" posture is favored by Feldman, in which Israel would declare publicly that it possesses a nuclear weapons delivery capability and would use it to protect its vital interests.[16]

U.S. extended deterrence could be coupled to Israeli nuclear disclosure only with great difficulty, if at all. Acknowledged Israeli nuclear capabilities could weaken rather than strengthen the U.S. commitment to protect Israel since these capabilities would reduce dependence. This could affect most profoundly the deterrence of Soviet direct involvement, which would leave any contest to the test of strength and will between Israel and its regional adversaries. Israeli nuclear forces would be viewed by many in the U.S. Congress, State Department, and public as destabilizing, however logical the case for their deployment on other grounds.[17] Disbelief in the unwillingness of Israel to use those weapons save in dire emergency would be increased by Arab suggestions that Israel's motives were aggressive rather than defensive. Loosening of the U.S. commitment to assist Israel by many means, including direct combat involvement if necessary, could be a by-product of the disclosed Israel nuclear deterrent.

U.S. potential involvement with the policies of its nuclear armed Mideast ally could provide leverage for the Soviets in their efforts to isolate the West from the Persian Gulf. The Saudis would almost certainly react to a disclosed Israeli nuclear deterrent by demanding improved conventional and possibly nuclear capabilities. Soviet overtures to provide those capabilities to Riyadh might be attractive to the latter. The opening wedge of Soviet penetration of the economies and political systems of Arab conservative monarchies would be provided by the ability of the Soviet Union to play upon Arab fears of Israeli nuclear preemption. Once penetrated, those countries would be neutralized as barriers to a more provocative Soviet policy in the Gulf and the Indian Ocean, one which might entertain the possibility of strangulation of sea lanes and forceful acquisition of a warm water port.

From the perspective of extended deterrence, American encouragement of an explicit Israeli deterrent only makes sense if it is assumed that we have no other options for deterring the Soviets and their clients from war. The history of Arab–Israeli war suggests, however, that we do. Diplomacy and conventional deterrence have provided for periods of peace in this region, and those same ingredients are not precluded from further contributions. A disclosed Israeli nuclear deterrent risks the gains of conventional deterrence and conflict resolution for a temporary and risky technological "quick fix."[18] Rather than facilitating U.S. extended deterrence in the region, it could preclude it. U.S. reluctance to commit itself to Israeli prewar diplomacy (fearing nuclear involvement) could backfire into Arab expectations of victory and the onset of war.

If the U.S. extended deterrence problem in the Middle East is intimately connected to the situation in the Gulf, it is also the case that extended deterrence in Europe is related to Mideast scenarios. War in the Gulf, or in the Middle East which expands to the Gulf would potentially affect the continuation of Europe's oil supplies. A disclosed Israeli nuclear deterrent could provoke a larger and more militant coalition of conservative and confrontationist Arab states, using economic leverage against Israel's Western patrons as their best strategy. Direct Western intervention against Arab efforts to twist the economic noose could be precluded by uncertainty about the role of Israeli nuclear weapons.

An Israeli deterrent might provide a convenient excuse for European members of NATO to separate their Middle Eastern policies from those of the United States, to the extent that they identified the United States as Israel's primary security guarantor. The U.S. position in the Western alliance vis-à-vis deterrence of Arab or Soviet hostilities in the Middle East could be an increasingly isolated one. It might turn out that no North Atlantic Treaty Organization ally would support U.S. efforts to guarantee the sovereignty of Israel if Israel announced an explicit policy of nuclear deterrence. This is especially problematical for the United States if European NATO members perceive the Israeli deterrent as provocative to the USSR, and as likely to hasten the escalation of war in the Third World to war in the First.

In terms of explicit comparison between "bomb in the basement" and disclosure policies for Israel, considerations of extended deterrence are not one sided. The balance favors unacknowledged capabilities, but not so strongly as it did with regard to the issues surrounding crisis stability. Unlike crisis stability, extended deterrence must take into account the multiplicity of other commitments that the superpowers have made outside the region. U.S. capabilities to provide conventional deterrence in Europe are influenced by, and influence, U.S. expectations for conventional deterrence in the Middle East and Persian Gulf. Similar, although not identical, is the case of Soviet commitments to Warsaw Pact allies, in terms of their implied or expressed commitments to Arab states. Notwithstanding these acknowledgments that a net assessment is more complicated in the case of extended deterrence, compared to crisis stability, the net assessment is not dissimilar. Unacknowledged capabilities for nuclear preemption or reprisal offer Israel more security than does open disclosure of an intention to go nuclear.

In fact, there is a significant likelihood that U.S. extended deterrence with regard to Israel could be weakened after Israeli disclosure. U.S. policymakers would have to grapple with domestic turbulence over the issue and with undoubted discontent within NATO. Arab states, which have in the past provided limited cooperation to the United States with regard to overflight rights, expedient basing, and cooperative training ventures, would be unlikely to do so unless the United States repudiated certain commitments to a nuclear armed Israel. The drift of "moderate" Arab states such as Egypt and Jordan into a marriage of convenience with the more "radical" regimes in Libya and Syria, for example, would remove U.S. diplomatic leverage from important parts of the Middle East and Southwest Asia chessboard. Forced to choose between commitments to Israel, in the face of unanimous Arab hostility toward those commitments, and the avoidance of European and Soviet hostility, the United States might easily choose the latter option. If Israeli disclosure were to bring about this second outcome, it would be more unfortunate for the Israelis than for the Americans, although a net loss for both.

Escalation Control

The control of escalation from the U.S. perspective requires the dampening of mutual alarms between U.S. and Soviet political and military leaders during a crisis.[19] If deterrence fails, escalation control requires the selective targeting and flexible use of strategic and other nuclear forces while seeking war termination at the lowest possible level of violence consistent with policy objectives.[20] To extend the process of escalation control into prewar deterrence and postwar bargaining, when more than two adversaries are involved, implies a coalition management problem for both superpowers which may be beyond their capabilities.

According to experts, it is not clear that U.S. nuclear forces can be alerted safely—that is, consistent with the simultaneous requirements for maintaining "positive" and "negative" control.[21] Positive control implies that the forces will be responsive to alert commands when those commands are received from authorized political leadership. Negative control should prevent accidental or unauthorized alerts, or overcompensations which could provoke excessive alerts on the other side.[22] Paul Bracken, John D. Steinbruner, and other expert analysts of U.S. command and control have found the system deficient in peacetime and during crises on these very points.

Steinbruner notes that the U.S. strategic command, control, and communications (C^3) system is more vulnerable to destruction than the retaliatory forces themselves.[23] Some 100 properly targeted Soviet warheads could destroy fixed command posts, communication links between warning sensors and the command posts, or cause other disruption which could prevent Emergency Action Messages from reaching U.S. ICBMs, SLBMs, and bombers. Paul Bracken discusses at length the horizontal and vertical integration which has taken place in the organizations for warning, attack assessment, intelligence, and force command in the U.S. C^3 system.[24] Horizontal integration has led to the creation of centrally coordinated war plans embodied in the Single Integrated Operational Plan (SIOP).[25] Vertical integration means that warning, intelligence, force commands, and National Command Authorities are tightly coupled into a system which is inundated with "real time" instantaneous information feedback. This vertical integration can result in the gross perturbation of the entire system by small and unrelated stimuli.[26]

In normal peacetime conditions, single American accidents such as failed chips in the computers of the North American Air Defense Command (NO-

RAD) do not lead to catastrophic failures because other parts of the system create checks and balances against overreaction. Under crisis conditions, it is less clear that the tightly coupled system would interpret correctly coincidental inputs. It might attribute casual relationships to discrete events, leading U.S. decisionmakers to maximize alerts which would be observed by Soviet leaders making pessimistic worst-case estimates.[27]

That this tightly coupled system could fail under the multiple stresses of unprecedented superpower crises is disconcerting enough. The superpowers have to some extent compensated for this possibility by providing for mutual emergency communications via the "Hot Line" and (in the U.S. case) by avoiding gratuitously provocative actions during crises. The Kennedy administration, for example, went to great lengths to reassure the Soviet Union during the Cuban missile crisis that removal of the Soviet missiles from Cuba was the sole objective of the U.S. navel "quarantine."[28] The originally proposed blockade perimeter was drawn in after the crisis began to provide to the Soviet leaders more time to consider the gravity of attempts to run the blockade. Secretary of Defense Robert S. McNamara wanted to be reassured by the navy that no unnecessarily provocative acts would be committed against Soviet surface or subsurface craft.[29] In this event, the crisis was defused on terms very favorable to the United States, but several unexpected events escaped presidential control, including the straying of a U-2 spy plane into Soviet airspace.[30]

Stresses to maintain escalation control after war began would be more pronounced. Soviet military doctrine is alleged to express disinterest in U.S. concepts of flexible targeting and escalation control during war.[31] As Benjamin Lambeth has noted, the important "threshold" for Soviet planners is the decision to go to war in the first place, and not the comparatively unimportant (for them) decision whether to escalate from conventional to nuclear war.[32]

Although Soviet literature has apparently recognized the possibility that war in Europe might begin with a prolonged conventional phase, this does not foreclose their option of preemptive use of nuclear weapons if it seems advantageous, or to avoid what might otherwise appear as unsupportable losses.[33] Soviet capabilities for flexible countercombatant targeting have increased in recent decades, but their expectations for controlling escalation during a major war in Europe are not optimistic.[34] Raymond Garthoff has noted that the Soviet Union should not be misperceived as optimistic that it can "win" a strategic nuclear war against the United States in the classical sense. Rather, Soviet leaders would enter such a war only reluctantly, but once engaged, it would use both offensive and defensive forces for maximum military advantage.[35] Robert Berman and John Baker note that Soviet military doctrine and force structure are prepared for short or long wars, using conventional or nuclear weapons, as their perceived necessity dictates.[36]

These reviews of U.S. and Soviet predilections for crisis management and postattack escalation control imply serious cautions for U.S. allies relying upon explicit nuclear deterrent threats. Given the understanding of weaknesses in the U.S. command structure and the contours of Soviet military doctrine and planning, the expectation that regional nuclear use could be contained to the Middle East given superpower involvement seems improbable. Only an Arab–Israeli conflict which somehow escaped serious attention and commitment by either superpower could be counted on to remain confined despite Israeli or Arab nuclear use.

A Soviet preemptive strike to disarm an Israeli nuclear deterrent without specific provocation seems unlikely and risky.[37] But this "worst-case" possibility is too easily rejected. Soviet expectations that a nuclear armed Israel might preempt against the Arab allies of the Soviet Union during a crisis is more pertinent. This could trigger higher levels of alert in the Soviet Union and compensatory reactions by the United States. As Bracken has noted, U.S. command systems and their Soviet counterparts are also "coupled" during crises by the increased attentiveness of both sides to moves that in other times might be ignored as innocent or inconsequential.[38] The danger is not hypothetical. During the 1973 war between Israel, Egypt, and Syria, a Soviet threat of unilateral intervention provoked a Defense Condition 3 alert of U.S. forces. Analysts believe this was the most serious U.S.–Soviet confrontation since the Cuban missile crisis.

The possession of nuclear weapons by Israel might deter Arab states from making incredible threats to destroy Israeli forces or society by a "bolt from the blue." The bolt from the blue is not the principal concern in this instance, just as it is not the principal concern of U.S. planners fearing escalation and war. More probable is the expansion of a limited war into a confrontation in which both Israel and its regional antagonists felt the ultimate values of survival for either side were at stake. It is difficult to imagine Israeli leaders who possessed usable nuclear forces not using those forces in such conditions, and it is equally difficult to imagine that Arab and Soviet expectations would not be pessimistic. Thus the threat to use nuclear weapons by Israel could deter premeditated Arab attacks but have the opposite effect during a crisis, even without offsetting nuclear capabilities in the hands of Israel's opponents. Arab attackers contemplating war would have to assume pessimistic Israeli perceptions should the war go against Israel in its early stages. The incentive to attack massively with conventional forces, rather than to launch a limited objectives attack, would be increased.[39]

If deterrence failed as it did in 1967 and 1973, U.S. efforts to persuade Israel not to threaten or use nuclear weapons might not succeed. Expectations by U.S. leaders of Israeli first use would lead to heightened alerts and visible tensions in the U.S.–Soviet relationship. Soviet leaders might not fear U.S. attack against their forces or allies, but they would worry about desperation plans to rescue Israel from conventional defeat in order to preclude Israeli nuclear strikes. U.S. efforts to contain the war below the nuclear threshold could project U.S. conventional forces directly into the conflict, with the possibility that they might actually oppose Israeli forces.

If the Soviet Union anticipated that the United States could not contain Israeli nuclear use, or if Soviet leaders assumed that we desired Israeli nuclear preemption against Arab states, their "worst-case" assessment of American motives could be a self-fulfilling prophecy. There is the fortuitous possibility that U.S. and Soviet leaders would join in dissuading Israeli nuclear strikes. This collaboration could be explicit or tacit. Tacit collaboration could take the form of Soviet threats to punish Israel (with diplomatic or military means) to which the United States responded with silence. Threatened punishments could range from conventional war waged by Soviet surrogates to direct Soviet conventional involvement. Soviet–U.S. collaboration against expansion of the Suez War in 1956 provides some precedent.

Much would depend upon the status of U.S.–Soviet relations at the outbreak of Arab–Israeli war. In the absence of other issues of equally disputatious content, U.S. and Soviet leaders could share the perception that escalation to superpower confrontation would benefit neither party. But this avoidance of escalation would be conditional. If Israeli nuclear strikes against Arab cities were perceived as a challenge to Soviet security guarantees, some Soviet response independent of U.S. wishes could be provoked. Soviet military options short of nuclear or massive conventional involvement of their own forces are foreseeable. One of these is the transfer to Arab allies of tactical nuclear weapons delivery systems from land, air, or sea-based platforms. Anticipatory transfers of this sort could deter Israeli first use even before war began and might be chosen by the Soviet Union as a prewar option. Israeli nuclear attacks against Arab capitals would likely be followed by Arab nuclear retaliation.

The political setting for postattack escalation control between Israel and its nuclear-armed opponents is not promising apart from the potential for superpower involvement. Even without superpower forces used by proxies or by the United States or Soviet Union themselves, Israeli nuclear strikes would bring only temporary advantage. Defeated Arab states would regard countercity attacks against their homelands as another holocaust. Their revenge with superior forces, including nuclear weapons, would be planned from the first days after their capitulation. This long-run perspective on Israeli nuclear use suggests that it would eventually be self-defeating, however temporarily "satisfying." An Arab war of revenge might begin with their "bolt from the blue" attacks against Israel, and it would not require many bombs exploding over Israeli soil to destroy its unique civilization.

From the U.S. perspective, Israeli nuclear deterrence can work to its advantage only if the outstanding political grievances between Israel and her neighbors were resolved. Recognizing this, Shai Feldman has suggested that Israel adopt a declaratory policy of nuclear deterrence while contracting its borders to pre-1967 lines. In his judgment, this would remove the casūs belli from the Arabs unless they sought only the destruction of Israel for its own sake. For that Arab objective, an Israeli nuclear deterrent is a necessary and sufficient condition in his judgment.[40]

The difficulty with this analysis is that it would not be obvious in all cases that Arab war aims were limited, even if the Arabs perceived them to be. A state of Israel's size can perceive ultimate threats in contingencies regarded by its opponents as less than total. There is little space to trade for time in Israel's case, and benevolent assumptions about Arab intentions after war begins are not a prudent basis for war plans. Once committed to a nuclear deterrent behind shrunken borders, Israeli leaders will be under duress to use that deterrent as a compellant to stop Arab attacks which by definition would now threaten Israel's very existence.

Even if successful under these conditions of restricted borders, a disclosed Israeli deterrent might preclude overt aggression at the cost of intensified Palestinian and other covert aggression. As Robert Friedlander points out in the next chapter of this book, PLO and other guerrillas would have the advantage of potentially provoking nuclear conflict between Israel and Arab states, bringing down the house on both. The appeal of this to the more fanatical terrorists among displaced Palestinians, Syrian surrogates, and Iranian proxies cannot be disregarded. Of course, many Palestinian Arabs in Israel would be among the victims of any major war which included nuclear exchanges in the region. This might dissuade Israel and Arab states more than terrorists, however, since the latter have less to lose from a destruction of the status quo. The provocation of catalytic war between Israel and Arab states has been on the agenda of terrorists in the past, and there is no reason to suppose that the objective has been removed from their catalogue.[41]

In terms of implications for escalation control, summary comparison of the two options, "bomb in the basement" or disclosure, is scenario dependent. If the Arabs are determined to acquire nuclear weapons in any case and to persist in intermittent attempts to regain territory lost in 1967 or to damage Israel itself, disclosure could reinforce Israeli deterrence of Arab first use. The intentions of Arab states are sometimes difficult to ascertain in the present, let alone in the future. Israeli worst-case analysts could also argue that, should deterrence fail, a disclosure policy would be no worse than a de facto or undisclosed policy of nuclear retaliation. Opponents of Israel might be less willing to escalate a war begun over limited territorial gains into an attack against Israel's survival if it were known that Israel would respond to the latter kind of attack with nuclear reprisals.

The danger for escalation control lies not only within the Middle East, but also outside of it. First use of nuclear weapons by Israel may cross a new threshold in the relationships between Arab and Jew, between Third World nationalism and perceived "neocolonialism," and between the superpowers. Except in retaliation for Arab first use, or in the case of a lost conventional war which would end with Israel's annihilation, Israel's first use of nuclear weapons would have systemic and negative connotations. Its subsequent exclusion from international forums within and outside of the United Nations system would be a foregone conclusion. Distance between U.S. and Israeli foreign policy objectives would grow. Although novelty wears off and "getting used to" the existence of nuclear weapons is something that the world has learned to do, the fact is that the first use of nuclear weapons since Nagasaki would be a jolt. No subsequent regional war in the Middle East or Southwest Asia would ever begin in quite the same psychological climate.

Assuming Arab nuclear weapons, it is difficult to see how the superpowers would control the use of nuclear weapons by their allies once they were introduced into a Mideast war. The character of Arab and Israeli nuclear forces (assuming one would follow the other) would not facilitate escalation control. Undoubtedly vulnerable to the superpowers' overwhelming arsenals, Arab and Israeli nuclear forces might also be vulnerable to one another. This mutual vulnerability of nuclear forces would have the opposite effect compared to the mutual vulnerability of cities, but not forces, in the U.S.–Soviet relationship. In the latter case, vulnerable cities and invulnerable forces are thought to contribute to deterrence and escalation control. In the case of vulnerable forces, the reverse is true. And the relationship between vulnerable forces or cities involves symmetry or reciprocity, if it is to preserve deterrence or control escalation. A one-sided Arab or Israeli vulnerability to the opponent's first strike could tempt that attack in the belief that an opponent disarmed of its nuclear forces would surrender.

This consideration of vulnerable forces versus vulnerable cities raises another issue relevant to choice between the options of disclosure or deliberate ambiguity. That related issue is the matter of targeting priorities for any disclosed or unacknowledged force. The basic distinctions in the literature are between counterforce targeting against the opponent's military forces or political and military command structure, versus countervalue targeting of cities and other societal values.

Such distinctions can be meaningful if applied to large countries with immense land areas and in which some of the strategic nuclear forces do not have to be co-located with major population centers. Only the superpowers and possibly the People's Republic of China can hope to achieve some significant measure of dispersion for part of their strategic forces, relative to probable threats to their survivability. Even in Europe, comparatively smaller land areas pose almost insurmountable problems for those who wish to make such distinctions between counterforce and countervalue targets.

Israeli disclosure would beg the question of where these weapons were targeted and when—that is, which targets would be struck first and which withheld for later attack. Some categorical pronouncements would be expected and some required, unless Israel were to be charged by its critics with a "genocide bomb" aimed only or solely at cities. Publicity aside, the targeting dilemmas are real, and distinctions between counterforce and countervalue targets, as Louis René Beres suggests in the introduction to this book, would be difficult to make and enforce during war. Thus it might come about that the attempt to control escalation, by threatening that first strikes would be launched against enemy military forces (by Israel or the Arabs), would promote escalation. This could happen if asymmetric expectations of the contending sides led them to evaluate differently the consequences of escalation control by attacking forces and sparing cities.

Thus, if regional escalation control were judged contributory to Israeli defeat, it would no longer commend itself to Israeli leaders. This situation could develop after the first exchanges of "tactical" nuclear weapons on both sides. The small land area of Israel and the concentration of much of its population within a few major cities makes it *strategically* vulnerable to *tactical* bombardments. Thus Israeli leaders must treat invasion of Israel within its pre-1967 borders as an imminent holocaust, especially if tactical nuclear weapons delivered by air or surface-to-surface missile were known to exist in Arab arsenals. If Israel chooses nuclear disclosure, the Arab incentive to nuclear preemption would increase. Notice that the tail wags the dog here in the presence of an acknowledged Israeli deterrent. Having declared its intention to retaliate with nuclear weapons against serious provocations, Israel invites the Arabs to engage in nuclear preemption if deterrence fails. The problem with this invitation is that it may be dissuasive to the Israelis as well as to the Arabs. The reason for the problematic character of this temptation to Arab preemption is that Arab and Israeli vulnerabilities are not the same. One or two bombs dropped on major Israeli cities would be a holocaust, morally and politically. It might spell the end of the State of Israel. It seems difficult for Israel to pose a comparable threat to the political viability of all its Arab neighbors, *especially* if Israel is struck first. The larger number of Arab states, and their attendant populations and land areas makes them relatively less vulnerable to Israeli nuclear strikes. This asymmetric societal vulnerability between Arabs and Israelis, once nuclear war begins, almost guarantees loss of escalation control.

For escalation control to work successfully in the context of Arab–Israeli conflict, a policy of Israeli nuclear nondisclosure would be preferable to overt disclosure. Disclosure of Israeli nuclear capabilities would call for decisions about declaratory and employment policies which, if made explicit, would inflame the Arab world and alienate Israel's friends. If those decisions are not made explicit, then uncertainty will work to unleash escalation rather than to control it. This is the case because the probability of escalation involves both controllable and uncontrollable risks, the latter based on interactions between the antagonists and idiosyncrasies beyond their control. Israeli disclosure would remove some uncertainties which now contribute to deterrence and escalation control, and substitute others which may have the reverse effects.

Conclusion

A disclosed Israeli nuclear deterrent is not without its appeals to a state with Israel's security problems, but only if those problems are defined without reference to superpower relationships. More inclusive considerations, including the U.S. commitment to Israel and the possible escalations from initial nuclear threats or use, do not commend such disclosure. If Israel is resolved to move toward nuclear disclosure within the next decade, the U.S. should use its diplomatic and military influence to prevent such a choice.

From the U.S. perspective, an Israeli nuclear deterrent invites expansion of regional war and superpower confrontation in crises during which the United States and the Soviet Union might otherwise stand aside. Dissuasion of the Israelis from nuclear declaratory and employment policies may require more limited U.S. extended deterrence commitments to Israel when it is faced with the possibility of conventional war. Israel's threat to cross the threshold of explicit nuclear deterrence policies may force Washington to reconsider previous "evenhandedness" in its security commitments. The best option for Israel remains discreet silence about its nuclear capabilities. Both superpowers have every interest in encouraging discretion rather than valor on the issue of Israeli nuclear disclosure.

10
The Armageddon Factor:
Terrorism and Israel's Nuclear Option

Robert A. Friedlander

To understand nuclear politics in the Middle East is to be able to distinguish between certainties and probabilities. Although there is no hard evidence, some informed commentators hold that Israel is not only capable of developing a successful nuclear technology, but has already produced atomic arms.[1] This is a possibility shunned by almost every Middle East analyst and specialist, as well as one being muted by the Israelis themselves. Current predictions are that an Islamic bomb, long in the making, is not far from completion—most likely by Pakistan—and that the Iraqis, recovering from Osiraq, are back on the road to producing nuclear weapons.[2] That is another Mideast prospect that the free world, in particular, is reluctant to recognize.

Possession of nuclear weapons is one thing; fashioning a workable nuclear strategy is quite another. In the Middle East politics often control state decisionmaking. Yet, pragmatic policy is essential to any rational defense posture, which also enters probability and unintended consequences into the overall equation. According to Edward Teller, member of the Committee on the Present Danger and adviser to President Ronald Reagan, "Defense, if the national peacekeeping aim is successful, serves to prevent the outbreak of war."[3] Defense in the atomic era holds to the same national objectives as in past centuries of conventional warfare: (1) to deter aggression whenever and wherever possible; (2) if not successful in the primary task, then to limit the extent of damage to the defending armed forces and the national interest.[4] There are those who would argue, at least from the Israeli perspective, that a nuclear deterrent in the Middle East is a matter of national survival.[5]

Scientist Freeman Dyson argues that effective control of nuclear weapons will not occur until the nuclear powers agree "upon a coherent concept of what the weapons are for."[6] If not clearly apparent with respect to the superpowers, the role of the nuclear option is very obvious in terms of contemporary Middle East politics. For Israel, the "bomb in the basement" represents a delimiting deterrence upon the military ambitions of her sworn enemies and a safety mechanism to ensure the continuing support of her avowed major ally, the United States. For the rejectionist Arab states, such as Iraq and Libya, an Islamic bomb could represent a way to neutralize both Israel's conventional dominance and its suspected nuclear superiority, perhaps cowering the Israelis into a supine diplomatic and political posture. In the mind of Muammar Khadafi, the Islamic bomb (or to be more precise, a Libyan bomb) may at long last allow him to obliterate the hated Israeli infidels, whatever the cost.[7]

Deriving a passive protection from their still undisclosed nuclear weaponry, which many knowledgeable experts concede to exist,[8] Israel currently is in the enviable position of maintaining a nuclear deterrent without disclosure. Even if credibility does not require an open acknowledgment, disclosure remains a key issue. If Israel were to disclose a nuclear weapons capability, would this hasten Arab proliferation? In other words, if Israel were to bring the bomb out of the basement and into the light of day, would the result be the accelerated development of a counter Islamic bomb? And would another consequence be rising levels of terrorism directed against Israel?

Economist Robert Powell defines deterrence as an agreement by one adversary in a confrontation "to lose," even though possessing the ability to destroy the other side.[9] This is, admittedly, a curious view. The traditional military and political meaning of deterrence is the ability to strike a heavy, decisive retaliatory blow at an enemy, one that would inflict such a magnitude of losses that any potential victimizer will not risk a first strike, or, in conventional terms, to undertake an invasion. Deterrence can also be psychological. The mere threat of annihilation may be enough to introduce a measure of stability into an unstable regional or world order.[10] Iran, after the fall of the Shah, did not meet these minimal standards and, hence, Iraq's invasion.

On the other hand, journalist and nuclear commentator Jonathan Schell maintains that for the superpowers, "In the Middle East, the military policy is either one of nuclear first use or nothing."[11] Schell is wrong in this assertion, as he is wrong on many other claims. The Soviet Union did approach the threshold of high risk-taking during the 1973 October War,[12] and the United States responded with a Defense Condition 3 Alert,[13] but Egyptian prudence vis-à-vis the Soviet Union and U.S. pressure on Israel helped to defuse the crisis. Soviet rebuilding of the smashed Syrian war machine in the Bekaa valley during the winter of 1982–83 paralleled U.S. pressure upon Israel to deescalate its Lebanon intervention.[14] In neither case was there a direct threat of nuclear confrontation, and in both instances superpower intervention actually led to a de facto stabilization between Israel and its Arab adversaries.

Improbabilities represent a much greater danger to the Middle East than do current controversies. It is traditional to believe, as does former U.S. Secretary of Defense James Schlesinger, that "a nuclear war would probably get started only by miscalculation."[15] This is the leader-loses-control-of-events theory.[16] But an equally logical postulate is that of risk competition—taking risks for a competitive or decisive edge, knowing full well what the costs of such gambles might be.[17] Bringing a Middle East bomb up from the basement might have the advantage of intimidating Israel's state adversaries in a major diplomatic or military conflict. The credibility of the bomb holder might be temporarily enhanced. The long-range implications, however, could include fragmented alliance structures while increasing the likelihood that a future confrontation would ignite a nuclear war. Moreover, Israeli disclosure would likely encourage adversaries to step-up state-supported terrorism, especially where disclosure might accelerate regional nuclearization.

Since time and distance in the Middle East are microcosmic rather than macrocosmic, the nature of any threat and the type of protective response are greatly accelerated. Once a bomb is brought into the open, it then becomes an effective part of a nations' permanent defense arsenal. Inevitably, given the volatile politics of the Middle East and the historic role of force as a first resort, the possibility of nuclear conflict via escalation rather than mistake is not inconceivable. Israel prides itself on the theory of flexible response. Former Secretary of State Henry Kissinger, in reacting to a statement that the North Atlantic Treaty Organization alliance has adopted an unarticulated policy against the first use of nuclear weapons, retorted that such an approach "creates the dangerous impression that we are willing to be defeated with conventional weapons."[18] If this philosophy is applied to a situation where there is a disclosed and credible Israeli or Islamic bomb, the chances for nuclearization of any interstate belligerency are increased many fold.

A *New Republic* editorial presciently warns that "the biggest real-life danger of a nuclear war is not the breakdown of deterrence between the superpowers, but a spiraling crisis triggered by the use of a nuclear bomb by a Third World country or terrorist group."[19] Several years ago, the International Peace Research Institute headquartered in Stockholm, on the tenth anniversary of its founding, predicted that within a decade some thirty-five countries would have the ability to produce atomic weapons. Such a development, the Peace Research Institute direly warned, would make nuclear war inevitable.[20] A short time after, the General Assembly of the United Nations requested the secretary-general to appoint a Group of Experts on a Comprehensive Study on Nuclear Weapons. Its report was issued in 1980, somewhat more cautiously predicting that the capability to develop nuclear weapons was "within the reach of 20 to 25 non-nuclear-weapon states."[21]

In terms of nuclear technology, the Middle East is an unmonitored arena. Proliferation raises the nuclear ante in any game of power politics. Although there are no guarantees, Israel could contribute to nonproliferation efforts by maintaining its policy of deliberate ambiguity.

William G. Hyland, editor of *Foreign Affairs*, draws a chilling analogy between the events of 1914 and the diplomacy of the contemporary world.

"There would be no rival alerts," he observes, "no one backing down, no one wanting to fight, but a mounting confrontation that could lead to fighting."[22] In other words, there is an escalation threshold beyond which events take control over those who had precipitated them. For reasons such as this, and because Israel was suspected of possessing a weapon which the Moslem states did not possess (or at least the capability of producing one), first Iran and then Egypt proposed a Middle East nuclear-weapon-free zone in 1974. The U.N. General Assembly, in support of this proposal, called on all states in that region either to accede to the Nuclear Non-Proliferation Treaty or to give solemn assurances to the U.N. Security Council that they would not acquire or develop nuclear weapons. Israel rejected both propositions.[23] Iraq ratified the Non-Proliferation Treaty in 1969, but, as Avi Beker points out in chapter 8, ratifications and good faith implementation are not always synonymous in the world arena.

On June 7, 1981, sixteen Israeli F-15 and F-16 jet fighter-bombers dropped sixteen MK.84 iron bombs on the Osiraq nuclear reactor in Baghdad, knocking it out of commission, ending the threat—for the time being—of a second Jewish Holocaust, and letting loose a firestorm of protest in the international community.[24] The Arab reaction was predictable and imaginative. A resolution of the Arab League presented to the U.N. Security Council labeled Israel's attack "an act of state terrorism." Kuwait's foreign minister accused Israel of "acts of terrorism and piracy." Even British Prime Minister Margaret Thatcher characterized Israel's conduct as "a grave breach of international law."[25]

The Arab League also called for compensation in addition to condemnation, but resolution 487 voted by the U.N. Security Council, calling the Israeli attack "a clear violation of the Charter of the United Nations and the norms of international conduct," was mild indeed.[26] In fact, the General Assembly resolution adopted more than three years later, on November 21, 1984 (a curious time to resume debate on the Osiraq reactor bombing), not only reiterated the claim of a charter violation, but called for measures to ensure Israel's compliance with resolution 487 and further placed "Israeli aggression against the Iraqi nuclear installations" on the provisional agenda for the fortieth session of the General Assembly.[27] The Israeli response at the time of the June 1981 Security Council debate was blunt and straightforward: Israel had exercised "its inherent right of self-defense as understood in general international law and as preserved in Article 51 of the United Nations Charter."[28]

Traditional international law allows a victim of armed attack or threatened aggression to utilize force in self-defense, as long as the force is proportional to the threatened harm. Article 51 of the U.N. charter has codified that right, as long as the act or acts in question are a response to an armed attack or armed aggression. The International Court of Justice has implicitly en-

dorsed this view in the *Certain Expenses* case (1963) by supporting the freedom of action by states, when that freedom is not violative of basic charter
principles.[29] The key issue in any situation involving the use of force is
whether the target state should be required to wait for an undisputed attack
against it, or whether an intended victim can strike first at its impending
assailant. Article 2 (4) of the U.N. charter obligates member states to refrain
from the use of force or the threat of force directed against the territorial
integrity and the political independence of another state party. In a much
quoted remark delivered at the annual meeting of the American Society of
International Law almost twenty years ago, former Secretary of State Dean
Acheson caustically observed: "The survival of states is not a matter of
law."[30]

Israel was convinced that elimination of the Osiraq nuclear reactor was
a matter of its national survival.[31] One distinguished American legalist, in the
aftermath of the bombing, defended the Israeli action as one of self-preservation, permitted by international law.[32] In a reconsideration published two
years later, he analogized "Operation Babylon" (as the Israelis termed it) to
the doctrine of humanitarian intervention as practiced in the famed Entebbe
raid.[33] Humanitarian intervention, however, was designed for different purposes and has been used solely as legal justification for a rescue operation, in
addition to being a controversial but still valid remedy.[34] Surprisingly, the
same author rejects outright the theory of anticipatory self-defense,[35] which
undoubtedly provides the best explanation for Israel's motives in unleashing
the attack.

From the Arab perspective—and in this instance rhetoric and sincerity
are more than likely intertwined—the Israeli strike was an act of state terrorism directed at the entire Arab world.[36] Since terrorism is frequently in the
eye of the beholder, the Moslem feeling of outrage for the most part was a
genuine one, although it was clear in the U.N. corridors and at diplomatic
dinner tables that several Arab governments were not altogether unhappy to
see a predatory Iraq temporarily defanged of its nuclear teeth.[37] From the
Israeli perspective, the feeling of terror was also genuine, despite the Begin
government's attempt to draw political advantage from the Osiraq raid.[38]
Israel's ultimate alternative was either bomb or be bombed.

According to Carl von Clausewitz, the character and scope of any war
should be based upon the elements of political probabilities.[39] The same holds
true for the use of force short of military conflict. Israel's bombing raid on
Iraq's nearly completed nuclear reactor was indeed a preemptive strike, but
it was also a carefully calculated act of deterrence, faced with the prospect of
an Arab nuclear weapons capability.[40] Operation Babylon was undeniably an
attempt to buy time, but to the Israelis, faced with potential catastrophe, time
was of the essence. From June 7, 1981, to the present date, the Middle East
peace process has inched forward, with great difficulty and much agony, but

there are developments which would not have been possible with a nuclear-ized Iraq. "If nuclear proliferation to the Middle East is inevitable, it is pref-erable that it occur *after* the central issues dividing Israel and the Arabs have been settled."[41] A major problem of Middle East conflicts, and almost every interstate confrontation, is that "the consequences are never as predictable and the moral calculus is never as clear-cut as war advocates contend."[42] (Witness the Israeli invasion and occupation of Lebanon from Israel's point of view then and now.)

Brian Jenkins, a leading U.S. authority on many aspects of terrorism, warns that "terrorists emulate states," and that it is within the realm of pos-sibility for a terrorist group to "go nuclear." Responding to Israeli disclosure of a nuclear option, terrorists could conceivably feel compelled to "go nu-clear" themselves. Moreover, taking into account the imitative factor vis-à-vis other terrorist groups, one nuclear terrorist incident, or even a major cred-ible threat, could quite literally set off a chain reaction of similar events.[43] Professor Geoffrey Kemp, a security specialist, admits that "it is not difficult to imagine a situation where Palestinian demands were backed up by nuclear blackmail."[44] The Palestine Liberation Organization (PLO) is the main can-didate for unleashing such a threat, but events in Lebanon over the past few years have demonstrated beyond question that radical Moslem fanaticism might intentionally seek to bring about a nuclear armageddon.

Concern over the possibilities of nuclear terrorism by knowledgeable commentators is well-documented.[45] With respect to nuclear terrorism in any conceivable form, the real question is not one of probability, but that of cred-ibility. This applies to individuals and organizations as well as to nonstate actors. Investigative reporter Ovid Demaris concludes his well-researched study of international terrorist organizations with a dire warning: "Nuclear terrorism is the wave of the future."[46] With the proliferation of nuclear weap-onry and the incremental growth of states capable of developing a nuclear military technology, the mathematical chances of a terrorist group stealing, adapting, or constructing a nuclear device is not beyond the realm of reason-able prediction. British security agencies reluctantly concede that a potential terrorist nuclear incident is undeniably credible. In their view, the issue is no longer *if* such an event is feasible, but rather *when* an episode of mass de-struction will finally occur.[47]

In this type of scenario, deterrence is a useless concept. How does a gov-ernment retaliate against nuclear terrorists? Should nuclear blackmail lend itself to a strategy of counterterror? Hardening targets is not sufficient pro-tection. Intelligence, group penetration, use of rapid counterforce, and an effective technology are but some of the means tried by the various govern-ments which have been subjected to audacious acts of terror-violence, but these measures pale under the dark shadow of the nuclear cloud. And what of a sponsoring state with respect to a nuclear terrorist group? Would retaliation by a victimized government with access to nuclear weapons increase or decrease the possibilities of a nuclear exchange, especially in the volatile Middle East?

One cannot overlook the past history of the PLO acting as a terrorist organization when surveying the potential for atomic disaster. The PLO has never ceased to embrace murder and barbarism as the prime means of attaining its objectives (whatever they may be), even if the battleground happens to consist of a grade school, a kibbutz nursery, or a toy store. The PLO campaign of terror-violence waged against Israel and the West for the past two decades has violated every extant human rights declaration and convention. To the PLO leadership the end justifies the means, and the means appear to be open-ended. Would the PLO, or the fragmented radical Palestinian leadership, go nuclear if it had the chance? The answer is, of course, mere speculation, but the historical record does not seem to be very encouraging.[48] An Israeli shift toward nuclear disclosure would likely heighten the prospect of nuclear terrorism against Israel.

Small wonder, then, that the U.S. Senate on June 15, 1984, by a vote of 82 to 0, recommended establishment of a nuclear risk reduction center by the governments of the United States and the Soviet Union. The recommendation was based in part upon the fear that a terrorist group in possession of nuclear materials or nuclear weapons could literally trigger an atomic war between the superpowers.[49] A U.S.–Soviet Hot Line has been established and upgraded,[50] and the fear of a nuclear terrorist incident was one of the major reasons for its employment. But direct confrontation between the superpowers is less of a probable threat than the perceived need to come to the aid of an embattled ally, who may be on the verge of either targeting or being the target of some form of nuclear weaponry.

Despite Israel's repeated pledge since 1962 that it will not be the first country to introduce nuclear warfare into the Middle East,[51] it was reported by some sources that the Israeli government was ready to utilize nuclear arms against Soviet-backed Egyptian forces in the October War of 1973.[52] If this had been attempted, the 1914 analogy may have become much more than a mere academic theory. The balance of terror in the Middle East is today, as it has been in the past, a very precarious one to say the least. Joseph Stalin once remarked that a nuclear weapon was something which is used to frighten people with weak nerves.[53] Many, many people throughout the globe are already frightened, even those with very strong nerves.

Although the precise nexus between Israel's nuclear strategy and nuclear proliferation in the Middle East is impossible to determine, one relationship seems clear: an overt Israeli move from "basement" to disclosure would hasten the spread of nuclear weapons among Israel's adversaries. Together with the understanding that "deliberate ambiguity" already provides Israel with a measure of enhanced deterrence—and does this without needless provocation of the Arabs—this suggests that Israel should continue with its present commitment to ambiguity. In so doing, it would reduce the risk not only of nuclear war, but also of a greater incidence of terrorism (especially state-supported terror-violence) against Israel.

Politically and historically, the Middle East has been a crucible for crises and conflict in the twentieth century. This was true long before the nuclear Armageddon factor became a harsh reality. In our volatile contemporary world, the specter of the ultimate nightmare comes not only from the shadows cast by states, but also from atrocities committed by individual nonstate actors.

Terrorism has been a way of life and a way of death in the Middle East for such a sustained period of time that the world community has come to accept it as normal practice. While Israeli nuclear strategy is only one variable in determining the future course of terrorism in the region, prudent consideration of available options supports the maintenance of "deliberate ambiguity." With such a policy, Israel stands a better chance to achieve real security and to ward off the remorseless embrace of a Final Conflict.

11

Israel's Choice:
Nuclear Weapons or International Law

Burns H. Weston

Introduction: The Normative Framework

During the next several years, the State of Israel and her enemies confront a fateful choice: whether or not, in an area of continuing instability and conflict, to extend existing forms of military competition into the nuclear realm.[1] Should these Middle Eastern adversaries decide to "go nuclear," the prospect of egregious violations of international law would arise. Despite the fact that the world community has yet to enact an explicit treaty or treaty provision generally prohibiting the development, manufacture, stockpiling, deployment, or actual use of nuclear weapons, certain of the laws of war, both treaty-based and customary, would prohibit virtually all likely uses of these weapons. Simply put, the general laws of war count when it comes to nuclear weapons and warfare.

Of course, the fact that there does not yet exist a general treaty ban on the use and threat of use of nuclear weapons is not lost on those who would defend the legality of nuclear weapons. They admit to a series of important treaties prohibiting nuclear weapons in Antarctica, Latin America, outer space, and on the seabed beyond the limit of the national territorial seas.[2] They acknowledge the Partial Test Ban Treaty outlawing the testing of nuclear weapons in outer space, under water, and within the earth's atmosphere.[3] They do not deny that the U.N. General Assembly has on various occasions declared the use of nuclear weapons to be "a direct violation of the Charter of the United Nations,"[4] "contrary to the rules of international law and to the laws of humanity,"[5] "a crime against mankind and civilization,"[6] and therefore a matter of "permanent prohibition."[7] And they recognize that in the *Shimoda Case*,[8] a much too neglected decision, a Japanese tribunal felt compelled to condemn as contrary to international law the only instance of actual belligerent use of nuclear weapons to date, the United States bombings of Hiroshima and Nagasaki. Nevertheless, consistent with the traditional state-centric theory of international legal obligation, which requires that prohibitions on international conduct be based on the express or implied consent of states, they rest their claim, in substantial part, on the proposition drawn from the World Court decision in *The Case of the S.S. Lotus*,[9] to wit, that states are free to do whatever they are not strictly forbidden from doing.[10] Indeed, consistent with Cicero's oft-quoted maxim *inter arma silent leges* (in war the law is silent), some go so far as to contend that nuclear weapons have made the laws of war obsolete.[11]

But this is not the end of the matter. While the lack of an explicit ban may mean that nuclear weapons are not illegal per se,[12] the fact is that restraints on the conduct of war never have been limited to explicit treaty prohibitions alone. As stated by the International Military Tribunal at Nuremberg in September 1946:"The law of war is to be found not only in treaties, but in the customs and practices of states which gradually obtained universal recognition, and from the general principles of justice applied by jurists and practiced by military courts."[13] The law of war, like the whole of international law, is composed of more than treaty rules, explicit and otherwise.

Taking my lead from the Nuremberg Judgment, I have undertaken to consider what the conventional and customary laws of war have to say about our topic; and what I have found are at least six core rules that strike me as prima facie relevant.

1. That it is prohibited to use weapons or tactics that cause unnecessary or aggravated devastation and suffering;[14]

2. That it is prohibited to use weapons or tactics that cause indiscriminate harm as between combatants and noncombatant military and civilian personnel;[15]

3. That it is prohibited to effect reprisals that are disproportionate to their antecedent provocation or to legitimate military objectives, or that are disrespectful of persons, institutions, and resources otherwise protected by the laws of war;[16]

4. That it is prohibited to use weapons or tactics that cause widespread, long-term, and severe damage to the natural environment;[17]

5. That it is prohibited to use weapons or tactics that violate the neutral jurisdiction of nonparticipating states;[18] and

6. That it is prohibited to use asphyxiating, poisonous, or other gases, and all analogous liquids, materials, or devices, including bacteriologic methods of warfare.[19]

Of course, these humanitarian rules of armed conflict, as I choose to call them, are general rules, and like all general rules, which are susceptible to differing contextual as well as linguistic interpretation, they harbor exceptions. Also, each traditionally has involved, particularly the first three, a balancing of the customary principles of military necessity and humanity, with "the line of compromise," as McDougal has written, tending to be "closer to the polar terminus of military necessity than to that of humanity."[20] The relative tolerance heretofore extended to "scorched earth" and "saturation bombing" policies and to incendiary and V-weapons, for example, probably attest to this observation. Nevertheless, even after subjecting these core rules to the standards of sophisticated jurisprudence, as I have attempted to do elsewhere for the purpose of determining their precise jural quality,[21] one may reasonably accept their pertinence to nuclear weapons and warfare.

More precisely, one may reasonably reach the following three conclusions about these rules: first, that they continue as a vital civilizing influence upon the world community's warring propensities; second, that, as presently understood, they are endowed with an authority signal that communicates their applicability to nuclear as well as to conventional weapons and warfare; and finally, that there exists on the part of the world community as a whole—evidenced, thankfully, more in words than in deeds—an unmistakable intention to have them govern the use of nuclear weapons should ever that terrible day arrive again. To be sure, the extent to which this control intention could in fact be fulfilled is ambiguous, and this ambiguity will persist as long as the distribution of the world's effective power remains as oligarchic as it now is. But it would be error to conclude from this ambiguity that there is no prescription or law placing nuclear weapons and warfare under the legal scrutiny of the humanitarian rules of armed conflict. Moreover, in view of the horrifying and potentially irreversible devastation of which nuclear weapons are capable, not to mention the very little time their delivery systems allow for rational thought, it is only sensible that all doubts about whether they are subject to the humanitarian rules of armed conflict, as a matter of law, should be answered unequivocally in the affirmative, as a matter of policy. Such a response seems mandated, in any event, by a world public order of human dignity, in which values are shaped and shared more by persuasion than they are by coercion.

In sum, despite an erosion over the years of legal inhibitions regarding the conduct as well as the initiation of war, there remains even in this nuclear age an inherited commitment to standards of humane conduct within which the reasonable belligerent can operate,[22] a commitment to the fundamental principle from which all the laws of war derive, namely, that the right of belligerents to adopt means and methods of warfare is *not* unlimited.[23] It is, I think, not unreasonable to contend that nuclear weapons are illegal per se, within the terms of rule 6 prohibiting the use of chemical, biological, and "analogous" means of warfare. Perhaps not all nuclear weapons conceivable, but certainly all nuclear weapons now deployed or planned, manifest radiation effects that for all intents and purposes are the same as those that result from poison gas and bacteriological means of warfare. In any event, the 1925

Geneva Gas Protocol is so comprehensive in its prohibition that it may be said to dictate the nonuse of nuclear weapons altogether.[24] But in the absence of a specific prohibition, one is expected to ask the same basic question that the conscientious belligerent is obliged to ask in any given conflict situation: Is resort to this means or method of warfare proportionate to a legitimate military end?[25]

Illegality in Context

In most if not all nuclear warfare situations, the answer to the foregoing question must be given, I believe, in the negative. It is hard to imagine any nuclear war, except possibly one involving a very restricted use of extremely low-yield battlefield weapons, where this vital link between humanity and military necessity—that is, proportionality—would not be breached or threatened in the extreme. And it is especially hard to imagine in the face of the "countervalue" and "counterforce" strategic doctrines that would be embraced by Israel and her adversaries in a nuclearized Middle East. Considering the millions of projected deaths and uncontrollable environmental harms that would result from any *probable* use of nuclear weapons, it seems inescapable that nuclear warfare is manifestly contrary to the core precepts of international law.

But the point here is not to deal in generalities. Rather, it is to investigate how and to what extent the humanitarian rules of armed conflict actually operate in concrete nuclear weapons contexts.[26] After all, a proper appreciation of any legal prescriptions, whether explicitly or implicitly formulated, cannot be had without a conscious understanding of the "real world" contexts within which it has to function.

Let us first be clear, however, that the overall issue we are addressing, is *not* the lawfulness of using or threatening to use nuclear weapons as part of a campaign or single act of aggression (as that term is defined in the 1974 U.N. General Assembly Resolution on the Definition of Aggression).[27] Whatever the exact legal status of the Kellogg–Briand Pact[28] and U.N. charter article 2(4),[29] particularly after the deafening silence that greeted the 1980 Iraqi invasion of Iran, an act of aggression is unlawful irrespective of the kinds of weapons used. Thus, recalling the customary right of individual and collective self-defense (now enshrined in U.N. charter article 51), and noting that all the nuclear weapons states admit to no other rationale for their arsenals, the question ultimately before us must be whether any *defensive* use or threat of use of nuclear weapons may be considered contrary to international law, hence prohibited. The issue subdivides, first, in terms of the actual first- or second-strike defensive use of these weapons for "strategic" or "tactical" purposes; and, second, in terms of the threat of their use by way of research and development, manufacture, stockpiling, or deployment for any defensive use or purpose.

First Defensive Use of Nuclear Weapons

Strategic Warfare: Countervalue Targeting. Nuclear weapons designed for countervalue or city-killing purposes tend to be of the strategic class, with known yields of deployed warheads averaging somewhere between 2 to 3 times and 1500 times the firepower of the bombs dropped on Hiroshima and Nagasaki. (In the Middle East of course, such weapons would likely be at the lowest level of this range.) Further, they are "dirty" bombs, capable of producing severe initial nuclear radiation, spatially and temporally dispersed residual radiation (or radioactive fallout), and, in addition, wide-ranging electromagnetic pulse (EMP) effects. Further still, their CEP (circular error probable) currently averages somewhere between 300 and 2500 meters (0.3 to 2.5 kilometers), which is to say that they lack pinpoint accuracy.[30] Thus, in addition to violating the rule 6 prohibition against chemical, biological, and "analogous" means of warfare, their capacity for violating all the other prohibitory rules noted, and on a truly awesome scale, seems self-evident.

However, when evaluating this defensive option, what really matters, in a certain sense, is less the fact that nuclear weapons would violate one or another of the prohibitory rules mentioned than the fact that massive nuclear warfare, as a defensive measure, would be unleashed most probably in response to a conventional warfare provocation. By any rational standard, this would constitute a gross violation of the cardinal principle of proportionality. Assuming even the so-called worst-case scenario (for example, a concerted Arab assault against Israel), where is the military necessity in incinerating entire urban populations, defiling the territory of neighboring and distant neutral countries, and ravaging the natural environment for generations to come simply for the purpose of containing or repelling a conventional attack? From the point of view of international law, a failure to provide for an adequate conventional defense does not excuse these probable results. If so, then we are witness to the demise of Nuremberg, the triumph of *Kriegsraison,* the virtual repudiation of the humanitarian rules of armed conflict in at least large-scale warfare. The very meaning of "proportionality" becomes lost, and we come dangerously close to condoning the crime of genocide as a military campaign directed more towards the extinction of the enemy than towards the winning of a battle or conflict.[31]

It is, of course, conceivable that a city-killing first strike might be in response to a perceived but as yet unexecuted threat of nuclear attack—an imminent one, we must assume. Indeed, it is conceivable that the threatened attack would be equivalent in character. Thus, howevermuch the anticipatory or preemptive strike would run afoul of the rules against aggravated and indiscriminate suffering (rules 1 and 2), it might nevertheless be argued to meet the test of proportionality in some rough way.

But the argument would be, I think, deceptive. A preemptive strike of the sort contemplated here, particularly if surface bursts are involved, still would inflict large-scale collateral harms beyond the place and moment of immediate conflict. In addition to violating the rule 6 ban on chemical, biological, and "analogous" weapons, it would likely violate also the minimal safeguards extended to internationally protected persons (rules 2 and 3), the natural environment (rule 4), nonparticipating neutral states (rule 5), and consequently by these excesses would strain severely the principle of proportionality. Moreover, to the extent that U.N. charter article 51 admonishes recourse to minimally coercive and nonviolent modes of conflict resolution, including resort to the collective conciliation functions of the United Nations, a preemptive strike probably would disproportionately violate rules 1 and 2 as well. After all, the threat still would be unexecuted. In any event, the principle of proportionality surely would require that the burden of policy proof be shouldered by those who would unleash the preemptive countervalue strike, and that burden would be a heavy one considering the massive and extended deprivation potentially involved. It is difficult to conceive of any nuclear threat that could not be met by some lesser preemptive mode—except, of course, in the case of foreign policies lacking in creative imagination and insensitive to the magnitude of the human values at stake.

Strategic Warfare: Counterforce Targeting. Involving the same strategic weapons with the same odious capabilities relied upon for countervalue targeting, a counterforce first strike, like a countervalue first strike, faces the test of proportionality with many presumptions against it. Even if intended for essentially military targets alone, it still would have far-reaching EMP and radiation effects that could not be confined to the place and moment of immediate confrontation, thus violating not only the rule 6 ban on chemical, biological, and "analogous" weapons, but, as well, the rights of great numbers of innocent and neutral—including distant—third parties both living and unborn. And, howevermuch actually restricted to essentially military targets, it still would consist of a massive nuclear retort to what likely would be only a conventional war provocation.

Concededly, because counterforce strategy is a policy of targeting the military, especially nuclear, forces rather than the cities of the other side, there is at least surface plausibility in the argument that a counterforce first strike would not unduly trample upon the rule 2 prohibition against indiscriminate injury to noncombatant persons and property. Indeed, a lure of counterforce doctrine is that it makes nuclear weapons more credible as instruments of war in part because, at least theoretically, it is less subject to the legal and moral criticisms that can be leveled against countervalue doctrine. The plausibility of this argument quickly vanishes, however, when it is matched against the available data. An oft-cited Office of Technology Assessment study published in 1979, for example, quotes U.S. government studies indicating that between two million and twenty million Americans would be killed within thirty days after a countersilo attack on U.S. intercontinental ballistic missile (ICBM) sites, due mainly to early radiation fallout from likely surface bursts.[32] Needless to say, in the Middle East, where distances are short and population centers very close to military facilities, the test of proportionality would be even more severely strained.

Indeed, when all the dynamics of an actual counterforce first strike are taken into account, the test of proportionality seems to be abrogated completely, particularly when both of the opposing sides are nuclear powers. In the first place, unless the counterforce attack were an all-out "disarming first strike" aimed at the total incapacitation of the enemy's nuclear forces (a likely achievement in the Middle East), it would virtually guarantee retaliation and therefore greater and more widespread devastation and suffering. Second, notwithstanding voguish theories of "intrawar bargaining," "intrawar deterrence,"and "controlled escalation," it is highly improbable that the opposing sides would or could restrict themselves to fighting a "limited" rather than "total" nuclear war, as if somehow governed by the rules of the Marquess of Queensbury. Finally, it seems fairly clear that counterforce capabilities, insofar as they might involve missiles that never have been tested over their expected wartime trajectories, are neither as accurate nor as reliable as publicly claimed.[33]

Again, however, it remains to be asked whether different conclusions might not obtain in the case of an anticipatory counterforce first strike as distinguished from an initiating one. Such a strike, designed to preempt, say, an imminent devastation of equivalent or greater dimension, conceivably could meet the test of proportionality precisely because it would be directed, pursuant to counterforce doctrine, against only military targets. This might particularly be the case where the statistical probability of accurate warhead delivery would be fairly high—that is, where the CEP of the preemptive strike would be fairly low (within 100–200 meters by current standards). This logic is based, however, on a calculation of statistical probability, and probabilities, let us be clear, are not certainties. In addition, it suffers from all the disabilities concerning proportionality that we noted in connection with both the preemptive countervalue strike and the initiating counterforce strike. Again, therefore, it is reasonable to conclude that the test of proportionality would not be met or that, at the very least, those who would unleash the preemptive counterforce strike would have the burden of proving otherwise.

Tactical Warfare: Theater/Battlefield Targeting. There is no clear borderline between so-called tactical and so-called strategic nuclear weapons, with the yields and consequent effects of the former commonly rising to the level and impact of the latter. Accordingly, it is logical to conclude that the first-strike use of tactical nuclear weapons above, say, the 13- to 22-kiloton range of Hiroshima and Nagasaki should be subject to the same legal judgments that attend the first-strike use of strategic nuclear weapons (both countervalue and counterforce). The first-strike use of such high-yield tactical nuclear weapons, just as the first-strike use of their strategic (particularly counterforce) equivalents would appear to violate in the same way and to similar degree, separately and in combination, not only all or most of the humanitarian rules of armed conflict listed in the introduction to this chapter, but also the fundamental principle of proportionality that mediates among them.

But what of tactical nuclear weapons below the 13- to 22-kiloton range of Hiroshima–Nagasaki? Would the first-strike use of such lower yield weapons, particularly those in the 1- to 2-kiloton or subkiloton range, equally violate the prohibitory rules discussed above? Would such a strike equally violate the principle of proportionality, on the grounds that, like its strategic counterparts, it probably would be in response to a conventional warfare provocation—indeed, in likely contrast to its strategic counterparts, probably in response to a conventional warfare provocation by a *nonnuclear* adversary? By common definitional agreement the term "tactical nuclear weapons" is intended generally to refer to those weapons systems that are designed or otherwise available for use against essentially military targets in intermediate "theater of war" and more limited "battlefield" situations.

In theory, I agree, the answers to these questions must depend, inter alia, on the characteristics and capabilities of the tactical weapons in question. For example, though the provocation might be a conventional one or, indeed, at the hands of a nonnuclear opponent, it is possible at least to conceive of a low-yield, relatively "clean," and reasonably accurate nuclear weapon or weapon system whose tactical first defensive use actually would save lives and protect property within the meaning of military necessity—that is, without violating the principle of proportionality. This "best-case" scenario, however, appears to be a limited one. Judging from the state of the art as so far publicly revealed, no such option is available among existing intermediate-range theater weapons, although some "progress" in this direction appears to be taking place in connection with limited-range battlefield weapons. The possibility of minimizing destruction and of avoiding indiscriminate harm consonant with rules 1 and 2 may be present, but not without substantial and, I submit, disproportionate cost in most circumstances relative to internationally protected persons (rules 2 and 3), the natural environment (rule 4) and nonparticipating neutral states (rule 5), due to initial and residual radiation. Moreover, except by a process of interpretation that is uninformed by the basic assumptions of a world public order of human dignity, there is no getting around the rule 6 prohibition of chemical, biological, and "analogous" weapons. By its very nature, a fission weapon must be regarded as "dirty"; and even if a pure fusion weapon with no fission were developed, its explosion in the air and, of course, at ground level still would result in some radioactive contamination, albeit not as extensive as when nuclear technology was less "tailored" than it is today.

But what is truly damning of the first defensive use of tactical nuclear weapons, whether in theater or battlefield operations, is less the nature of the weapons themselves than the nature of tactical nuclear warfare as a whole. In the first place, as should be apparent to all, if a military campaign defined in part by a first-strike use of nuclear weapons were ever to take place, it surely would not be limited to one or two nuclear strikes, even if only the first user were a nuclear power. Likely as not, tactical nuclear warfare, at least at theater level, would result in hundreds and thousands of nuclear explosions and, consequently, untold immediate and long-range, long-term collateral harm. In addition, once unleashed, the probability that tactical nuclear warfare could be kept at theater or battlefield level would be small. A crisis escalating to the actual first use of even relatively small nuclear weapons would bring us dangerously close to the ultimate stage, a "strategic exchange," particularly if one of the two sides saw itself at a disadvantage in a drawn-out "tactical exchange." In sum, once out of the bottle, likely as not even the tactical nuclear genie would quite literally cause "all hell to break loose"; and this fact, in combination with the observations already made regarding the humanitarian rules of armed confict, would seem by any rational analysis to run hard up against the principle of proportionality upon which the doctrine of military necessity is premised.

Thus, the first use of nuclear weapons again would appear contrary to the basic laws of war as now understood. It need only be added that, for all the reasons noted previously, but especially the last two relative to the essential uncontrollability of tactical nuclear warfare in general, this conclusion may be seen to apply to the preemptive first use of tactical nuclear weapons as well as to their initiating first use.

Second Defensive Use of Nuclear Weapons

Would a second defensive use of nuclear weapons—one undertaken as a *claimed* "legitimate reprisal" in response to a prior attack unlawfully initiating the use of such weapons—equally or similarly violate the humanitarian rules of armed conflict? In view of the numerous qualifying reservations now attached to the 1925 Geneva Gas Protocol, conditioning adherence to it upon reciprocal observance of its terms,[34] it may be that the rule 6 ban on chemical, biological and "analogous" means of warfare would not stand in the way. On this point, concededly, there is ambiguity. But what about the rule 3 prohibition of reprisals that are disproportionate to legitimate belligerent objectives or that are disrespectful of persons, institutions, and resources otherwise protected by the laws of war? Is there ambiguity here as well?

Strategic Warfare: Countervalue Targeting. In the case of a second use of nuclear weapons characterized by countervalue targeting, there is, I submit, no ambiguity. For at least three reasons, such a use may be said to violate the humanitarian rules of armed conflict as contemporaneously understood, especially rule 3.

In the first place, a retaliatory city-killing attack would flagrantly trample upon guarantees extended to civilians and civilian populations, among other internationally protected persons, by the most recent formal statements on the laws of war. Article 51(6) of 1977 Protocol I Additional to the 1949 Geneva Conventions, for example, is characteristically unequivocal: "Attacks against the civilian population or civilians by way of reprisals are prohibited."[35]

Second, except to destroy enemy morale, which is clearly an impermissible objective under the laws of war,[36] and the more so, one would think, when the result is to terrorize an enemy community through the infliction of literally overwhelming—perhaps irremedial—societal destruction, it is difficult to see how a retaliatory countervalue strike would serve any military necessity whatsoever. To the contrary, even if the antecedent first use were likewise countervalue-destructive in character, it would appear to serve mainly the purposes of vengeance rather than the values of proportionate policing (given, at least, the present essentially rural deployment of the world's strategic forces).

Finally, if the history of belligerent reprisals is any indication, there is the near certainty that a retaliatory countervalue strike would lead not to a reduction of hostilities nor to a moderation of tactics but to an escalatory spiral and spread of countervalue exchanges.[37] At this point, virtually everything for which the principle of proportionality is supposed to stand, including the integrity of the natural environment and the inviolability of neutral state territory, would be threatened; the humanitarian rules of armed conflict would become all but obsolete.

Strategic Warfare: Counterforce Targeting. The case of a second counterforce use of nuclear weapons is not so clear-cut. Because such a response would be directed, pursuant to counterforce doctrine, against the military (especially nuclear) forces rather than the cities of the first user, and because the laws of war do not invite national suicide, there is room to contend that such a strike would be compatible with prohibitory rule 3 and the other humanitarian rules of armed conflict, provided that it not be patently excessive relative to the antecedent attack and the goal of law—compliance or nonrecurrence. Indeed, paradoxical though it may seem, it might even be argued that, to ensure a minimum destruction of cherished values (preferably the values of freedom and equality), a nuclear counterstrike of this kind would be required. On the other hand, bearing in mind the characteristics and capabilities of the weapons and weapon systems that constitute today's counterforce arsenals, there remains the problem of reconciling the rights of states not party to the conflict and of persons and property expressly shielded by the law of reprisals and the more general laws of war. "Clean bombs" and "surgical strikes," especially in relation to strategic warfare, exist more in the minds of military planners than they do in reality. Additionally, there is the customary injunction that reprisals be taken only as measures of last resort. In the context of nuclear war, this injunction is all the more imperative.

Thus, the permissibility of a counterforce second strike under the humanitarian rules of armed conflict may be regarded as ambiguous. Of course, because of the essentially uncontrollable dangers involved, one must assume that such a second use, if permissible, would be authorized only in response to an antecedent attack of equivalent or greater proportion—that is, a prior counterforce or countervalue attack. But even then, because of the unrefined nature of the weaponry involved and the likelihood of crisis escalation and spread, the burden of policy proof would again weigh heavily on those who would retaliate in this manner. Let us be candid. As Roger Fisher has written, "Honestly, each of us would prefer to have our children in Havana, Belgrade, Beijing, Warsaw, or Leningrad today than in Hiroshima or Nagasaki when the nuclear bombs went off."[38]

Tactical Warfare: Theater/Battlefield Targeting. If there is a case to be made for the use of nuclear weapons consistent with the humanitarian rules of warfare, it is here, in respect of the second use of tactical nuclear weapons. Arguably, a second retaliatory use of a low-yield, "clean," and reasonably accurate intermediate- or limited-range nuclear weapon directed only at a military target could be said to meet the requirements of proportionality (or military necessity) that govern the law of reprisals as presently understood.

When making the case beyond this highly circumscribed option, however, at least two major complexities arise. First, to the extent that a retaliatory second use would involve theater or battlefield weapons around or above the 13- to 22-kiloton range of Hiroshima–Nagasaki, there is the problem of having to deal with all the ambiguities and qualifications noted in connection with a second counterforce use of nuclear weapons. And second, regarding all tactical nuclear weapons, including those in the 1- to 2-kiloton or subkiloton range, there is the problem of establishing upper limits on the number of retaliatory strikes that could be launched at any time without doing violence either to the rights of internationally protected persons (rules 2 and 3) and neutral states (rule 5) or, more generally, to the principle of proportionality. In other words, except in the narrowest of circumstances, the unrefined and unpredictable nature of nuclear weapons and weapon systems in general continues to cloud the legality of their second use even in tactical warfare. Add to this the extreme dangers that would attend a likely escalatory spiral once the process of reprisal and counterreprisal were set into motion, and again the burden of proving that this retaliatory approach should be favored over other means of deterring the enemy becomes very heavy.

Threat of First or Second Defensive Use

If a given use of nuclear weapons is properly judged contrary to the humanitarian rules of armed conflict, then logically any threat of such use—including not only an ostentatious brandishing of arms (such as a menacing "demonstration burst"), but also their research and development, manufacture, stockpiling, and deployment—should be considered contrary to the humanitarian rules of armed conflict as well. In view of our preceding discussion, the threat at least of a strategic first strike, a tactical first strike, a second countervalue strike, and possibly also a second counterforce strike as well as most tactical second strikes would fit this logic.

A distinct problem with this thesis, however, is that nothing in the traditional rules of warfare prohibits the preparation in contrast to the actual use of weapons and weapon systems. Also, it flies in the face of the deterrence doctrines that are said to have kept the peace, at least between the superpowers, for the last thirty-odd years—a difficulty of major significance because, to be minimally credible, a policy of deterrence requires the research and development, manufacture, stockpiling, and deployment of the weapons upon which it is premised. It is true that the nuclear deterrence policies currently practiced, between the superpowers especially, may be criticized in numerous ways: for involving unacceptably high risks; for building upon an inherently unstable balance; for terrorizing populations and holding them hostage as a consequence; for detracting from acceptable solutions or alternatives in case of failure of deterrence; and so forth. But because of the widespread perception, however much open to debate, that the prevention of widespread conflict rests on nuclear deterrence and that this system is, in turn, dependent on credible nuclear threat, it would be difficult to conclude that measures short of actual use would violate the humanitarian rules of armed conflict as presently understood. Not even U.N. General Assembly resolution 1653 (XVI) or 2936 (XXVII), which declare the use of nuclear weapons, respectively, "a crime against mankind and civilization" and a matter of "permanent prohibition," seek to outlaw measures short of actual use.

Nevertheless, to facilitate a comprehensive outlook, at least three qualifying observations should be borne in mind. First, a number of pathbreaking treaties do specifically prohibit nuclear weapons preparations short of actual combat use: the 1959 Antarctica Treaty,[39] the 1963 Partial Test Ban Treaty,[40] the 1967 Treaty of Tlatelolco,[41] the 1967 Outer Space Treaty,[42] the 1971 Seabed Arms Control Treaty,[43] and the 1979 Draft Moon Treaty.[44] Second, where "demonstration bursts" or equivalent menacing tactics are involved, there is always the possibility of violating the rule 6 ban on chemical, biological, and "analogous" weapons and, in addition, the other humanitarian rules of armed conflict designed to safeguard internationally protected persons, the natural environment, and neutral states. Finally, because of the high risks and monumental dangers involved, any nuclear weapons measure short of actual use, but especially those of particularly ostentatious or provocative nature, must be taken with extreme caution. The history of war is riddled with well-meaning doctrines gone out of control, and the possibilities of war increase in direct proportion to the effectiveness of the instruments of war we adopt. It is, no doubt, this viewpoint that lies behind article 36 of 1977 Geneva Protocol I Additional to the 1949 Geneva Conventions: "In the study, development, acquisition or adoption of a new weapon, means or method of warfare, a High Contracting Party is under an obligation to determine whether its employment would, in some or all circumstances, be prohibited by this Protocol or any other rule of international law applicable to the High Contracting Party."[45]

Conclusion

While no treaty or treaty provision specifically forbids nuclear warfare per se, except in certain essentially isolated whereabouts, almost every use to which nuclear weapons might be put in the Middle East, appears to violate one or more of the laws of war that serve to make up the contemporary humanitarian law of armed conflict, in particular the cardinal principle of proportionality. Whatever legal license is afforded appears restricted, at most, to the following:

> Essentially cautious, long-term preparations for preventing or deterring nuclear war, short of provocative "saber-rattling" activities;

> Very limited tactical—mainly battlefield—warfare utilizing low-yield, "clean," and reasonably accurate nuclear weapons for second use retaliatory purposes only; and

> Possibly, *but not unambiguously* (until as yet undeveloped technological refinements are achieved), an extremely limited counterforce strike in strategic and theater-level settings for second use retaliatory purposes only.

In other words, applying the humanitarian rules of armed conflict to different nuclear weapons options or uses, in the Middle East and elsewhere, tends to prove rather than disprove the illegality of these weapons generally. And when one adds to this the conclusion at Nuremberg that the extermination of a civilian population in whole or in part is a "crime against humanity,"[46] plus the spirit if not also the letter of the 1948 Convention on the Prevention and Punishment of the Crime of Genocide,[47] then a presumption of illegality and a commensurate heavy burden of contrary proof relative to the use of nuclear weapons on *any* extended or large-scale basis seems beyond peradventure. To be sure, ambiguities exist here and there, especially in the case of limited tactical uses where the venerable test of proportionality must struggle between increasingly "tailored" military technologies and the human propensity for escalatory violence. But, overall, the law opposes resort to these instruments of death, and to argue otherwise on the basis of the arguable permissibility of some essentially restricted use is to engage in the highest form of sophistry.

Of course, as I stated at the outset, it would be naive to expect that the law alone can make the progressive difference, particularly when, as in the Middle East, it touches sensitively upon prevailing notions of national security. But more and more the strategic planners among prospective nuclear-weapon states must learn to recognize the hazards and uncertainties of nuclearization. More and more they must come to see the essential incompatibility of nuclear weapons with the core precepts of international law. More and more they must come to understand that adherence to these precepts is the surest path to genuine safety.

12
Deterrence, Holocaust, and Nuclear Weapons: A Nonparochial Outlook

Avner Cohen

Israel's position on the question of nuclear weapons is fundamentally ambiguous. Although Israel has never made public details about its nuclear program, it is generally believed to have acquired an "undisclosed nuclear option." This vague phrase is usually meant to suggest that Israel is only a "screwdriver away" from the bomb, if not already in secret possession of it (the "bomb-in-the-basement" posture). Israel itself, however, has been quite careful neither to confirm nor to deny the widely circulated speculations about its nuclear capability.[1]

Although Israel signed and ratified the Nuclear Test Ban Treaty, it has steadily resisted political pressures to sign the Non-Proliferation Treaty (NPT).[2] Its official policy, formulated first in the early 1960s and held ever since, is nevertheless strongly antiproliferation. This policy maintains that Israel will not be the first nation to introduce nuclear weapons into the Middle East conflict.[3]

By implication it also denies actual Israeli possession of nuclear weapons.[4] The ambiguity of this policy became more apparent after the midsixties, when Israel inserted a conditional clause to this stance, saying that though Israel will not be the first to introduce nuclear weapons into the Arab–Israeli conflict, it will not be the second either.[5] In June 1981 this equivocal clause received a straightforward expression when Israel, adhering to its antiproliferation policy, conducted a successful preemptive strike on the Iraqi Osiraq nuclear reactor near Baghdad.[6]

This unprecedented action—the world's first preemptive strike on a nuclear facility—was a clear demonstration of Israel's total opposition to the nuclearization of Middle East conflict. As to Israel itself, whatever the actual status of the Israeli nuclear capability, its historical record is unambiguous: Israel has never issued any nuclear threats. Even at the early stages of the Yom Kippur War, when Syrian armor columns were overlooking the Galilee, no nuclear threats were made.[7]

This is not to say, of course, that Israel has not made certain political uses out of its ambiguous posture. But to the extent that the nuclear dimension has been involved in the Israeli general deterrence position, it has been strictly limited to the uses of ambiguity and uncertainty.[8] Hence, if it is fair to call it a nuclear deterrent posture at all, it is a very peculiar one: *capability without threats.*[9]

At the level of national security policy Israel's nuclear dilemma is often presented as the question of ambiguity vis-à-vis disclosure: the choice between covert and overt nuclear postures. Would Israel be better off by converting its present policy of nuclear ambiguity into an open regime of nuclear deterrence, built upon a modified version of the superpowers' regime of global nuclear deterrence? Would it also be *morally* acceptable?

For many years the dilemma was hardly discussed in Israel. A veil of official secrecy surrounded all aspects of the Israeli nuclear program. Though this program is known to have been operational for twenty years at least, Israel's nuclear strategy (that is, what the program is *for*) has never been under any public scrutiny. In fact, the dilemma has been treated by all Israeli decisionmakers (in and out of office) as if it simply does not exist.[10] Until the present day, Israeli officials refrain from making any public references to the very existence of such a dilemma. The official silence has been extended to almost all vehicles of public discussion, including the media and the Knesset.[11]

In recent years, however, the dilemma has been brought out of the woods, at least as a matter of academic discourse. Some Israeli (as well as non-Israeli) academic strategists, influenced by new pro-proliferation theoretical arguments, have openly put forward the idea of a nuclear shift in Israel's national security policy, arguing that Israeli nuclear disclosure could stabilize the Middle East conflict and possibly even lead to its political resolution.[12] Not surprisingly, this idea has received little public attention in Israel, but it nevertheless opened the door for a moderate academic debate on the subject.[13] As expected, other academics rejected this idea, arguing that it would be too risky, because of its ill-conceived analogy with the superpower nuclear regime, as well as the standard global arguments against nuclear proliferation.[14]

But the interesting thing about this debate is not only the matter of disagreement, but also the matter of agreement. To begin with, all the contenders in the debate seem to share a "primitive" faith in the very idea of nuclear deterrence—a certain tacit approval, at times even endorsement, of the "logic" of global nuclear deterrence. In general, they view the institution of nuclear deterrence between the superpowers as an *advantageous* mechanism to preserve global peace.[15] Hence, the genuine areas of disagreement relate only to questions of whether, from Israel's standpoint, it would be prudent to follow the steps of the superpowers and to apply the concept of nuclear deterrence to the context of the Middle East; whether such Israeli nuclear disclosure would be destabilizing. Another distinctive feature of the debate is its amoral tone; none of the contenders raised any *moral* qualms about the significance of the initiative to introduce nuclear weapons into a new area. The debate is distinguished by its value-free attitude toward nuclear deterrence.

My aim in this chapter is to argue *against* the idea of Israeli nuclear deterrence, but for reasons, I believe, that are quite different in scope and approach from those usually mentioned among the strategists. In a way, my own starting point is diametrically opposite to the one of the strategists—it rests on both moral and prudential rejection of the very idea of nuclear deterrence.[16] Hence, I will approach the Israeli security dilemma from a nonparochial perspective, from the broader perspective of the *nuclear predicament* at large—the nuclear predicament as a radical turning point in human history, and its vast implications for all pragmatic and ethical appraisals of nuclear weapons policies.

My argument, then, will begin by examining some of the distinct and peculiar features of the nuclear predicament, particularly the "logic" of nuclear deterrence. The regime of nuclear deterrence (in *all* of its manifestations) is fraught with danger, I will argue, not *only* because of some specific discrepancies between the classical theory of nuclear deterrence and actual strategic postures, or because of some specific destabilizing geopolitical factors peculiar only to the Middle East conflict. The very nature of nuclear deterrence thinking is paradoxical. The problem of nuclear deterrence is more serious than what strategists have recognized thus far: we lack an adequate conceptual and empirical understanding of what nuclear deterrence is, how it really works and affects world politics, under what political circumstances it is likely to fail, and above all how to assess its overall worth.

The argument has strong skeptical overtones. It is not that we know, as a matter of fact, that nuclear deterrence thinking is utterly irrational; rather, it is that our ignorance about nuclear matters is too encompassing while errors are unaffordable. Here is the *moral* imperative of the nuclear age: where nuclear war is concerned, probabilities and likelihoods are not enough (if they make any sense at all); we need moral certainties. And this is precisely what the theory of nuclear deterrence cannot provide. This skeptical lesson has, I believe, an alarming significance for the Israeli dilemma.

The Nuclear Predicament

The nuclear era has distinctive *emergent* features.[17] The invention of nuclear weapons was one of those moments in human history at which a unique and distinctly new causal factor emerges, whose actual and symbolic consequences affect humanity far beyond its immediate historical context.[18] With their coming into existence a new predicament was on its way, a predicament that only now, almost four decades after its dawn, is sufficiently unfolded to distinguish its sui generis features.

As early as 1946, at the very dawn of the nuclear age, Einstein had foreseen the formation of the new predicament. "The unleashed power of the atom," he said, "has changed everything save our modes of thinking, and we thus drift towards unparalleled catastrophe."[19] This is true now more than ever before. Though it has been recognized that nuclear weapons systems no longer have the qualities of genuine (politically significant) weapons, humanity is still driven to think of them—and, worse, to treat them—as proper and legitimate instruments of politics and strategy.

War is a distinct species of violence. In contrast to other forms of mass violence, war is the only one that has been reconciled with the purposes of organized society. We think of war as the activity of armed violence performed for a political community by its military organization. Both these societal elements—a political community and a military organization—are indispensable to our understanding of the phenomenon of war. Accordingly, we may define war as large-scale armed conflict between *political* communities. As such, war is essentially a rule-governed societal practice.

The institutional nature of war is evident in its normative (moral) dimension. Within the limits of the humanitarian rules of international law, acts of war are considered neither deviant nor criminal; they are, above all, *socially approved* activities of mass violence. Since war is waged on behalf of a political community, it receives its legitimacy from it. Unlike other forms of violence, the institution of war has been associated with rich, value-laden, culturally significant moral and legal vocabularies. Throughout the ages, warring cultures have developed special spheres of moral discourse—normative codes of rights and wrongs—for times of war.[20]

But even a stronger claim can be made. The phenomenon of war is not only indigenous to civilization but parasitic on it. To put it differently, war is fundamentally a *creation* of civilization; genuine war is possible only within conflict situations peculiar to politicized societies. The institution of war, along with international politics, is a relatively new human "invention," made possible through the transition to civilization. The marriage between politics and war is not accidental; it is a matter of historical development. Both are by-products of the emergence of civilization, and particularly the rise of the city-state as a new social entity. The urban revolution, like the nuclear revolution, is one of these unique thresholds in human history where a single, distinguishable development has profound and lasting consequences for human consciousness well beyond its immediate impact. Since the invention of politics, the predicament of war has become an intrinsic feature of the political system of sovereign states.

But with the emergence of the nuclear predicament everything has changed. The delicate relationships between civilization and war now reach a full dialectical turn. War, born out of the emergence of civilization, has developed to the point where it has become a *threat* to civilization; what was "invented" jointly with the "invention" of politics now threatens the very existence of a political system based on sovereign states.[21] The nuclear predicament negates the essence of the institution of war—its essential link with politics.

This point can be shown from another angle. If the phenomenon of war makes sense at all, it does so only because war is essentially a corporate human activity; its rationality lies in individuals adhering to the collective interests of their particular political community.[22] The institution of war, then, is intimately linked to a hierarchy of collective goals (that is, national interests) all formulated in the language of politics.

Thus the success of war is traditionally measured by the achievements of those objectives. Nations go to war to save, preserve, or promote their national interests; never to lose them. But this way of thinking no longer fits the characteristics of the nuclear age.

The nuclear predicament came into being as technology was pushed to new limits by the human mind unaware of the coming consequences of those limits.[23] As it turned out, these consequences have *outdated* the very politicostrategic and moral presuppositions that gave rise to the nuclear technology in the first place. Our prenuclear intuitions appear inadequate to comprehend the eventuality of nuclear war; its utter irrationality explodes everything with it, including the prudential and moral thinking that had made it possible.

The argument from the nuclear predicament is twofold. It considers both nuclear war and nuclear deterrence. Just as our conception of nuclear war, if we have one, departs from our traditional intuitions about the institution of war, so does the regime of nuclear deterrence outdate our traditional intuitions about military deterrence and politics. The crux of the argument is the essential link between deterrence and war; if we reject the possibility of nuclear war we must also reject the regime of nuclear deterrence.

Nuclear War: Thinking the Unthinkable

There are some prima facie emergent features of nuclear warfare which suggest that their significance is irreducible to the physical properties of the bomb itself. First and foremost is the recognition that nuclear weapons are not mundane instruments of warfare; they are, and ought to be, substantially different from all other weaponry humanity has known before. Consider the distinction between *conventional* and *nuclear* weapons.

Ever since 1945 it has been a fundamental distinction; it is the conceptual foundation for the entire secular theology of nuclearism. Though from the standpoint of technology this distinction is not necessary, and, in fact, could have been easily blurred (it is technically possible to design nuclear warheads of even lower yields, and perhaps even very low radioactive impact), it is essential for military, political, and moral thinking. The difference between dynamite explosion and nuclear detonation is something that anyone must notice, and which everyone should trust the other to notice as well.[24] It enables us to install absolute thresholds separating the mundane from the profane; crossing the threshold means a violation of a sacred taboo. Since Hiroshima and Nagasaki no state has dared doing so.

The political lesson of the nuclear age is clear and indisputable: nuclear weapons should not be used at all. Violating the nuclear taboo will instantly make any nation an outlaw in the community of civilized nations. But in the real world this recognition is not comforting.

Nuclear weapons are still here, and as long as they are around, they *can* always be used. Indeed, they are likely to be used if nuclear powers should find themselves in a moment of a surpreme national danger. What makes them so dangerous is the fact that their presence alone is enough to aggravate a crisis. Nuclear weapons inspire so much fear that this could inspire an aggressive act of preemption. As the historical record surely shows, the very emergence of a new nuclear power is sufficient to evoke all kinds of preemptive ideas.[25] Such ideas would obviously be especially threatening in a volatile climate of sustained crisis or protracted conflict.

This dual recognition—the imperative that nuclear weapons ought not to be used and the knowledge that they can be used—has had a profound, and admittedly encouraging, impact on nuclear proliferation. Realizing that nuclear weapons may invite attack, rather than deter it, many highly developed nations have decided that it is not their interest to "go nuclear." Though the technology to produce fission bombs is widely understood, only six nations have so far been declared nuclear powers, and only one (India) during the last twenty years of the nuclear age.

The nuclear taboo was extended from *use* to *possession*. Nonnuclear nations who desire to cross the possession threshold may also be regarded as outlaws among the community of nations. This strong antiproliferation sentiment is, no doubt, one of the positive legacies of the nuclear age. But there is no guarantee that this trend will continue in the long run.[26]

What makes nuclear warfare sui generis, so radically different from all other wars humanity has known before? The answer, I think, lies more in our ignorance than in our knowledge. Since we have had no experience of nuclear warfare, we don't really know what it could be like.

In fact, the situation is even worse, because we don't know how much we do or do not know about it. All we have are various kinds of speculations and guesses, which can never be tested unless we actually cross the nuclear threshold. Let me elaborate on this point a bit further. The unique status of nuclear warfare lies not only in the unprecedented extent of *actual* devastation that any single strategic nuclear detonation (even the smallest one) is bound to leave behind it, but, and most importantly, also in its unprecedented *potential* for all kinds of unpredictable catastrophes.

To cross the nuclear threshold is to enter into the land of the unknown; at that point all strategic doctrines (when, where, why, how, and which nuclear weapons ought to be used) would fade into absurdity. One thing, however, is quite clear: no matter what nuclear war might be, it would not be the kind of rule-governed practice earlier defined as war. This element of unpredictability is one of the most important emergent features of the nuclear weapons regime.

It is true, of course, that any eruption of large-scale violence, such as war, is bound to produce further waves of disorder. Carl von Clausewitz's well-known dictum about war deserves repeating here: "In war more than anywhere else in the world, things happen differently to what we had expected, and look differently when near, to what they did at a distance."[27] Nevertheless, in the case of nuclear war the unknown exceeds all the uncertainties traditionally associated with war.

Another emergent feature of the nuclear weapons regime is what Thomas Donaldson calls "technological recalcitrance," the tendency of modern nuclear weapons systems to be *recalcitrant* to the intentions of their users.[28] The more advanced and technologically sophisticated the system becomes, the less room it provides for full human control. The problem of technological recalcitrance is particularly apparent in the area of command, control, communication, and intelligence (C^3I).

All nuclear doctrines must rely heavily on adequate functioning of C^3I. If nuclear deterrence is to be credible, there must be reliable procedures to properly verify nuclear attack, the extent of damage inflicted, and how to communicate retaliatory orders. But the incredible speed and destructiveness of modern nuclear weapons systems have raised a variety of issues of great concern regarding the proper functioning of C^3I, to the extent that some people speculate that they render futile all nuclear war fighting doctrines. Consider the following four points of grave concern:[29]

1. An unprecedented reliance on highly sophisticated nonhuman elements (such as computers and sensors) of C^3I along the entire chain of command

2. A drastic temporal compression of the formerly distinct levels of political and military decisionmaking

3. Unprecedented institutionalized pressures for a very rapid use of nuclear weapons at time of crisis, lest the opportunity to use them at all be lost permanently ("use 'em or lose 'em")

4. The impossibility of testing the proper functioning of the entire system prior to their actual use

While in past wars weapons were relatively accident-free (and if an accident did occur there was never so much at stake), today's technologically recalcitrant weaponry has raised the unprecedented possibility of accidental nuclear wars. Reliance on a strategy of "launch on warning" could invite disaster, if, say, warning sensors mistakenly indicate a full-scale nuclear attack. Further, technologically recalcitrant systems tend to frustrate, even to foreclose, political options of control during war. This drawback is especially critical today, when political compromise is all the more needed.

To sum up, we do not really know how to *conceive* of nuclear warfare as a concrete actuality, how it could be properly kept under control and how it might be brought to termination. In the absence of any experience of nuclear war, no one can responsibly claim to know whether or how such war could be managed, controlled or concluded. Leaving aside the many grave questions concerning physical survivability of C^3I systems, doubts still remain about the human and organizational factors involved in the proper operating of these systems, at both political and military levels.

We have very little *relevant* experience even to speculate about how individual decisionmakers, from the officers in the silos to the president himself, would react to the first news about nuclear detonations, let alone how the chain of command would respond as an integrated system to the pressures and stresses of nuclear warfare. As to the more societal, long-term effects of nuclear war (ecological, economic, demographic, social, and political), we can predict even less.[30] The point is general: Because the event of a nuclear war would be sui generis, no positive generalizations about it can make any sense.

Much of what I have said is particularly relevant to the recent talk of "limited nuclear war" (LNW). Even in the nuclear era, many nuclear strategists argue, one must distinguish between "limited" and "total" uses of military forces (for example, counterforce versus countervalue strategies). Insisting on the significance of this distinction, the idea of LNW has become the standard response to the fundamental dilemma of the nuclear age: how to think the unthinkable, how to incorporate the reality of nuclear weapons into traditional modes of strategic thinking.[31] Doctrines of LNW have risen and fallen time and again during the four decades of thinking of nuclear strategy, but the basic motivation behind them is always the same: to "humanize" nuclear war—that is, to make it more warlike, less apocalyptic.[32] After all, only if LNW is a feasible strategic option can nuclear deterrence maintain its political credibility.

Attempting to fight a LNW would be a total gamble in circumstances of *complete uncertainty.* Accordingly, no one has the moral right to be engaged in such planning.[33] All we do know is that even a few small nuclear warheads in a strictly counterforce operation would kill and wound millions of human beings. As McGeorge Bundy puts the matter, "Of course, no one can prove that any first use of nuclear weapons will lead to general conflagration; but what is decisive is that no one can come close to proving that it will not."[34] The problem, however, is that the doctrine of nuclear deterrence *requires* this irrational and immoral act as a necessary condition for its credibility.

The Logic of Nuclear Deterrence

Ever since the dawn of the nuclear age the idea of nuclear deterrence has been advanced as the answer to the questions about the political rationale for the existence of nuclear weapons. Nuclear deterrence is said to be a *new* type of deterrence, a unique invention of the nuclear age. Its stated purpose is solely to avert the possibility of war between the nuclear powers.

In the nuclear age, so goes the argument, a *credible* and *stable* posture of mutual nuclear deterrence is the only guarantee against the horrors of nuclear war between the superpowers; the more credible the policy of nuclear deterrence, the more assured we are against its failure. In a world in which nuclear weapons are inevitable facts of life, the only legitimate purpose they may have is by forming a new kind of bilateral strategic stability, a world order that rests on a mutual balance of terror. This has been the standard justification for the existence of nuclear weapons. What makes nuclear deterrence work is precisely the fear of nuclear war; nuclear deterrence, therefore, must be rational.

But is it so? Is this reasoning sound? Is nuclear deterrence a coherent idea at all? Can it be "the ultimate peacekeeper" of the nuclear age as its theory requires? In the following two sections I will argue for the contrary, that the idea of nuclear deterrence is in theory and practice a confused and incoherent idea based on contradiction. To show this, I will analyze the idea of nuclear deterrence as built on two basic principles: the *principle of classical deterrence* and the *principle of the singularity of nuclear weapons.*

Deterrence is one of the most fundamental species of threat system used in politics.[35] As a general mechanism to control social behavior, its roots can be traced to very primary, biologically programmed, postures of animal behavior. The basic idea of deterrence is quite simple: it is a way of convincing an adversary *not* to act in a certain way by threatening the infliction of severe harm should the adversary so act. Considered in its purest form, deterrence is a threat distinguished by its negative aspect. While an ultimatum, for example, is a threat designed to coerce an adversary to act in a certain way, or undo something already done, deterrence is the use of threats to *prevent* an act from being committed in the first place.

What is it that makes a deterrent system successful? The immediate answer is, of course, *credibility*. In order to be effective, deterrent threats must be credible in the eyes of the threatened; the threatener must be perceived as having the *capability* and the *will* to carry out the threats if need arises.

As such, deterrence is an inherent feature of the Hobbesian regime of sovereign states. In the sphere of international politics, deterrence is the instrument that keeps political conflicts stable; it contains conflicts within the boundaries of threats only. If the threats are successful, they are neither executed nor tested, they simply deter. As such, deterrence is an indispensable element in the political arrangement of world order among sovereign states.

Significant implications follow from this essential link between deterrence and politics. First, deterrence is liable to intrinsic uncertainties that are due to the very nature of political power—its amorphousness and temporal fluctuations. The international system is fundamentally dynamic. Geopolitical changes in the structure of world-orders, particularly fluctuations in the strategic balance of power between nations (through an arms race, for example), are inevitable for the long run. In principle, no world-order arrangements can ever be fully stable or final in the long run.

Further, while threats of legal punishments are explicit and relatively invariant through time, the threats involved in military deterrence are often ambiguous, mostly implicit, and subject to interpretation. The notorious problem of the "hermeneutic circle," typical of any interpretative acts, is present in politics as well. The meaning assigned to an isolated deterrent threat is dependent on the *entire* interpretation of the opponent's foreign and defense policy (intentions, interests, policies, commitments and so forth). As such, deterrence is not only ever liable to misinterpretations and miscalculations in ways that may unexpectedly lead to its failure, but systematic biases of all kinds are, in fact, inevitable.[36]

Another important feature of deterrence has to do with the inherent uncertainties about their scope of application. In international politics boundaries of threats are hard to spell out in detail prior to the occurrence of a crisis in which the threats are actually challenged. Indeed, the history of nations is abundant with wars resulting from miscalculations due to insufficient credibility of deterrence postures. The lesson of our analysis is clear: as long as we continue to rely on the mechanism of deterrence, the phenomenon of war cannot be excluded. The principle is defined as follows:

The Principle of Classical Deterrence. Deterrence is the primary and indispensable regulatory mechanism available in international politics to prevent war.

But in addition to the principle of classical deterrence, the idea of nuclear deterrence must also contain the unique lesson of the nuclear age:

The Principle of the Singularity of Nuclear Weapons. Nuclear weapons are sui generis in the sense that their actual use is unacceptable.

Now we can formulate the principle of nuclear deterrence. As an idea nuclear deterrence is an attempt to reconcile principles (1) and (2), each by itself appears to be an indispensable and self-evident truth:

The Principle of Nuclear Deterrence. Threatening to do what would serve no political purpose is the only way to avoid nuclear war; nuclear deterrence is both indispensable and sui generis.

According to this principle, the only proper political role for nuclear weapons is deterrence, that is, ensuring that they will never actually be used. Since they have the capacity to bring an unprecedented holocaust on both sides, the use of this capacity does not make any sense. Thus, the sole purpose of nuclear weapons is to ensure that the other side will never forget the unique imperative of the nuclear era.

The problem, however, with the principle of nuclear deterrence is that it is made up of incompatible intuitions—the view that the nuclear situation is unique, and the view that it is largely continuous with prenuclear reality. This conceptual difficulty is demonstrated by two problems:

1. *The Usability Problem.* The more deterrentlike we make nuclear deterrence, that is, the more "usable" we make the weapons for the sake of the threat's credibility, the more likely it is that the weapons will be used.

2. *The Credibility Problem.* The more we treat nuclear weapons as sui generis, that is, as "unusable," the more incredible the threat to use them becomes, and the more likely the threat will fail.

Both problems appeared in a concrete form as criticism of specific nuclear strategic deterrent postures. The first is a problem for the principle of nuclear deterrence, and the second is a problem for the principle of singularity.

Consider the former. The starting point of all deterrence thinking is that the institution of war is an inevitable and indispensable phenomenon of international politics. This means that within the regime of sovereign states the possibility of war cannot be excluded. Credible deterrence, therefore, depends on demonstrating a genuine readiness and resoluteness to carry out the threat. Hence *credibility of the deterrent threat requires the usability of the weapons.* Otherwise, the threat would be seen as ineffective.

But the more usable we make the weapons, the more we treat them as mundane, and the more likely they are to be used. Since threatening with usable weapons is more credible, it generates more incentive for a preemptive strike at times of crisis. In general, the more nuclear deterrence comes to resemble conventional deterrence, the more likely it is to have all the weaknesses and uncertainties that characterize conventional deterrence. Further, as emphasized earlier, no deterrence system could ever guarantee its absolute future success, since geopolitical changes and errors are inevitable. But with nuclear weapons we cannot afford even a single error.

Let us move now to the second problem. According to the principle of singularity, best manifested in the notion of mutual assured destruction (MAD), the uniqueness of nuclear weapons lies in the fact that their use can serve no political purpose. But once we recognize nuclear weapons as sui generis, the threat to retaliate with them becomes *incredible.* There are two cases to consider. First is the threat of nuclear retaliation against a conventional attack or a limited nuclear strike by a nuclear adversary. This threat may not be credible because nuclear retaliation in such circumstances would likely bring a full-scale nuclear response, whether immediately or by escalation.

The second case concerns the threat of nuclear retaliation against a full-scale nuclear first strike. If the raison d'être of this threat is just to prevent such a first strike from being launched, what reason, political or military, would remain to launch a second strike once deterrence had failed? As Jonathan Schell puts it, "The logic of deterrence strategy is dissolved by the very event—the first-strike—that it is meant to prevent. Once the action begins, the whole doctrine is self cancelling."[37]

Given that retaliation in response to a full-scale first strike could serve no purpose, the threat of such retaliation is problematic. Moreover, attempts to solve this problem by adopting a more counterforce nuclear strategy is vitiated by the usability problem of the first kind. Any attempt to adopt a strategy of nuclear deterrence is bound to face these difficulties, either the one or the other.

What these problems demonstrate is that when the principle of classical deterrence and the principle of singularity are combined into the principle of nuclear deterrence, *paradox* results. If one makes nuclear deterrence more like conventional deterrence, nuclear war is rendered more likely; but if one makes nuclear deterrence less like conventional deterrence, nuclear war is still made more likely. The lesson is obvious. There is a fundamental incompatibility between traditional forms of military deterrence and the unique features of nuclear weapons. The classical forms of military deterrence depend on *war*, on its possibility to make the threat credible, and on its actuality to achieve the potential goals should the threat fail. The unique features of nuclear war make it unable to play either role.

We noticed already that in the nuclear age the dialectical relationship between war and civilization has come full circle. Nuclear war would be a peculiar form of primitive warfare for which the motivation would be backward-looking revenge rather than forward-looking deterrence. But what we can notice now is that the argument about the unique aspects of nuclear war makes nuclear deterrence conceptually incoherent as well. If nuclear war becomes irrational, so is the threat of nuclear war; for the effectiveness of the threat depends on the execution of the threat as a political option. We can rely neither on nuclear war nor on the threat of nuclear retaliation as a policy, that is, as a way of achieving political goals such as national security.

This illustrates Einstein's warning about the fundamental discontinuity between the nuclear reality and the way in which we think of this reality. If we admit (as we should) the uniqueness involved in the eventuality of nuclear holocaust, we can no longer retain our old political intuitions about deterrence and war; while if we decide to continue thinking of the nuclear reality in traditional politicomilitary terms we must fail to recognize the singular nature of nuclear weapons. In essence, the principle of nuclear deterrence is incoherent for attempting to preserve *both* our prenuclear intuitions about politics and war and our postnuclear understanding.

Does Nuclear Deterrence Prevent Wars?

There is, however, one nagging question that must surely arise as a counterargument to my criticism of the "logic" of deterrence: if nuclear deterrence is so bad, why has it been so effective in preventing nuclear war? Of course, this question assumes that nuclear deterrence is the sole (or primary) explanation for the fact that there have been no great wars between the superpowers in the last four decades. The claim does not imply, of course, that ideological-political conflicts between the superpowers have miraculously disappeared in the nuclear age. It does say, however, that *due* to nuclear deterrence, patterns of international conduct among the great powers have changed in such a way that conflicts are now handled with extra caution.[38] It postulates a certain causal connection between the dynamics of nuclear weapons and the dynamics of international politics.

This kind of reasoning, implicit in the principle of nuclear deterrence, constitutes the standard defense of nuclear weapons: it is nuclear weapons that have enabled us to enjoy the comfort of peace.[39] It assumes that recent history has indeed verified empirically the rationality calculus behind the principle of nuclear deterrence—it has changed the most fundamental patterns of international politics. The conclusion is one of moderate optimism: reliance on nuclear deterrence, once made with care and prudence, is advantageous to keep political conflicts under control. Nuclear weapons can serve as the primary cause for bipolar global strategic stability. This kind of reasoning is also the basic rationale behind the recent proposals for Israeli nuclear disclosure.

This *probabilistic* argument, however, is far from being valid, and obviously it does not render the moral certainty we require for dealing with nuclear weapons systems. It is based on one big confusion between factual-descriptive statements and inferential-causal statements, in addition to its strong inductivist biases. To acknowledge (factually) that patterns of conflict management in global politics have radically changed in the nuclear age is one thing, and to say (inferentially) that nuclear deterrence is the sole cause behind these changes is another. The former does not imply the latter; one can accept the former and reject the latter as its direct explanation. The fact that no great wars have broken out between nuclear powers is not enough to confirm the reliability of nuclear deterrence. In fact, this lucky state of affairs could have obtained in spite of the risks of nuclear deterrence, not because of it, and surely there is nothing to necessitate its continuance. The reasons for this skepticism are more than the standard Humian objections to inductive inferences into the future; they have to do with the unverified nature of deterrence.

To begin with, general deterrence is not an isolated act whose effectiveness can be tested independently of the other elements composing the national security policy; it is the entire national security posture. Since deterrent threats are always tied up with the *entire* corpus of foreign policy objectives, it is hard, perhaps theoretically impossible, to assess the *exclusive* contribution of each threat in preventing war. This is a general methodological problem of *general* deterrence: the link between deterrence and political stability is not something to be empirically verified. Hence, the absence of wars is not necessarily due to the deterrent postures; it could exist *in spite of* these postures. It is only the specific deterrence posture at crisis time, what Morgan calls "special deterrence," that can give some empirical measure about the credibility of deterrent threats in preventing wars.[40]

The main point is this: since general deterrence is ever-present in international politics, it is not something to be observed at work; it is something to be interpreted against the entire political background. Such interpretation should consider the strategic objectives of the nation in question, as well as the configuration of the political system as a whole.

But this problem is, in a sense, even worse once nuclear deterrence is considered. Since, fortunately enough, our experience in actual nuclear crises is overwhelmingly limited, there is no empirically decisive way to determine the role of nuclear postures in shaping new patterns of international relations, including the avoiding of crises.[41]

It is true, of course, that so far circumstances for East–West direct military confrontations have been carefully avoided. But how should we interpret this historical fact? Can we simply say inferentially that this fortunate state of affairs has been achieved *due* to nuclear deterrence? Does it reveal the *intrinsic* stabilizing nature of nuclear deterrence?

I don't think so. In fact, one could make the opposite case. It can be argued that the most significant stabilizing factor in East–West relationships during the last forty years—the division of the European continent into two spheres of influence—was achieved prior to and independently of the advent of nuclear deterrence as a significant political factor.[42] Whatever the contribution of nuclear weapons to global stability may be, it has been achieved within a political context that has already encouraged stabilization.

From the General Argument to the Israeli Dilemma

Nothing beyond hints and hunches has been said thus far about the Israeli nuclear dilemma in particular. At this point, the relevance of the general argument to the Israeli case is just like any other relationship between a general argument and a particular case. But a stronger case can be made.

In two significant respects the general argument is more relevant to the Israeli case than to the superpower situation. First, the specific geopolitical features of the Middle East conflict enhance the general antinuclear line even further than in the general case. Second, it is *only* in an as yet nonnuclearized region, such as the Middle East, that antinuclear arguments can carry some significant *political* and *practical* weight, in addition to their basic moral weight. Since in the Middle East the ultimate proliferation decisions have probably not yet been made, there are still realistic chances to prevent nuclear spread in that region. This final section, therefore, is devoted to a brief strategic characterization of the Arab–Israeli conflict in order to apply our general antinuclear argument to the pertinent context of the Middle East.

Consider the following peculiar features of the Arab–Israeli conflict:

The Cultural-Emotional Dimensions of the Conflict. The Arab–Israeli conflict has deep cultural and emotional dimensions beyond the political one. Essentially, it is a violent conflict between two cultural entities over territorial rights. By and large the Arab world, excepting only Egypt, still denies Israel's right to exist as a sovereign state. It is the legitimacy of Israel as a neighbor and partner that is still unacceptable for the Arabs. Israeli and Arab perceptions of each other's peaceful intentions are abysmally low, while on the side of warlike designs the distrust is even worse.

The totality of the conflict has a profound impact on military thinking of both sides. Israel, having features of a pariah state, tends to perceive its wars as having the potential to become all-out confrontations, if only its opponents will have the chance.[43] And just as Israeli perceptions of the Arab threat are influenced by images from Jewish history, so also Arab perceptions of their threat are fed by their vision of the Zionist expansionist ambitions.[44] This climate of the conflict is particularly dangerous in the context of nuclear weapons—it evokes fears of holocaust.

The Intensity of the Conflict. Since the establishment of the State of Israel (1948) the Arab–Israeli conflict has been marked by five major wars (1948, 1956, 1967, 1973, 1982), while subwar violence has dominated the periods between wars. Remarkably, three of these wars (1956, 1967, 1973) began with a surprise attack, a fact that traumatized both sides.[45] This fact is essentially significant for Israel, whose geopolitical inferiority and demographic vulnerability (see next item) are primary reasons for its tendency to rely on preemptive strategy.[46] Obviously, such geopolitical constraints only contribute to Israel's basic sense of insecurity.

The Geopolitical Asymmetries of the Conflict. The Arab–Israeli conflict is built upon basic geopolitical and demographic asymmetries. The Arab side is composed of multinational, multipolar coalitions of states. The Arab–Israeli conflict is a significant element in inter-Arab politics, but not exclusive. The steady Arab political pattern of forming and reforming loose and short-lived alignments might have further destabilizing consequences once nuclear weapons were introduced.[47]

In considering these fundamentals of the Arab–Israeli conflict, one recognizes instantly many important differences between the multipolar system of the Middle East and the bipolar rivalry of the superpowers. Each of these fundamentals implies a specific set of obstacles for *long-term* stability of the system. This point can be made in another way.

Those strategists who believe that real stability could be achieved via nuclear deterrence insist upon a certain set of conditions. Among these conditions are the following: (1) bipolarity of the political system, (2) symmetric strategic relationships, (3) mutual recognition and communication, (4) relative separation between nuclear deterrence and conventional deterrence, (5) invulnerability of second-strike nuclear forces. None of these stabilizing elements is currently in place in the Middle East. And considering the history of the region, it is unlikely that they would appear shortly after any move toward nuclear disclosure.[48] In fact, based on the history and geopolitical constants of the region, one can make "informed" speculations to the contrary. The very act of nuclear disclosure by any state in the Middle East would cause drastic destabilizing effects for the entire region (for example, pressures for military preemption, grand realignment of the Arab world, formations of nuclear coalitions).

All current scenarios for a nuclearized Middle East reflect the fundamental tension between the traditional patterns of military and political behavior in the region and the presence of nuclear weapons. They pose the same old fundamental dilemmas of nuclear deterrence: either to make nuclear weapons politically relevant (consistent with conventional deterrence), but then too "usable," or to make them for deterrence only (inconsistent with traditional politics), but then incredible. The "usability" and "credibility" problems would arise again, but this time in a region too volatile to actually test nuclear deterrence.

Of course, the fact that the Middle East has a long tradition of violence and political instability does not *prove* that nuclear weapons could not alter the situation as the nuclear advocates expect. It is not impossible that nuclearization might bring a measure of stability and moderation to the Middle East that the conventional balance has not brought, and probably cannot bring. But to say this is to say very little. This is so *simply* because in the field of human affairs there are no absolute proofs *at all;* there are only "informed speculations" about the future. But if we are not clear about the role of nuclear weapons in stabilizing the East–West situation in the *past,* we can say much less about a volatile region that has no nuclear experience at all. It may well be, as Paskins argues, that global nuclear deterrence has not yet shown its danger simply because nuclear proliferation has not yet affected new regions.

To sum up, the real issue about the Israeli dilemma is not whether or not we can make predictions for the future—obviously nobody can, though everybody claims to have informed guesses—but (1) whether one has *justifiable grounds* (in terms of the risk assessment calculus) to prefer the nuclear option over that of deliberate ambiguity, and (2) whether one has the *moral* right to propose to take the risk. As far as I can see the answer to both questions is absolutely NO.

Final Reflections

In world history the term *Holocaust* is automatically associated with a unique event—Nazi Germany's genocidal plan to bring a "final solution" to the Jewish people. This unprecedented catastrophe was a deliberate and calculated attempt to bring a full human culture into physical extinction. Out of this tragedy, the most traumatic event in Jewish history, the State of Israel was established. Indeed, this catastrophe defines Israel's ultimate moral raison d'être.

Ever since Hiroshima and Nagasaki, a new vision of holocaust has overshadowed our entire world civilization. Nuclear holocaust would be the ultimate of all holocausts. For four decades we have been living under a new regime of nuclear threats built upon huge bureaucratic and technological organizations. It is known as the regime of nuclear deterrence. This regime signifies our lack of political imagination and moral courage to overcome outdated patterns of thought and behavior. This lesson should never be forgotten.

Nuclear weapons have distinctive Promethean features. Once they have been created, they cannot be "disinvented." It is impossible to regain our innocence. Nuclear weapons are the postmodern era Golem: they are manmade, invented to put an end to terrible violence, but now threatening even greater violence.

In this chapter I raised the *general* case against nuclear deterrence. Admittedly, as a general argument it has little *political* weight. At the present time no politically feasible alternatives to nuclear deterrence appear on the horizon. Nevertheless, nuclear proliferation has not yet spread all over the globe as many experts predicted some twenty years ago.[49] As far as nuclear proliferation is concerned, the antinuclear line has gained some political (and moral) weight.

If Israel has actually developed a nuclear option, it did so out of the conviction that another Jewish holocaust *must* be prevented. Its decisionmakers may have felt that Israel should always be in close proximity to a weapon of last resort. But Israel has also been sensitive to the lessons of the nuclear age: it has totally rejected the idea of nuclear deterrence as a national security posture. One should be reminded again, despite all of the international speculations, that Israel's record is absolutely clear. It has never issued any nuclear threats, not even during the darkest hours of the Yom Kippur War.

On all conceivable prudential and moral grounds, Israel is obliged to maintain its antinuclear policy and *not* to introduce nuclear weapons politics into the Middle East. Deliberately taking the nuclear path would be mistaken. One should hope that it will never take place.

Notes

Chapter 1
Introduction

1. From 1965 to the present, Israel has adopted the cautious formula: "Israel does not have nuclear weapons and will not be the first to introduce them into the region." Presumably, however, this formula is not meant to suggest that Israel will sit idly by if its adversaries "go nuclear." In this connection, Yigal Allon's comment is instructive: "Israel will not be the first to introduce nuclear weapons into the Middle East, but neither will it be the second." For more on this "refinement" of Israeli policy, see Yair Evron, "The Relevance and Irrelevance of Nuclear Options in Conventional Wars: The 1973 October War," *Jerusalem Journal of International Relations* 7, nos. 1–2(1984):146.

2. See chapters 4, 5, and 6 in this book.

3. *The Babylonian Talmud,* Order Zera'im, Tractate Berakoth, IX.

4. Even the balance of power generally, of which the balance of terror is a particular variant, has never been very durable, never more than a facile metaphor. Indeed, it has never had anything to do with equilibrium. Since it is always a matter of individual and arbitrary perceptions, adversary states are never really confident that strategic conditions are well balanced. Rather, each side always fears that it may be just a little bit behind. The net effect of this search for balance, therefore, is inevitably disequilibrium and insecurity.

5. In this connection, success is defined very narrowly in terms of the avoidance of nuclear war. Where the workings of nuclear deterrence are considered more broadly in terms of effects on day-to-day life under the threat of nuclear annihilation, however, they can hardly be termed "successful." For example, the prevailing system of "deadly logic" has had corrosive effects on ordinary human feelings of care and compassion. In the United States, small but growing bands of Americans dubbed "survivalists" are arming themselves and learning how to kill in a postapocalypse milieu. Going far beyond the self-help aspect of the bomb shelter movement of the 1950s and 1960s, this retreat to medieval thinking entails a heightened form of social Darwinism, a generally accepted willingness to kill neighbors to survive.

6. In this connection, one of the significant hazards of proliferation in the Middle East lies in the increased likelihood of "catalyzing" nuclear war between the su-

perpowers. There is evidence that this hazard has been prefigured by conventional wars in the region. For example, it has been alleged that toward the close of the Yom Kippur War, the Soviet Union prepared to send a very substantial force into the Middle East, and that an ad hoc team of the U.S. National Security Council decided, on the night of October 24, 1973, to place a part of the U.S. armed forces on a Defense Condition 3 alert. (There are five degrees of Defense Condition alert that can be declared in the U.S. armed forces, degree 5 being the lowest and degree 1 the highest. Strategic Air Command (SAC) forces are routinely in a state of degree 4 readiness.) Although a partial alert, this included, inter alia, the SAC forces and the fleet of Polaris submarines. The U.S. administration explained that the "precautionary alert" order was intended to make it clear to the Soviets that the United States would not acquiesce to "any unilateral move on their part to move military forces into the Mideast." (See President Nixon's news conference of October 26, 1973, and Secretary Kissinger's news conference of October 25, 1973.) For a fuller elucidation of these events, see Yona Bandmann and Yishai Cordova, "The Soviet Nuclear Threat Towards the Close of the Yom Kippur War," *Jerusalem Journal of International Relations 5*, no. 1(1980):94–110. According to the authors, "At the beginning of November 1973, a week after the superpower confrontation of October 24–25, fuller details began to appear in the American press on the background to the alert in the U.S. armed forces. From these reports, it appeared that the USSR also had made use of an atomic threat in the Middle East in the last stage of the Yom Kippur War" (p. 97).

7. Even if its strategy remained "countervalue," Israel's perceived willingness to use nuclear weapons in retaliation would be problematic, since civilian populations would be intentionally targeted (unlike a counterforce strategy, where civilian injuries and fatalities are "collateral damage"). But there would be no sensible reason for Israel to opt for a countervalue posture.

8. Nuclear proliferation refers not only to the actual production of nuclear weapons by states not yet members of the nuclear club, but also to the further spread of the capability to manufacture nuclear weapons. Since a very close relationship exists between civilian nuclear power programs and the capacity to develop nuclear weapons (such programs may provide access to weapons-usable materials, facilities, and expertise), the spread of these programs is an integral part of the proliferation problem. A state, of course, might also seek entry into the nuclear club with a research reactor to make weapons-grade plutonium or through the enrichment of uranium 235 to weapons-grade levels. In comparison to the plutonium that is made from power reactors, the plutonium from research reactors is cheaper, faster, and of higher weapons-making quality. For information on the relevance of civilian nuclear power programs to the proliferation of nuclear weapons, see especially Albert Wohlstetter et al., *Swords from Plowshares: The Military Potential of Civilian Nuclear Energy* (Chicago: University of Chicago Press, 1979); and *Nuclear Proliferation and Civilian Nuclear Power*, 9 vols., A Report of the Nonproliferation Alternative Systems Assessment Program, DOE/NE-0001, U.S. Department of Energy, Washington D.C., December 1979, 153 pp.

9. See Shai Feldman, *Israeli Nuclear Deterrence: A Strategy for the 1980s* (New York: Columbia University Press, 1982), p. 46. Feldman's argument is merely a specific instance of a more general position, one that has been with us for a long time. In this view, nuclear proliferation is seen as potentially stabilizing because it might

enlarge the number of states with credible deterrence postures. See, for example, Kenneth Waltz, *The Spread of Nuclear Weapons: More May Be Better,* Adelphi Papers, no. 171 (London: International Institute for Strategic Studies, 1981); and Pierre Gallois, *The Balance of Terror: Strategy for the Nuclear Age* (Boston: Houghton Mifflin, 1961). For a critical appraisal of this position in general theoretical terms, see Louis René Beres, *Reason and Realpolitik: U.S. Foreign Policy and World Order* (Lexington, Mass.: Lexington Books, 1984), ch. 4, U.S. Nuclear Strategy: Proliferation.

10. A state that *believes* it has achieved some measure of active and/or passive defense might have additional reason to consider preemption.

11. Even if we could assume that leadership behavior were always rational, this would say nothing about the accuracy of the information used in rational calculations. Rationality refers only to the *intention* of maximizing specified values or preferences. It does not tell us anything about whether the information used is correct or incorrect. Hence, rational actors may make errors in calculation which lead them to nuclear war. Daniel Frei speaks of these errors in terms of "unintentional nuclear war." According to Frei: "What is being envisaged here is not accidental nuclear war, but rather nuclear war based on false assumptions, i.e., on misjudgment or miscalculation by the persons legitimately authorized to decide on the use of nuclear weapons. Substandard performance by decision-makers in crisis situations is particularly common." See Daniel Frei, *Risks of Unintentional Nuclear War* (Geneva: United Nations Institute for Disarmament Research, 1982), p. ix.

12. See Feldman, *Israeli Nuclear Deterrence,* p. 87.

13. Ibid., pp. 30–31.

14. Ibid., p. 31.

15. In this connection, Israel cannot hope to repeat its Osiraq strategy against every adversary that develops nuclear reactor facilities, even though such facilities might be used clandestinely to manufacture nuclear weapons. Indeed, in September 1984 Israel pledged that it would not attack nuclear facilities dedicated to peaceful purposes and that it would abide by any international agreement on protecting such facilities from military assault.

16. See "Excerpts from Iraqi Leader's Speech," *New York Times,* June 24, 1981, p. 6. See also "Israeli Attack on Iraqi Nuclear Facilities," Hearings before the Subcommittee on International Security and Scientific Affairs on Europe and the Middle East and on International Economic Policy and Trade of the Committee on Foreign Affairs, House of Representatives, 97th Congress, 1st sess., June 17 and 25, 1981 (Washington, D.C.: U.S. Government Printing Office, 1981).

17. See Stephen M. Meyer, *The Dynamics of Nuclear Proliferation* (Chicago: University of Chicago Press, 1984). By late 1984, Belgium was seriously considering a $1 billion offer from Libyan leader Muammar Khadafi to help that country build its first nuclear power plant. At issue is a standard-size nuclear power plant which Libya hopes to begin building on the Gulf of Sidra in June 1986. The Soviet Union has promised to supply Libya with the nuclear heart of the reactor, including the fuel. See Gary Yerkey, "Belgium Consults Allies As It Weighs Libyan Bid for Nuclear Power Plant," *Christian Science Monitor,* October 31, 1984, p. 28.

18. For example, Pakistan—described by an authoritative report issued by the Carnegie Endowment for International Peace as having reached the "nuclear weapons threshold"—is concerned preeminently with India (the two countries have fought

three wars since the Indian subcontinent became independent from Britain in 1947). See Leonard S. Spector, *Nuclear Proliferation Today,* a Carnegie Endowment Book (New York: Vintage Books, 1984). It should also be noted that Pakistan might be willing to supply nuclear weapons to a major ally such as Saudi Arabia.

19. See Uri Bar-Joseph, "The Hidden Debate: The Formation of Nuclear Doctrines in the Middle East," *Journal of Strategic Studies 5,* no. 2 (June 1982):208.

20. See A. H. Cordesman, *The Gulf and the Search for Strategic Stability: Saudi Arabia, the Military Balance in the Gulf, and Trends in the Arab–Israeli Military Balance* (Boulder, Colo.: Westview Press, 1984), p. 760.

21. On this point, see Rodney W. Jones, *Small Nuclear Forces,* Washington Papers, no. 103 (New York: Praeger Publishers, 1984), p. 54. As Jones points out, this special vulnerability would flow from small nuclear force size, a lack of familiarity with nuclear military options, inadequate early warning systems and weak or unreliable command, control, communication, and intelligence (C^3I) links.

22. See Avi Beker's chapter (8) in this book.

23. It is significant to point out here that most Israeli authorities, as well as the general public, would regard any concerted military effort to destroy Israel as more than war. Nurtured by a Jewish history overstocked with martyrs, they would view such an effort as genocide. After the June 7, 1981 Israeli destruction of the Osiraq reactor on the outskirts of Baghdad, then Prime Minister Begin defended the raid as a "supreme moral act" to save the Jewish state from "another Holocaust." In my judgment, this suggests that if it should be faced with the "end of the Third Temple," Israel would fire whatever nuclear weapons it might have at its disposal.

24. The importance of a continued reliance on conventional deterrence is examined by the Yaniv, Eytan, Dowty, Steinberg, and Inbar essays herein.

25. In this connection, we must also consider that the effects of such an Israeli attack would also be felt in other noncombatant countries. As yields exceeded 30 kilotons, part of the cloud of radioactive debris would "punch" into the stratosphere, affecting states that were not intended targets. The expectation of such unintended effects would, of course, have to be factored into Israel's decision concerning nuclear attack.

26. This conclusion suggests reconsideration of Clausewitz's principle that war should always be conducted with a view to sustaining the "political object." According to Clausewitz: "War is only a branch of political activity; it is in no sense autonomous. . . . It cannot be divorced from political life—and whenever this occurs in our thinking about war, the many links that connect the two elements are destroyed, and we are left with something that is pointless and devoid of sense." See Carl von Clausewitz, *On War* (Princeton, N.J.: Princeton University Press, 1976) book VIII, chapter 6B, War Is an Instrument of Policy.

27. For additional information on the concept of a nuclear winter, see Richard P. Turco, Owen B. Toon, Thomas P. Ackerman, James B. Pollack and Carl Sagan, "The Climatic Effects of Nuclear War," *Scientific American, 251,* no. 2 (August 1984): 33–43: Paul R. Ehrlich et al., "Long-Term Biological Consequences of Nuclear War," *Science 222* no. 4630 (December 23, 1983): 1293–1300; R. P. Turco et al., "Nuclear Winter: Global Consequences of Multiple Nuclear Explosions," *Science 222,* no. 4630 (December 23, 1983): 1283–92; Carl Sagan, "Nuclear War and Cli-

matic Catastrophe: Some Policy Implications," *Foreign Affairs 62,* no. 2(Winter 1983–84): 257–92; Curt Covey et al., "Global Atmospheric Effects of Massive Smoke Injections from a Nuclear War: Results from General Circulations Model Simulations," *Nature 308,* no. 5954(March 1, 1984): 21–25; and Carl Sagan, "The Nuclear Winter," published by the Council for a Livable World Education Fund, Boston, 1983, 10pp. See also *The Effects on the Atmosphere of a Major Nuclear Exchange,* a report issued on December 11, 1984 by the National Research Council, National Academy of Sciences, Washington, D. C., 193 pp. Commissioned by the Department of Defense, this report supports the main lines of argument and the principal findings of the 1983 nuclear winter research team headed by Carl Sagan. The NAS research panel, chaired by Dr. George F. Carrier of Harvard University, stressed that its findings implied no threshold. A smaller war would produce smaller effects, but the study did not disclose exactly how small a nuclear exchange would have to be to avoid a nuclear winter.

28. The issues of arbitrariness and unpredictability also raise the standards of international law as they pertain to nuclear war. According to these standards, any resort to nuclear weapons would be contrary to the principles of *jus in bello* (justice in war). Although no specific treaty exists that outlaws nuclear weapons per se, any use of these weapons would be inherently indiscriminate and disproportionate—characteristics that violate the codified and customary laws of war. Further support for the argument that any use of nuclear weapons would be in violation of international law can be found at book III, ch. 11 of Hugo Grotius's *The Law of War and Peace (1625).* Here, Grotius speaks of the need to allow innocents an opportunity to escape from carnage, an imperative that is itself drawn from Old Testament accounts of ancient Israel. According to Grotius: "The Jewish interpreters note that it was a custom among their ancestors that, when they were besieging a city, they would not completely encircle it, but would leave a sector open for those who wished to escape, in order that the issue might be determined with less bloodshed." A similar argument was made by Polybius *(Punic Wars)* with his account of Scipio Aemilianus' proclamation upon the destruction of Carthage: "Let those who wish, flee." And by the judgment of Tacitus, "To butcher those who have surrendered is savage." For a fuller elucidation of these issues, see the chapter by Burns Weston in this book.

29. According to a recent analysis by the Jaffee Center for Strategic Studies in Tel Aviv, Israel is already losing its military edge over the Arab states. In the words of Major-General Aharon Yariv, who now heads the Center, special notice must be made of Syria, which is driving for "strategic parity" with Israel and which is well on its way toward acquiring offensive capacity against Israel. See "Study Says Israeli Edge Over Arabs Is Waning," *New York Times,* Wednesday, February 13, 1985, p. 1.

30. See Yehoshafat Harkabi, *The Bar Kokhba Syndrome: Risk and Realism in International Politics* (Chappaqua, N.Y.: Rossel Books, 1983), p. 118.

31. In this connection, special attention should be given to Charles E. Osgood's very promising *graduated and reciprocated initiatives in tension-reduction* (GRIT) strategy. For information on this strategy, see Osgood's "Psycho-Social Dynamics and the Prospects for Mankind," presented to the Peace Science Society (International) in 1977 and to a United Nations' colloquium in 1978; and his "The GRIT Strategy," *Bulletin of the Atomic Scientists 36,* no. 5(May 1980): 58–60.

Chapter 2
Going Public with the Bomb: The Israeli Calculus

1. Robert Harkavy, *Spectre of a Middle Eastern Holocaust: The Strategic and Diplomatic Implications of the Israeli Nuclear Weapons Program*, Monograph Series in World Affairs (Denver: University of Denver Press, 1977).

2. Shai Feldman, *Israeli Nuclear Deterrence: A Strategy for the 1980s* (New York: Columbia University Press, 1982), pp. 123, 126.

3. Ibid., pp. 103–21, 129–36.

4. P. Schroeder, "Letter to the editor," *Commentary* 61 (February 1976): 8–14.

5. J. Bowyer Bell, "Israel's Nuclear Option," *Middle East Journal* 26 (Autumn, 1972): 379–388; Avigdor Haselkorn, "Israel: From an Option to a Bomb in the Basement?", in R. M. Lawrence and J. Larus, eds., *Nuclear Proliferation: Phase II* (Lawrence: University Press of Kansas, 1974), pp. 149–82.

6. Steven J. Rosen, "Nuclearization and Stability in the Middle East," *Jerusalem Journal of International Relations* 1 (Spring 1976):1–32; Feldman, *Israeli Nuclear Deterrence*, pp. 188–191.

7. Fuad Jabber, *Israel and Nuclear Weapons: Present Options and Future Strategies* (London: Chatto and Windus, 1971), pp. 141–44, believed that Israel would use its nuclear capability to preserve its 1967 territorial gains. Others argue in one form or another that overt nuclear status and territorial withdrawal go hand-in-hand. See Rosen, "Nuclearization and Stability in the Middle East"; Feldman, *Israeli Nuclear Deterrence*, pp. 228–32; and Shlomo Aronson, "Nuclearization of the Middle East: A Dovish View," *Jerusalem Quarterly* 1(Winter 1977): 27–44.

8. Thomas S. Schelling, *The Strategy of Conflict* (Cambridge, Mass.: Harvard University Press, 1960), p. 196; Haselkorn, "Israel"; Yair Evron, "Israel and the Atom: The Uses and Misuses of Ambiguity," *Orbis* 17(Winter 1974):1326–43.

9. Robert Tucker, "Israel and the United States: From Dependence to Nuclear Weapons?" *Commentary* 60 (November 1975):29–43.

10. Feldman, *Israeli Nuclear Deterrence*, p. 91.

11. The latest to do so is Peter Pry, *Israel's Nuclear Arsenal* (Boulder, Colo.: Westview Press, 1984), pp. 113–16.

12. Feldman, *Israeli Nuclear Deterrence*, p. 101.

13. Ibid., p. 145.

14. Ibid., pp. 9–24. Feldman also argues that it is risky to wait until the last moment to unveil a nuclear deterrent, as it might be taken for a bluff or lead to other bad judgments under the crisis conditions of a "last resort." But as Feldman points out repeatedly in his book, it is precisely in these circumstances—that is, fighting ostensibly for survival—that the nuclear threat becomes most credible. In any event, it is difficult to imagine an Arab state so certain of Israel's nuclear innocence as to push matters to this pass, or of such a situation developing without time to disclose the deterrent, partially or entirely, in a more deliberate fashion. Finally, a demonstrative explosion should be effective if other methods of gaining attention failed, leaving Israel in approximately the same situation it would be in had it conducted an open test earlier.

15. Alan Dowty, "Israel and Nuclear Weapons," *Midstream* 22(November 1976):6–7.

16. Pry, *Israel's Nuclear Arsenal.*

17. Central Intelligence Agency, "Prospects for Further Proliferation of Nuclear Weapons," DCI NIO 1945/74, September 4, 1974, p. 1., quoted in Leonard S. Spector, *Nuclear Proliferation Today* (New York: Vintage Books, 1984), pp. 128–29.

18. Francis Perrin, quoted in Steve Weissman and Herbert Krosney, *The Islamic Bomb: The Nuclear Threat to Israel and the Middle East.* (New York: Times Books, 1981), esp. pp. 69–70.

19. "Dayan Says Israelis Have the Capacity to Produce A-Bombs," *New York Times,* June 25, 1961.

20. Aronson, *Conflict and Bargaining in the Middle East, 1965–1976* (Baltimore: Johns Hopkins University Press, 1978), pp. 165–66.

21. For more on this issue, see chapter 8, by Avi Beker, in this book.

22. Feldman, *Israeli Nuclear Deterrence,* p. 242.

Chapter 3
Deliberate Ambiguity: Evolution and Evaluation

1. "Dayan Calls for Nuclear Option," *Jerusalem Post,* February 18, 1976; "Dayan for Golan Changes to End State of War," *Jerusalem Post,* February 29, 1976; *Ma'ariv,* February 20, 1976.

2. Shai Feldman, *Israeli Nuclear Deterrence: A Strategy for the 1980s* (New York: Columbia University Press, 1982.

3. *Ma'ariv,* April 8, 1976; "Saudis Pose Real Threat, Gur Says," *Jerusalem Post,* November 14, 1976.

4. "No Need for Nuclear Option—Allon," *Jerusalem Post,* September 9, 1976.

5. Alan Dowty, "Israel and Nuclear Weapons," *Midstream* 22 (November 1976): 7–22 and elsewhere in this book.

6. "White House Brushes Off Report of Israel A-blast (Briefing)" Eliot Marshall, *Science* 207 (March 14, 1980):1185.

7. W. Seth Carus, "The Bekaa Valley Campaign," *Washington Quarterly* 5, no. 4(1982).

8. Shlomo Aronson, *Conflict and Bargaining in the Middle East* (Baltimore: Johns Hopkins University Press, 1978), p. 42.

9. Mordechai Gazit, *President Kennedy's Policy toward the Arab States and Israel,* Shiloah Center for Middle Eastern and African Studies, Tel Aviv, 1983, p. 38.

10. Ibid. p. 52.

11. Aronson, *Conflict and Bargaining in the Middle East.*

12. The issue of inspections has arisen periodically in the course of U.S.–Israeli relations since then. In 1974, President Nixon declared his intention of bestowing nuclear power reactors on both Israel and Egypt. The United States then sought to apply "full scope safeguards" on all Israeli nuclear facilities, including Dimona, which Israel, of course, resisted. This and other factors eventually led the United States to abandon this effort.

13. Feldman, *Israeli Nuclear Deterrence,* p. 215.

14. William Quandt, *Decade of Decision* (Berkeley: University of California Press, 1977), pp. 66–67.

15. Robert E. Harkavy, *Spectre of a Middle Eastern Holocaust: The Strategic and Diplomatic Implications of the Israeli Nuclear Weapons Program,* Monograph Series in World Affairs (Denver: University of Denver Press, 1977), p. 15.

16. For different interpretations of this issue, see Shlomo Aronson, "The Nuclear Dimension of the Arab–Israeli Conflict: The Case of the Yom Kippur War," *Jerusalem Journal of International Relations 7,* nos. 1–2(1984), and Yair Evron, "The Relevance and Irrelevance of Nuclear Options in Conventional Wars: The 1973 October War," *Jerusalem Journal of International Affairs 7,* nos. 1–2(1984).

17. Harkavy, *Spectre of a Middle-Eastern Holocaust.* p. 11.

18. Hasanyn Haykal in *Al Ahram,* October 15, 1965, as cited by Feldman, *Israeli Nuclear Deterrence,* p. 256.

19. *Ma'ariv,* March 2, 1978.

20. *Ma'ariv,* December 2, 1974.

21. "Katzir: Let World Worry about Israel's Nuclear Potential," *Jerusalem Post,* December 3, 1974.

22. "Dayan: Atoms, Not Tanks, Should Defend Israel," *Jerusalem Post,* November 30, 1976.

23. *Ma'ariv,* April 8, 1976. Cited by Inbar in chapter 5 of this book.

24. "No Need for Nuclear Option—Allon," *Jerusalem Post,* September 9, 1976.

25. "Dayan: Israel Won't Be First or Last to Use Nuclear Weapons," *Jerusalem Post,* July 13, 1980.

26. "Dayan Says Israel Can Make Nuclear Weapons Quickly," *New York Times,* June 25, 1981.

27. See Feldman, *Israeli Nuclear Deterrence,* and Robert Tucker, "Israel and the United States: From Dependence to Nuclear Weapons?" *Commentary* (November 1975).

28. *The Military Balance, 1982/3* (London: International Institute for Strategic Studies, 1983).

29. Feldman, *Israeli Nuclear Deterrence,* p. 193.

30. Tucker, "Israel and the United States."

31. Feldman, *Israeli Nuclear Deterrence,* p. 12.

32. Fuad Jabber, *Israel and Nuclear Weapons* (London: Chatto and Windus, 1971).

33. "No Need for Nuclear Option—Allon," *Jerusalem Post,* September 9, 1976.

34. See, for example, Feldman, *Israeli Nuclear Deterrence.*

Chapter 4
Israel's Conventional Deterrent: A Reappraisal

1. This thesis challenges the not infrequent assertion of both Israeli and foreign scholars that Israel's conventional deterrent has been a failure. See for example Oz Chen, "Reflections on Israeli Deterrence," *Jerusalem Quarterly,* and John Mearsheimer, *Conventional Deterrence* (Ithaca, N.Y.: Cornell University Press, 1983). Shai Feldman's advocacy in *Israeli Nuclear Deterrence: A Strategy for the 1980s* (New York: Columbia University Press, 1982) also begins from the premise that Israel's conventional deterrence has been totally unsuccessful. Not surprisingly, Arab analysts

tend to concur with this evaluation. See Muhamad Abdul Mumin "Arab Deterrence and the Collapse of Israeli Strategy," *Shuun Philastinyia* (January 1974): 25–34.

2. Raymond Aron, *Peace and War* (New York: Doubleday, 1966), p. 404.

3. Raoul Naroll, Vern L. Bullough, and Frada Naroll, *Military Deterrence in History* (Albany: State University of New York Press, 1974). Bruce Russett, Alexander George, and Richard Smoke reached similar conclusions. See Bruce Russet, "The Calculus of Deterrence," *Journal of Conflict Resolution* 7 (1963):97–109, and Alexander George and Richard Smoke, *Deterrence in American Foreign Policy* (New York: Columbia University Press, 1974), esp. chs. 17–19.

4. This quality of Israel's administrative culture is reflected by the following "reconstruction" of the "Israeli view."

5. Yoram Peri, *Between Battles and Ballots: Civil–Military Relations in Israel* (Cambridge, England: Cambridge University Press, 1982), pp. 1–3.

6. For a definition of the scope of national security in Israel see my article "National Security and Nation-Building: The Case of Israel," *International Interactions 11*, no. 2, pp. 193–217. Also Peri, *Between Battles and Ballots*.

7. See David Ben-Gurion, *The Restored State of Israel*, vol. 1 (Tel Aviv: Am Oved, 1975), pp. 469, 509 (Hebrew); Yigal Allon, *The Making of Israel's Army* (London: Weidenfeld and Nicolson, 1970), p. 72; Ezer Weizman, *Thine the Sky, Thine the Land* (Tel Aviv: Am Oved, 1975), p. 172 (Hebrew).

8. See David Ben-Gurion, *The Restored State of Israel*, p. 537; Yigal Allon, *A Curtain of Sand* (Tel Aviv: HaKibbutz HaMeuhad, 1981), pp. 188–204 (Hebrew).

9. Yoav Ben-Horin and Barry Posen, *Israel's Strategic Doctrine*, Rand/R-2845-NA, The Rand Corporation, Santa Monica, Calif., September 1981.

10. On this see statement by (then) Israeli Minister of Defense Moshe Arens in *HaAretz*, June 5, 1984.

11. The most succinct Israeli analysis of perceptions of Arab goals remains Yehoshafat Harkabi's *Arab Strategies and Israel's Response* (New York: The Free Press, 1977). Harkabi was instrumental in bringing to the attention of many Israelis a statement by an Arab strategist advocating such a comprehensive war of attrition. See Y. Harkabi, ed., *The Arabs and Israel*, no. 5, (Tel Aviv: Am Oved, 1975) (Hebrew). This issue of the periodical includes an article by Hytham al Ayubi, a Syrian officer, under the title "Future Arab Strategy in Light of the 1973 War." The article is the most elaborate statement to date of the Arab strategy of multiple attrition.

12. Yuval Ne'eman, formerly Israeli Chief of Military Intelligence, once gave this perception a statistical expression and presented it in these terms to the Chief of Staff and to the Minister of Defense. He disclosed this years later in a symposium held at Tel Aviv University of December 14–17, 1981. See also Moshe Dayan, *Avnei Derekh* (Jerusalem: Idanim, 1976), p. 212 (Hebrew).

13. This point is stressed by Ben-Horin and Posen in *Israel's Strategic Doctrine*. It can be stated mathematically in the following way:

$$\frac{\Delta x(V)}{\Delta T} = D \frac{\Delta(D+N)}{\Delta T} = P$$

(V = victory; T = time factor; N = Normalization; P = peace; Δ = change). See my article "Deterrence or Defense in Israeli Strategy," *State, Government and International Relations 24*(Spring 1985) (Hebrew).

14. Ibid. Also Yigal Allon, *A Curtain of Sand*, pp. 235–64.

15. See Michael Handel, *Israel's Political-Military Doctrine*, Harvard Center for International Affairs, Cambridge, Mass., 1973, p. 65; Janice Gross Stein and Raymond Tanter, *National Decision-Making: Israel's Security Choices, 1967* (Columbus: Ohio State University Press, 1980), pp. 91–134; *Basic Facts: The IDF and the Security of Israel*, IDF, Tel Aviv, 1982 (Mimeo).

16. For explicit references to the security role of alliances see M. Bar Zohar *Ben Gurion* (Tel Aviv: Am Oved, 1977) (Hebrew), pp. 1152 ff. Ezer Weizman, *The Battle for Peace* (Jerusalem: Idanim, 1982), p. 62 (Hebrew). Israel Tal, "National Security," *The Jerusalem Quarterly* 27 (Spring 1983):10–11.

17. See my article, "Deterrence or Defense."

18. Dayan, *Avnei Derekh*, p. 356.

19. *Basic Facts*. The document was not written by Sharon. But it markedly bore his personal imprint.

20. Cf. Moshe Dayan, "Peacetime Military Operations," *Maarakhot 159* (1959). An English version of this important presentation of the logic of reprisals is available in Donald Robinson, ed. *Under Fire* (New York: W.W. Norton, 1968), pp. 120–23.

21. See commentary on this by then OC Northern Command and later Chief of Staff General David Elazar, quoted by Y. Hameiri, *On Both Sides of the Heights* (Tel Aviv: Levin Epstein, 1970), p. 38 (Hebrew). T. Schelling grasped this trait of Israeli conduct intuitively. See *Arms and Influence* (New Haven, Conn.: Yale University Press, 1966), p. 151.

22. Yaakov Bar-Siman-Tov, *The Israeli–Egyptian War of Attrition 1969–1970* (New York: Columbia University Press, 1980).

23. See Avner Yaniv and Robert J. Lieber, "Personal Whim or Strategic Imperative: The Israeli Invasion of Lebanon," *International Security 8*, no. 2(1983).

24. Cf. Meir Pail "On Purity of Arms—Without Hypocrisy," *HaAretz* (July 29, 1979); Yoav Gelber, "Purity of Arms," *Ma'ariv*, July 10, 1979; Zeev Schiff, "On Purity of Arms and Hypocrisy," *HaAretz*, July 20, 1979.

25. Yaniv, "Deterrence or Defense."

26. See Zeev Schiff and Ehud Yaari, *Israel's Lebanon War* (New York: Simon and Schuster, 1984), passim.

27. See Fuad Ajami, "The End of Pan Arabism," *Foreign Affairs 57*, no. 2 (Winter 1978–79):355–73.

28. On the "rules" of the Arab balance of power see Alan R. Taylor, *The Arab Balance of Power* (Syracuse, N.Y.: Syracuse University Press, 1982). On this particular point see ch. 6 of Taylor's book.

29. See Avigdor Haselkorn, "Israel: From an Option to a Bomb in the Basement?" in Robert M. Lawrence and Joel Larus, eds., *Nuclear Proliferation, Phase II*, (Lawrence: University of Kansas Press, 1974).

30. Yair Evron, "Israel and the Atom: The Uses and Misuses of Ambiguity," *Orbis 17*(Winter 1974):1326–43.

31. Feldman, *Israeli Nuclear Deterrence*, pp. 10–14.

32. Such a possibility looms very large in Israeli defense planning. For example, during the great debate on the defense budget in November-December 1984, Defense Minister Rabin alerted the Knesset Defense and Foreign Relations Committee to the

Table 4–1
Force Comparisons

	Israel	Total Eastern Front	Syria	Jordan	Iraq
Regular troops	170,000	833,300	313,000	80,300	440,000
Reserves	370,000	1,010,000	500,000	30,000	480,000
Total manpower	540,000	1,843,300	813,000	110,300	920,000
Combat planes	670	1,350	690	120	540
Transport planes	96	100	25	12	63
Helicopters	75	724	265	25	434
Armored divisions	11		5	2	
Mechanized divisions		35	3	2	23
Tanks	3,600	10,200	4,200	1,000	5,000
Armored personnel carriers	8,000	8,400	3,500	1,460	3,500
Artillery	1,000	6,350	2,300	550	3,500

Source: R. Pdahzur, "The Threats of the Eastern Front," *HaAretz*, November 25, 1984.

possibility that an Arab Eastern Front, consisting of Syria, Jordan, and Iraq might materialize. If that happened, Israel would be faced by a dangerously imbalanced correlation of forces, as table 4–1 demonstrates.

Chapter 5
Israel and Nuclear Weapons since October 1973

1. See Harvey Sicherman, "The United States and Israel: A Strategic Divide?" *Orbis* 24(Summer 1980):381–94; Efraim Inbar, "Sources of Tension between Israel and the United States," *Conflict Quarterly* 4(Spring 1984):56–65.

2. For a detailed analysis of the Rabin government national security policy, its great sensitivity to the "American factor," and Rabin's central role in it, see Efraim Inbar, *Problems of Pariah States: The National Security Policy of the Rabin Government,* Unpublished Ph.D. dissertation, University of Chicago, 1981, parts 2 and 3.

3. "Nuclear ambiguity" indicates that a country appears to have the ability to produce a nuclear device, but remains ambiguous as to its intentions. For an analysis of the Israeli ambiguity, its rationale, and its uses see Yair Evron, "Israel and the Atom: The Uses and Misuses of Ambiguity, 1959–1967," *Orbis* 17(Winter 1974):1326–43; Alan Dowty, "Nuclear Proliferation: The Israeli Case," *International Studies Quarterly* 22(March 1978):79–121 and his "Going Public with the Bomb," chapter 2 in this book. See also Gerald Steinberg's chapter.

4. Efraim Inbar, "The Israeli Basement—With Bombs or Without?" *Crossroads* 8(Winter-Spring 1982):81–106. Dowty "Nuclear Proliferation" is also doubtful of the existence of an Israeli nuclear force.

5. For a summary of the committee position and its gradually reduced activity, see the introduction to its literary legacy, *Israel–Arab States: Atom Armed or Atom Free* (Tel Aviv: Amikam, 1963) (Hebrew).

6. See Efraim Kishon, "We Have Lived for 26 Years under the Shade of Nuclear War," *Ma'ariv*, June 28, 1974; Shlomo Aronson, "To Live in the Shade of the Atom," *HaAretz*, June 30, 1974.

7. See A. Rappaport, "Nuclear Balance in the Middle East," *HaAretz*, July 26, 1974; Eliahu Galezer, "Israel and the Atom," *Ma'ariv*, December 17, 1974; Shlomo Aronson, "Nuclear Weapons: Reluctance and Deterrence," *HaAretz*, June 29, 1975; see also his "Deterrence in the Middle East," *HaAretz*, February 2, 1976.

8. See his "Israel and the United States: From Dependence to Nuclear Weapons?" *Commentary* 60(November 1975):29–43. He claimed a nuclear force would (1) eventually create a balance of terror and deter further major wars, (2) reduce Israel's dependence on the United States, (3) ease the burden on the Israeli economy, and (4) significantly reduce the risks in withdrawing from occupied territories. Other academicians also published in that period works viewing positively a nuclear Middle East. See, inter alia, Shlomo Aronson, "Nuclearization of the Middle East," *Jerusalem Quarterly* 2(Winter 1977):27–44; Steven J. Rosen, "Nuclearization and Stability in the Middle East," *Jerusalem Journal of International Relations* 1(Spring 1976):1–32.

9. See, inter alia, Hagai Eshed, "To Entrench Ourselves until Year 2000," *Davar*, December 19, 1975; Shlomo Aronson, "Deterrence in the Middle East," *HaAretz*, February 2, 1976; Avraham Schweitzer, "The Importance of the Nuclear Option," *HaAretz*, March 19, 1976. Schweitzer advocated such a policy as early as the 1960s (A. Schweitzer, *HaAretz*, August 14, 1962); Efraim Kishon, "Enslavement and Its Name Is Arms Race," *Ma'ariv*, April 12, 1976.

10. For reports of and quotations from his speeches, see *Ma'ariv*, February 20, 1976, March 11, 1976; *Time*, "How Israel Got the Bomb," April 12, 1976; D. Goldstein, "The Interview of the Week with Moshe Dayan," *Ma'ariv*, December 3, 1976. In this interview Dayan changed his position somewhat. He stated that Israel should not be the first to introduce nuclear weapons into the region, but hinted that Israel should publicly overcome the plutonium obstacle. In any case, the lasting impact of his previous statements could not be easily eradicated. Although Dayan, like Peres and many other Rafi activists (a group that split from the dominant socialist Mapai party in 1964) was suspected of "being receptive to Gaullist ideas," it was the first time Dayan came out publicly in favor of Israeli nuclear bombs.

11. For the most comprehensive pronuclear argument, see Shai Feldman, *Israeli Nuclear Deterrence: A Strategy for the 1980s* (New York: Columbia University Press, 1982). For a review of the arguments against nuclearization see Efraim Inbar, "The Nuclear Mirage," *Midstream* 27(March 1981) and Gerald Steinberg's, Avner Yaniv's, Avner Cohen's, and Zeev Eytan's chapters in this book.

12. The discussion over the proper reaction to the proposed U.S. sale of a nuclear reactor to Egypt in June 1974 had already provided some Israeli leftists with the opportunity to voice their opposition to nuclear weapons. Meir Pail and Uri Avneri called then for a nuclear-weapon-free zone in the Middle East. See *HaAretz*, June 20, 1974.

13. For his role in formulating Israel's security doctrine in the 1960s, see Gilboa, *Shesh Shanim, Shisha Yamim* 2nd ed. (Tel Aviv: Am Oved, 1969), pp. 29–30, 64–65

(Hebrew). Rabin was sensitized to the tension with the United States on the nuclear issue already when chief of staff (see Yitzhak Rabin, *Memoirs* (Tel Aviv: *Ma'ariv* Book Guild, 1979), pp. 127, 128–30) (Hebrew). Rabin, while prime minister, answered "no" in an ABC interview when asked, "Do you have a tactical nuclear weapon?" When further questioned about Israel's willingness to use the ultimate weapon, Rabin said, "No doubts that Israel is ready to [do] the ultimate for its defense, but we believe that we live in an era in which we can do it with conventional weapons" (Rabin, "ABC Interview" April 15, 1975, ABC transcript, p. IV-4). In October 1975 at an international symposium, Rabin again belittled the role of nuclear weapons and conveyed his conviction that conventional weapons will be decisive in a future Middle East war. See Louis Williams, ed., *Military Aspects of the Israel–Arab Conflict* (Tel Aviv: University Publishing Projects, 1975), p. 210. Rabin's statement at the symposium received little publicity.

14. *Ma'ariv*, March 15, 1976.

15. *Ma'ariv*, April 8, 1976 (emphasis added). Rabin expressed little apprehension of a change in the military balance, and even minimized the possibility of a preemptive conventional strike. "While we have the present lines there is no need for a preemptive strike. And as long as we will have the means to defend ourselves, that is to say, to get arms from our own sources and from the US. . . ." ("Rabin and Sadat," *NBC Interview*, April 5, 1975). This conditional formulation served also to remind the United States that Israel may adopt a more destabilizing posture under certain circumstances.

16. Moshe Gilboa, *Shesh Shanim, Shisha Yamim*, pp. 29–30. For Alon's views on the subject see his *Sand Curtain* (Hebrew) (Tel Aviv: HaKibbutz HaMeuhad 1959), pp. 400–402.

17. *Ma'ariv*, March 30, 1976.

18. *HaAretz*, September 9, 1976.

19. For Achdut Haavodah's view against nuclearization, see M. Brecher, *The Foreign Policy System of Israel* (New Haven, Conn.: Yale University Press, 1972), p. 191. Moshe Carmel, a long-time leader of Achdut Haavodah and a member of the Parliamentary Committee for Security and Foreign Affairs, attacked Dayan's views as potentially inciting an arms race in the Middle East and as ultimately damaging Israel. See his "Nuclear Potential and National Responsibility," *Yediot Achronot*, March 17, 1976.

20. Yoram Nimrod, "Israel and Nuclear Weapons," *Davar*, April 22, 1976. Sharon believed also that any Egyptian installations preparing a nuclear bomb will have to be wiped out (*New York Times*, February 8, 1975, p. 4).

21. Brecher, *Foreign Policy System of Israel*, p. 344.

22. "Interview with Shimon Peres," *Davar*, April 30, 1976. Peres spoke about the coming ten years.

23. Brecher, *Foreign Policy System of Israel*, p. 344. For Peres's views on possible uses of the option, see his interview with *Ot*, September 1966.

24. *HaAretz*, June 17, 1975.

25. Dov Goldstein, "Interview of the Week," *Ma'ariv*, December 24, 1976. Gur actually believed that a nuclear environment requires *greater* conventional forces than a conventional one (interview with Gur, June 29, 1979).

26. *Bemahane*, January 19, 1977. Gur's views were probably shared by other

high officers. Major-General Shlomo Gazit, Head of Intelligence (1974–1978) indicated that Israel has no intention of building nuclear weapons if there is no change in Arab nuclear capabilities or Israel's conventional ones. See Robert H. McKenzie-Smith, "Crisis Decision Making in Israel: The Case of the October 1973 Middle East War," *Naval War College Review* 29(Summer 1976):51n.

27. Interview with Rabin, November 18, 1979; interview with Allon, June 4, 1979; interview with Peres, June 18, 1979; interview with Galili, October 22, 1979. Rabin and Allon clarified to the Americans several times that Israel's formula meant "no explosion of a nuclear device" (interview with Allon).

28. *HaAretz,* June 16, 1974.

29. *Ma'ariv,* June 20, 1974.

30. *Ma'ariv,* December 4, 1974.

31. Interview with Rabin, March 25, 1979.

32. Interview with Allon, June 4, 1979.

33. For example: The parliamentary committee for Foreign Affairs and Security refrained from officially expressing deep concern so as not to cast a shadow on the president's visit (*Ma'ariv,* June 16, 1974).

34. *Christian Science Monitor,* December 3, 1974.

35. Interview with Shimon Peres, June 18, 1979; see also reports on government displeasure in *Ma'ariv,* December 9, 1974.

36. *Jerusalem Post,* August 12, 1975. For a discussion of the Tlatelolco Treaty (the Latin American NWFZ) see John Maddox, *Prospects for Nuclear Proliferation,* Adelphi Paper 113 (London: International Institute for Strategic Studies, Spring 1975), p. 7.

37. *Ma'ariv,* December 26, 1975.

38. Interview with Asher Ben Natan, August 28, 1979. Ben Natan served as the political advisor to Peres.

39. Williams, *Military Aspects,* p. 210.

40. "Allon's Address at the UN," *Jerusalem Post,* October 1, 1975.

41. *Ma'ariv,* January 28, 1976.

42. William Epstein, "Nuclear Free Zones," *Scientific American* 233(November 1975):31.

43. After the 1967 war, Israel seemed uninterested in arms control. For a discussion of Israel's position on nuclear and conventional arms control, see Evron, "Israel and the Atom," pp. 1335–36.

44. *HaAretz,* October 6, 1974.

45. Interview with Rabin and Allon.

46. After Egypt's turn to the West in the aftermath of the October 1973 war, Egyptian relations with Iran improved considerably. In May 1974, Iran decided to finance an oil pipeline from Suez to Alexandria, which could serve as a substitute for the Israeli Eilat–Ashkelon pipeline. Egyptian–Iranian cooperation was strengthened during the Shah's visit to Cairo in January 1975. Iranian–Egyptian relations caused concern in Israel. Iran was an Israeli regional ally and its main oil supplier. It was feared that a pro-Arab Iran might stop the oil flow to Israel and increase Israel's regional isolation. Furthermore, Israel was in the midst of negotiations with Egypt, which involved the possibility of withdrawal from the Abu Rudeis oilfields. Relinquishing the oilfields meant an increase in Israeli oil import requirements. The contin-

ued flow of Iranian oil was therefore extremely important to Israel, and thus Allon was sent to Teheran in February 1975 to receive assurances as to the continuation of Iranian oil sales to Israel (see Shmuel Segev, "The Oil Bridge between Iran and Israel," *Ma'ariv*, May 15, 1981). It seems that the Shah's promise to continue dealing with Israel was an important contributing factor to Israeli willingness to give up the Abu Rudeis fields already in the early stages of the negotiations. It should be noted that Iran, in spite of doing business with Israel, moved gradually closer to the Arab position in the Arab–Israeli conflict. This process was reinforced by the détente with Iraq, after the dispute over the water rights in the Shatt el Arab was resolved to Iran's satisfaction (March 1975).

47. *HaAretz*, October 16, 1975; see also his "Arab Forces Two Years after the Yom Kippur War," in Williams, *Military Aspects*, p. 194.

48. *Ma'ariv*, January 28, 1976; see also Shimon Peres, *Tomorrow Is Now* (Jerusalem: Mabat, 1978), p. 53. In the Rabin period the main Israeli concern was about the nuclear progress in Iraq. Only later did Pakistan also become a focus of Israeli concern.

49. Dov Goldstein, "Interview with the Foreign Affairs Minister, Itzhak Shamir," *Ma'ariv*, June 12, 1981. Some of this activity became known in the aftermath of the June 1981 Israeli attack on the Iraqi nuclear reactor.

50. Interview with Allon (Allon's emphasis).

51. Interviews with Israeli officials. It is not clear if there were precedents of such unofficial visits by American dignitaries.

52. *Ma'ariv*, August 6, 1976. The agreement included supervision of only U.S.-supplied installations. Interestingly, the United States insisted upon including an article preventing Israel from building the reactors in the administered territories. Israel had no intention of building them there and the obvious compromise was to specify the possible sites for the power reactors, all in the pre-1967 territory.

53. Interview with Shlomo Avineri, October 29, 1979; Professor Avineri served as the director general of the Ministry of Foreign Affairs from April 1976 to June 1977.

54. Disclosed by Professor Shimon Yiftah (*Ma'ariv*, March 14, 1976). Professor Yiftah served as the president of the Israeli Nuclear Sciences Society. In the 1960s, he served as chief scientist in the Ministry of Defense. It is not clear whether the Israelis were offered the Phoenix research reactors or a prototype nuclear power reactor.

55. See Inbar, Ph.D. dissertation, pp. 204–207.

56. See Inbar, "The Israeli Basement . . .", pp. 99–101.

57. *Jerusalem Post*, October 1, 1975.

58. *HaAretz*, April 10, 1975. Israel suggested reducing the Egyptian army by 200,000 soldiers to 400,000, in exchange for shortening the time served by Israeli conscripts from three to two years. Israel also demanded that some Egyptian units stationed on the Israeli front be transferred west.

59. "Rabin and Sadat," *NBC Interview*, April 5, 1975.

60. For Allon's statement see *Jerusalem Post*, October 9, 1975; for Peres statement see *Ma'ariv*, December 26, 1975.

61. Interviews with Rabin and Peres.

62. See Albert Wohlstetter, "Spreading the Bomb Without Quite Breaking the Rules," *Foreign Policy* 25(Winter 1976–77):88–179.

63. See "The Official Israeli Position," *New Outlook* (May 1982):68–72. This is an excerpt from Foreign Minister Yitzhak Shamir's statement to the U.N. General Assembly on October 1, 1981; a letter to the U.N. secretary-general from Israel Ambassador Yehudah Blum (October 27, 1981) and the concluding section from the Israeli White Book entitled, "The Iraqi Nuclear Threat—Why Israel Had to Act." See also Avi Beker's chapter in this book.

64. *HaAretz,* February 21, 1984. Ne'eman, a nuclear scientist, is one of the leaders of the right-wing Techia party. In the past he served, inter alia, as an advisor to Peres. See also *Ma'ariv* December 10, 1984.

65. For the Israeli shift to a system of casūs belli see Efraim Inbar, "Israeli Strategic Thinking after 1973," *Journal of Strategic Studies* 6(March 1983).

66. Ibid.

67. See his *The Next Stage,* 2nd ed. (Hebrew) (Tel Aviv: Am Hasefer, 1966), pp. 130–34.

68. For Sadat's doubts about the existence of Israeli nuclear weapons, see, inter alia, *Christian Science Monitor,* January 2, 1975, p. 1; Cl. Sulzberger, "Absence of War and Peace," *New York Times,* January 19, 1977, p. A-23; *Ma'ariv,* April 14, 1976; "Interview with Sadat," *Survival* 19(March-April 1977): 81. Asad holds similar views. See *Ma'ariv,* April 28, 1977. See also Feldman, *Israeli Nuclear Deterrence,* pp. 11–12. For Egyptian atomic inquiries during the peace process, see Eitan Haber, Zeev Schiff, and Ehud Yaari, *The Year of the Dove* (New York: Bantam Books, 1979), pp. 40, 102–103, 230.

69. For the difficulties of the Israeli nuclear casūs belli, see Inbar "Israeli Strategic Thinking after 1973," pp. 52–53.

Chapter 6
A Nuclear or Conventional Defense Posture?

1. When writing "threat" I mean a military threat.

2. An example of a threat not covered here would be: a threat to Israel by France in which France sends troops to fight on the Arab side in a future Arab–Israeli war. I estimate the probability of such an event as extremely low. There is a very low probability that the regime in France will change as it did in 1958, become more oriented toward revival of France's role in international affairs, and become more pro-Arab than at present. As such a chain of events is highly unlikely (though possible), I do not include it, and similar threats, be they Soviet, British, or other.

3. I would prefer to attach numerical values to probabilities between 0 (absolutely no chance of an event happening) and 1 (absolute certainty that an event will happen) but assume that we lack the capability to do so in this case. I take "probability" in the subjective Bayesian sense (another person may judge it to be different than I do). For the person making the probability estimate, appraisals, such as a probability of war, are directed by a consistent set of measures taken on the basis of the evaluation. A probability is not only an evaluation regarding an event which has happened in the past. It also covers events which have never happened, but could happen, such as President John F. Kennedy's estimate, during the 1962 Cuban missile crisis, that there was a 50 percent probability of a nuclear war breaking out.

4. Positive probability is anything above 0, say 0.001; a negligible probability is one low enough to be ignored, and this may be for one person 0.05, for another it may be 0.01 or any other probability, though no rational person will claim that a probability of 0.3 is negligible. Thus, a nonnegligible probability is one not to be ignored.

5. All of these countries have been listed as "near nuclear" in recent studies of proliferation. See Introduction and other chapters in this book.

6. Iraq's nuclear efforts have been displayed by Israeli destruction of the Osiraq reactor in 1981.

7. An example of what can be ignored: the probability of the PLO obtaining an ICBM and firing on Tel Aviv.

8. In an unavoidably arbitrary way, I have to define a "high probability" as being 50 percent or higher; a "low probability" as being less than 5 percent. This leaves an intermediate group, less than 50 percent and more than 5 percent. I remind the reader that these are my subjective estimates.

9. Shai Feldman, *Israeli Nuclear Deterrence:* A Strategy for the 1980s (New York: Columbia University Press. 1982), pp. 74, 79 on French uranium and reactor to Iraq; pp. 78–79 also cover Syrian and Libyan nuclear efforts.

10. *Ma'ariv* of June 6, 1983 quoted the *Reading Eagle* (Reading, Pa.) as having said that Pakistan had received uranium and $200 million from Libya in order to develop the Pakistani nuclear bomb, and in return will give Libya five nuclear bombs. There have been other reports regarding Libyan financial aid to Pakistan.

11. When the PLO shelled Israel in 1981 there were less than 20 fatal casualties. The casualties suffered by Israel between the 1967 and 1973 wars were around 800, many as a result of shelling. Israel suffered 257 casualties during the War of Attrition, from 1969–70 along the Egyptian front, many of whom were killed by artillery fire. See my "Shovakh Yonim: Tikhnun Mul Bitsua" *Ma'arachot* no. 276–777, October-November 1981, pp. 38–46 (Hebrew).

12. I agree with Efraim Inbar, elsewhere in this book, who assumes that "an already existing nuclear force during the period under discussion was not a self-evident fact requiring no proof" and views the "bomb in the basement" speculation with skepticism.

13. Professor Yuval Ne'eman is a renowned Israeli physicist who served as minister of science in Shamir's government until after the July 1984 elections. The citation in the text is a direct quote of an interview with Ne'eman on Israeli radio on December 11, 1984, recorded by me. Ne'eman stated that these same statements appeared in an article printed by the *Boston Globe* apparently on the previous day.

14. Israel is now seeking another $750 million in special economic emergency aid for each of the years 1985 and 1986. A U.S. administration resolution has been passed allocating $1.8 billion in military aid to Israel in 1986. I believe this is the limit; the U.S. government cannot go any further.

15. The inquiry in the United States in May 1985 regarding the alleged transfer of Krytrons to Israel confirms the hypothesis that a reduction in U.S.-Israel technological cooperation could result.

16. Shai Feldman, *Israeli Nuclear Deterrence*, p. 10 and passim. Feldman claims that the openly nuclear posture "would give Israel's nuclear deterrence far greater credibility" (as compared with the other policy options, including the "bomb in the basement").

Chapter 7
The Imperative to Survive

1. "Rise of Militancy by Moslems Threatens Stability of Egypt," *New York Times,* October 27, 1981, p. A1.

2. See Leonard Binder, "Egypt: The Integrative Revolution," in Lucian Pye, ed., *Political Culture and Political Development* (Princeton, NJ: Princeton University Press, 1965), pp. 409–411, wherein the powerful role of shame in Egyptian culture is discussed.

3. On a somewhat personal note, many years ago in taking my Ph.D. oral preliminary exams at Yale, I was queried by the late Harold Lasswell as to what I considered the most important understudied or ignored area of international relations. My candidate for that honor was the related themes of humiliation and vengeance, and their roles as impediments to conflict resolution. Nearly twenty years later I would now, if again asked that same question, give the very same answer. The perhaps sole exception is evidenced in H.W. Glidden, "The Arab World," *American Journal of Psychiatry 128* no. 8(February 1972):98–102. On p. 99:

> Shame is intensely feared among the Arabs, and this fear is so pervasive that Arab society has been labeled a shame-oriented one. This contrasts sharply with Judaism and with Western Christian societies, which are guilt-oriented. . . . Shame is eliminated by *revenge.* It is difficult to describe the depth of the Arabs' emotional need for revenge, but suffice it to say that Islam itself found it necessary to sanction revenge. The felt need for revenge is as strong today as it was in pre-Islamic times, as witnessed by the continued proliferation of vengeance-related feuds, murders, and so forth, for both private and political reasons, in the Arab Middle East.

It is, incidentally, my opinion that the works of Alroy (see the next reference) and Glidden stand almost alone as serious efforts at a beginning of an understanding of the Middle Eastern conflict.

4. See, for instance, Gil Carl Alroy, *Behind the Middle East Conflict: The Real Impasse between Arab and Jew* (New York: Putnam, 1975), esp. ch. 8; and Yehoshafat Harkabi, *Arab Attitudes to Israel* (Jerusalem: Israel Universities Press, 1972), esp. ch. 12.

5. See, for an elaboration upon this theme, Martin van Creveld, *Military Lessons of the Yom Kippur War: Historical Perspectives,* Washington Papers, no. 24 (Washington, D.C.: Center for Strategic and International Studies, Georgetown University, 1975). Arguing against the too early assumption of the demise of the tank was Avraham Adan, *On the Banks of Suez* (San Francisco: Presidio Press, 1980), ch. 35.

6. This is detailed in Seth Carus, "Military Lessons of the 1982 Israel–Syria Conflict," in R. Harkavy and S. Neuman, eds., *The Lessons of Recent Wars in the Third World* (Lexington, Mass.: Lexington Books, 1985).

7. See "Study Says Israeli Edge over Arabs Is Waning," *The New York Times,* February 13, 1985, p. 1.

8. Trevor DuPuy, "Measuring Combat Effectiveness: Historical-Quantitative Analysis," in Harkavy and Neuman, *Lessons of Recent Wars in the Third World,* and Michael Handel, "Numbers Do Count: The Question of Quality versus Quantity," *Journal of Strategic Studies 4*(September 1981):225–260.

9. This is discussed in historical and comparative context—in R.E. Harkavy,

Preemption and Two-Front Conventional Warfare, Jerusalem Papers on Peace Problems, no. 23 (Jerusalem: Hebrew University, 1977).

10. This perhaps tendentious (on my part) theme is pursued in numerous articles in *Commentary Magazine* in recent years; also, in the article by David Sidorsky in the Winter 1985 Symposium issue of *This World* on "Jews and American Politics," pp. 4–15.

11. Nuclear weapons are, of course, not the only types of weapons of mass destruction. For a recent analysis of the looming specter of proliferation of biological weapons, now to be based on the new recombinant genetic technologies, see Jonathan B. Tucker, "Gene Wars," *Foreign Policy* 57(Winter 1984–85):58–79. For one argument on behalf of a U.S. security guarantee to Israel, see Richard Ullman, "Alliance with Israel?" *Foreign Policy* 19(Summer 1975):18–33.

12. Much of the remainder of this chapter consists of updated summaries of the materials and arguments contained in R.E. Harkavy, *Spectre of a Middle Eastern Holocaust: The Strategic and Diplomatic Implications of the Israeli Nuclear Weapons Program,* Monograph Series in World Affairs (Denver: University of Denver Press, 1977). A now somewhat dated but still very useful bibliography is Donna S. Kramer, "Is Israel a Nuclear Power? Selected Bibliography, 1961 to the Present," Congressional Research Service, Washington, D.C., June 15, 1978.

13. See, for instance, Tad Szulc, "Murder by Proxy," *Penthouse Magazine,* August 1975, p. 46; "Tod aus der Textilfabrik," *Der Spiegel,* May 5, 1968; and "How Israel Got the Bomb," *Time,* April 12, 1976, pp. 39–40.

14. The relevant approximate calculations can be seen in Fuad Jabber, *Israel and Nuclear Weapons* (London: Chatto and Windus, 1971), p. 88.

15. According to *Aerospace Daily,* Vol. 133, Issue 1, May 1, 1985, Israel has already deployed Jericho II nuclear-armed intermediate-range ballistic missiles. The missiles reportedly are based in the Negev Desert and Golan Heights and are said to be installed on erector-launcher trucks. Allegedly supported by a network of underground, nuclear-hardened facilities featuring rail lines for reload and primary support areas, as well as for security alert and alert maintenance areas, the Jericho II missiles feature an inertial guidance system that was reportedly tested in unpopulated parts of Iran in the mid- to late-1970s. The range of the solid-propellant Jericho II with its nuclear payload is thought to be 700 kilometers.

16. This is discussed in "Military Lessons of the 1982 Israel–Syria Conflict," Carus, who cites claims that this missile has a radar homing-system and a range of 40 kilometers, far short of estimates for Jericho.

17. See "Israel Seen Holding 10 Nuclear Weapons," *Washington Post,* July 31, 1975, wherein Israel was said to be working on an advanced solid-fuel missile with a range of 500 to 900 miles.

18. See Harkavy, *Spectre of a Middle Eastern Holocaust,* pp. 39–41, for discussion of ranges of Israeli delivery systems in relation to various Arab cities and other key potential targets.

19. Though not explicitly related to SDI, the growing interest in devising military means to combat Nth country nuclear forces, including Israel's, is reflected in Rodney Jones, *Proliferation of Small Nuclear Forces* (Washington, D.C.: Center for Strategic and International Studies, Georgetown University, April 30, 1983), a report prepared for the Defense Nuclear Agency.

20. The following discussion is an updated summary of Harkavy, *Spectre of a Middle Eastern Holocaust*, pp. 57–58.

21. The term "triangular second-strike capability," which I devised earlier, refers to the capability by Israel to "absorb" a first nuclear strike from the Soviet Union, and to then subsequently retain the capability to launch a nuclear response against one or more Arab states which would result for the latter in "unacceptable" damage. It is thus an indirect form of the "normal" bilateral second-strike relationship.

22. Again, the technical possibilities for an Israeli biological warfare program are provided by Tucker, "Gene Wars."

23. In a related vein, there is considerable evidence that Nasser's instigation of the 1967 crisis was inspired by the fear of Israel's impending nuclear status, by the feeling that "the sands were running out" and that a preventive war was thus required. See the following *New York Times,* 1966, articles: "Warning on Bomb Given by Nasser," February 21, p. 8; "Nasser Assails U.S. and Britain," February 23, p. 2.; "Nasser Threatens War on a Nuclear-Armed Israel," April 18, p. 6; and "Nasser Cites Need for Nuclear Arms," May 9, p. 8.

24. In the 1976 *Time* article "How Israel Got the Bomb," Dayan is quoted as follows: "Israel has no choice. With our manpower, we cannot physically, financially, or economically go on acquiring more and more tanks and more and more planes. Before long, you will have all of us maintaining and oiling the tanks."

25. See Harkavy, *Spectre of a Middle Eastern Holocaust*, pp. 39–40.

26. The Insight Team of the *London Sunday Times, The Yom Kippur War* (Garden City, N.Y.: Doubleday, 1974), pp. 282–85.

27. See Lewis A. Dunn, "Some Reflections on the 'Dove's Dilemma,'" in George Quester, ed., *Nuclear Proliferation: Breaking the Chain* (Madison: University of Wisconsin Press, 1981), pp. 181–92.

28. See R. E. Harkavy, "Pariah States and Nuclear Proliferation," ibid., pp. 135–163.

29. See "Taiwanese Program at MIT Ended," *Washington Post,* July 16, 1976, p. A5; "Visit by Taiwan Leader to Saudis Underlines Bond between Nations," *New York Times,* July 11, 1977, p. 35; and "Taiwan Using Unofficial Diplomatic Ties to Avoid Becoming Outcast," *New York Times,* September 9, 1977, p. 2.

30. Jack Anderson, "Israel, Taiwan, South African Cruise Missile Program Cited," *Spokane Daily Chronicle,* December 8, 1980.

Chapter 8
A Regional Non-Proliferation Treaty for the Middle East

1. See, for instance, "The Fallout from Baghdad," editorial in the *New York Times,* June 16, 1981; Robert Gomer, "Baghdad," *Bulletin of the Atomic Scientists* (August/September 1981); George W. Ball, "No More Blank Checks," *Washington Post,* June 15, 1981.

2. The most explicit and updated statement on the subject was given by the Science and Development Minister in the Likud government, Professor Yuval

Ne'eman, early in 1984. Ne'eman, himself a nuclear physicist and a former member of the Israeli Atomic Energy Commission, said that it is not in Israel's interest to develop a nuclear deterrent to Arab aggression. Ne'eman noted that already in the early 1950s Israel decided to create a nuclear infrastructure in response to the fear that the Arabs would get the bomb from their superpower allies. "But we've never crossed the threshold into the nuclear weapons club," he said. *Jerusalem Post,* February 21, 1984, p. 1.

3. In chronologic order they are Robert W. Tucker, Steven J. Rosen, Shlomo Aronson, and Shai Feldman. See the complete sources in Efraim Inbar's notes herein.

4. For the views of Professor Harkabi see Lesley Hazleton, "One Year after Osiraq," *Moment,* June 1982, p. 6, and for the views of Ne'eman see: Steve Weissman and Herbert Krosney, *The Islamic Bomb* (New York: Times Books, 1981), pp. 306–7.

5. Shai Feldman, *The Raid on Osiraq—A Preliminary Assessment,* Memorandum no. 5, Center for Strategic Studies, Tel-Aviv University, August 1981, pp. 10–14. In his book *Israeli Nuclear Deterrence: A Strategy for the 1980s* (New York: Columbia University Press, 1982), Feldman emphasizes that he has no knowledge of the current stage of Israel's nuclear capability.

6. Feldman, *The Raid on Osiraq.* See also editorial in the *New York Times,* "The Fallout from Baghdad," and Gomer, "Baghdad," pp. 7–8.

7. Jed C. Snyder, "The Road to Osiraq: Baghdad's Quest for the Bomb," *Middle East Journal 37* no. 4 (Autumn 1983):570, 587.

8. IAEA/Vienna, PR 81/9, June 9, 1981.

9. "Nuclear Safeguards or Sham?" *Washington Post,* June 16, 1981.

10. For an extensive and documented presentation of Third World views on the NPT see Avi Beker, *Disarmament without Order—The Politics of Disarmament at the United Nations* (Westport, Conn.: Greenwood Press, 1985), ch. 6: "Nuclear Proliferation: 'Haves' and 'Have Nots'."

11. William Epstein, "Measures Necessary to Curb Nuclear Proliferation," in Seymour Maxwell Finger and Joseph R. Harbert, eds., *U.S. Policy in International Institutions: Defining Reasonable Options in an Unreasonable World* (Boulder, Colo.: Westview Press, 1978), p. 20; *A Short History of Non-Proliferation* (Vienna: IAEA, February 1976), p. 22.

The new IAEA director, Hans Blix, has gone on record saying that "you can't stop proliferation by safeguards." In addition he disclosed that the agency had made no progress in persuading Pakistan to allow additional monitoring facilities in its Karachi reactor, where "anomalies and irregularities" have been detected. See "U.N. Aide Sees Little to Curb Spread of Atom Arms," *New York Times,* February 18, 1982, p. 2.

12. SIPRI, *The NPT: The Main Political Barrier to Nuclear Weapons Proliferation* (London: Taylor and Francis, 1980), pp. 8, 21.

13. See the following articles in the *Bulletin of the Atomic Scientists* (October 1981): Sidney Moglewe, "IAEA Safeguards and Non-proliferation"; Roger Richter, "Testimony from a Former Safeguards Inspector"; S. Eklund, "The IAEA on Safeguards" (statement by the IAEA director-general in defense of the system of safeguards). Also the following reports in the *New York Times:* "Report on Bomb Safeguards: Gross Deficiencies," November 16, 1981, p. 8; "Nuclear Cheating: Why

the Experts Are Worried over Safeguards," December 22, 1981, Science Section, C1.

14. Moglewe, "IAEA Safeguards and Non-proliferation," p. 28.

15. "Nuclear Safeguards, Deemed Weak by U.S. Regulatory Commission," *New York Times,* December 1, 1981, p. 7. In a later report the Nuclear Regulatory Commission went beyond previous expressions of concern and determined that IAEA safeguards alone could not "reliably" warn of diversions of weapons-grade materials.

16. Mark F. Imber, "NPT Safeguards: The Limits of Credibility," *Arms Control 1,* no. 1(1980):192. See also Paul Szaz, *The Law and Practices of the International Atomic Energy Agency* (Vienna: IAEA, September, 1970), pp. 549, 564.

17. *Status of Multilateral Arms Regulation and Disarmament Agreements* (New York: United Nations, 1978), p. 94, n. 18.

18. Under article III of the NPT each party has to conclude a safeguards agreement with the IAEA. The fact that a party does not have known significant nuclear activities does not absolve it from observing this provision. In 1984, 76 of 118 parties to the NPT fulfilled this obligation.

19. *Non-Proliferation Treaty,* Hearings before the Committee on Foreign Relations, U.S. Senate 1968, pp. 27–28, 78.

20. "Baghdad Blocks Inspection of Its Nuclear Reactors," *Washington Post,* November 7, 1980, p. 10.

21. Fred Charles Iklé, "Bombs and Reactors: The Nuclear Divide," *Bulletin of the Atomic Scientists* (January 1980):42.

22. One example of a few others: "Raid on Iraqi Reactor Revives Issue: Can Nuclear Safeguards Ever Work?" *New York Times,* July 14, 1981, p. 11.

23. Senator John Glenn at Hearings before the Senate Subcommittee on Energy, Nuclear Proliferation and Government Processes, June 24, 1981, and John Glenn, "Nuclear Traffic: Toward Better Controls," *Washington Post,* June 29, 1981, p. 12.

24. IAEA, PR July 7, 1981.

25. "Ex-Inspector Asserts Iraq Planned to Use Reactor to Build A-Bombs," *New York Times,* June 20, 1981, p. 7. See Richter's testimony and Eklund's reply in *Bulletin of the Atomic Scientists* (October 1981).

26. *IAEA Safeguards: An Introduction* (Vienna, IAEA, December 1981).

27. "UN Aide Sees Little to Curb Spread of Atom Arms," *New York Times,* February 18, 1982, p. 2.

28. General Assembly Documents, *Status of Multilateral Disarmament Agreements—Report of the Secretary General,* A/39/454, September 6, 1984.

29. For background and analysis of the Tlatelolco Treaty, see "Measures Necessary to Curb Nuclear Proliferation," Epstein, pp. 55–60, 207–214. John R. Redick, "The Tlatelolco Regime and Nonproliferation in Latin America," in George Quester, ed., *Nuclear Proliferation: Breaking the Chain* (Madison: University of Wisconsin Press, 1981), pp. 103–34.

30. Jozef Goldblat, *Agreements for Arms Control: A Critical Survey,* SIPRI publication (London: Taylor and Francis, 1982), pp. 63–68.

31. One hundred twelve states, including Israel, signed the 1963 Partial Test Ban Treaty, which prohibits nuclear explosions in the atmosphere, outer space, or under water. Ten Arab countries have not yet joined the PTBT. Kuwait added, on its ratification of the PTBT, the regular Arab disclaimer on the nonrecognition of Israel, with an ominous reservation stating that the ratification does not "oblige it to apply the provisions of the Treaty as far as Israel is concerned."

32. See ch. 6 on the problem of regionalism in Inis L. Claude, *Swords into Plowshares* (New York: Random House, 1971).

33. *Comprehensive Study of the Question of Nuclear-Weapon-Free Zones in All Its Aspects*, Conference of the Committee on Disarmament, A/10027/Add.1, 1976.

34. Final Document of SSD I, July 1978, A/RES/S-10/2 para. 60–61.

35. Jean François Guilhaudis, "Nuclear Free Zones and Zones of Peace: The Regional Approach to Disarmament within Non-nuclearized Regions," *Arms Control* 1 no. 2(1981):205.

36. "Israel's Position on Nuclear Nonproliferation," as stated by Foreign Minister Shamir in the Knesset, July 30, 1980, mimeo (documented in the Knesset records).

37. *Comprehensive Study of the Question of Nuclear-Weapon-Free Zones*, annex 1, sec. 180.

38. The Independent Commission of Disarmament and Security Issues (Olof Palme, chairman), *Common Security—A Blueprint for Survival* (New York: Simon and Schuster, 1982), pp. 171–72. On the "pushful majority" approach to regional disarmament see Guilhaudis, "Nuclear Free Zones and Zones of Peace," pp. 207–11.

39. In the final document adopted by the sixth summit conference of the non-aligned in Havana, Cuba, September 1979, there was no reference whatsoever to the NPT in the 310 paragraphs of the Political Declaration. Sixth Conference of Heads of State or Government of Non-Aligned Countries, GAOR, A/34/542, October 11, 1979.

40. See for instance the Indian foreign minister on the NPT: GAOR, A/35/PV.23, October 3, 1980, p. 68. And on NWFZ: *The United Nations Disarmament Yearbook*, vol. 7:1982 (New York: United Nations, 1983), p. 483.

41. Paul F. Power, "Preventing Nuclear Conflict in the Middle East: The Free Zone Strategy," *Middle East Journal 37*, no. 4(Autumn 1983):619.

42. GAOR, A/C.1/35/PV.31, November 13, 1980, pp. 19–26.

43. Report of the Secretary General, "Israeli Nuclear Armament," A/36/43, September 18, 1981, p. 23. Ironically, this report was submitted on behalf of the group by Professor Ali A. Mazrui, a well-known proponent of the development of the so-called Islamic bomb, who has called several times for further proliferation of nuclear weapons in the Middle East and Africa: Ali A. Mazrui, "Changing the Guards from Hindus to Muslims: Collective Third World Security in a Cultural Perspective," *International Affairs 57*(Winter 1980–81):1–20; "Africa's Nuclear Future" *Survival* (March-April 1980), and "The Barrel of the Gun and the Barrel of Oil," *World Order Models Project*, no. 5 (New York: Institute for World Order, 1978).

44. A/C.1/35/PV. 32-33, November 18–19, 1980 and Iraq A/C.1/35/PV.16, October 28, 1980.

45. A/C.1/35/PV.36, November 20, 1980.

46. A/C.1/35/PV.37, November 20, 1980.

47. A/35/PV.15, September 29, 1980.

48. A/C.1/30/PV.36, November 20, 1980.

49. *Jerusalem Post*, February 21, 1984, p. 1.

50. Statement by Senator Alan Cranston before the Senate Foreign Relations Committee, Hearings, U.S. Congress, Washington D.C., June 18, 1981; also "Baghdad Blocks Inspection of its Nuclear Reactors," *Washington Post*, November 7, 1980, p. 10.

51. *Jerusalem Post,* February 21, 1984, p. 1.

52. George H. Quester, "Peaceful P.A.L.," ACIS Working Paper no. 9, Center for Arms Control and International Security, University of California, Los Angeles, November 1977.

53. Israel in Policy Shift to Seek Mideast Ban of Nuclear Weapons," *New York Times,* November 8, 1980, p. 1.

Chapter 9
An Israeli Nuclear Deterrent: Implications for U.S.–Soviet Strategic Policies

1. The phrase is Thomas Schelling's. See Schelling, *The Strategy of Conflict* (New York: Oxford University Press, 1960), and Albert Wohlstetter, "The Delicate Balance of Terror," *Foreign Affairs 37,* no. 2(January 1959):209–34.

2. Richard K. Betts, *Surprise Attack: Lessons for Defense Planning* (Washington, D.C., Brookings Institution, 1982) argues that U.S. strategic nuclear forces have been designed from the beginning under the assumption that they must withstand a "bolt from the blue" and still retaliate. Technology has made this possible since the 1960s.

3. Graham T. Allison, *Essence of Decision: Explaining the Cuban Missile Crisis* (Boston: Little, Brown, 1971).

4. Colin S. Gray, *The MX ICBM and National Security* (New York: Praeger Publishers, 1981).

5. President's Commission on Strategic Forces (Scowcroft Commission), *Report,* (Washington, D.C.: April, 1983). See also Louis René Beres, *Mimicking Sisyphus: America's Countervailing Nuclear Strategy* (Lexington, Mass.: Lexington Books, 1983).

6. Matthew Bunn and Kosta Tsipis, "The Uncertainties of Preemptive Nuclear Attack," *Scientific American 249,* no. 5(November 1983):38–47.

7. Colonel Thomas A. Fabyanic, "Strategic Analysis and MX Deployment," *Strategic Review 10,* no. 4 (Fall 1982):29–35.

8. John Steinbruner, "Nuclear Decapitation," *Foreign Policy 45*(Winter 1981–82):16–28.

9. Congress of the United States, Congressional Budget Office, *Strategic Command, Control and Communications: Alternative Approaches for Modernization* (Washington, D.C.: U.S. Government Printing Office, October 1981); Desmond Ball, *Can Nuclear War Be Controlled?* Adelphi Papers, no. 169 (London: International Institute for Strategic Studies, Autumn 1981).

10. See Paul Bracken, *The Command and Control of Nuclear Forces* (New Haven, Conn.: Yale University Press, 1983), and Peter Pringle and William Arkin, *SIOP: The Secret U.S. Plan for Nuclear War* (New York: W.W. Norton, 1983).

11. See Desmond Ball, "Counterforce Targeting: How New? How Viable?" *Arms Control Today 11,* no. 2(February 1981), reprinted with revisions in John F. Reichart and Steven R. Sturm, eds., *American Defense Policy* (Baltimore: Johns Hopkins University Press, 1982), pp. 227–34.

12. Bracken, *The Command and Control of Nuclear Forces,* p. 227 and passim.

13. Assessments of the degree of danger of direct superpower conflict, differ considerably. The author is inclined to agree with Phil Williams that the superpowers were actually cautious in both the 1967 and 1973 Middle East wars. See Williams, *Crisis Management: Confrontation and Diplomacy in the Nuclear Age* (New York: John Wiley and Sons, 1976), pp. 108–9.

14. See Williams, *Crisis Management,* pp. 108–9, and Betts, *Surprise Attack,* pp. 65–80.

15. John Mearsheimer, *Conventional Deterrence* (Ithaca, N.Y.: Cornell University Press, 1983) characterizes Sadat's strategy in 1973 as one of "limited aims."

16. Shai Feldman, *Israeli Nuclear Deterrence: A Strategy for the 1980s* (New York: Columbia University Press, 1982).

17. For one perception of the U.S. response to Israeli nuclear disclosure, see Feldman, *Israeli Nuclear Deterrence,* pp. 192–233.

18. The temptation to see in technology an escape from unavoidable dilemmas of strategy would parallel similar processes in the evolution of U.S. nuclear deterrence policies. See Lawrence Freedman, *The Evolution of Nuclear Strategy* (New York: St. Martin's Press, 1983).

19. For a discussion of mutual alarms and their implications for U.S.–Soviet conflict, see Thomas C. Schelling, *Arms and Influence* (New Haven, Conn.: Yale University Press, 1966).

20. For a statement of the Reagan administration position on this, see Caspar W. Weinberger, *Annual Report to the Congress: Fiscal Year 1985* (Washington, D.C.: U.S. Government Printing Office, February, 1984), p. 29.

21. See John Steinbruner, "Nuclear Decapitation," *Foreign Policy* 45(Winter 1981–82):16–28.

22. Potential conflicts between positive and negative control are discussed in Steinbruner, "Launch under Attack," *Scientific American,* January 1984, pp. 37–47, and Bracken, *Command and Control of Nuclear Forces,* passim.

23. Steinbruner, "Nuclear Decapitation," and Congress of the United States, *Strategic Command, Control and Communications.*

24. Bracken, *Command and Control of Nuclear Forces,* pp. 5–73.

25. Ibid., pp. 76–97, and Pringle and Arkin, *SIOP.*

26. Bracken, *Command and Control of Nuclear Forces,* pp. 56–57.

27. Ibid., pp. 61–68.

28. Allison, *Essence of Decision.*

29. Elie Abel, *The Missile Crisis* (New York: Bantam Books, 1966).

30. Ibid., pp. 172–73.

31. Fritz W. Ermath, "Contrasts in American and Soviet Strategic Thought," in Derek Leebaert, ed., *Soviet Military Thinking* (London: Allen and Unwin, 1981), pp. 50–69.

32. Benjamin S. Lambeth, "On Thresholds in Soviet Military Thought," in William J. Taylor, Jr., Steven A. Maaranen and Gerrit W. Gong, eds., *Strategic Responses to Conflict in the 1980s* (Washington, D.C.: Center for Strategic and International Studies, 1984), pp. 173–82.

33. John G. Hines and Phillip A. Peterson, "The Warsaw Pact Strategic Offensive: The OMG in Context," *International Defense Review* 10(October 1983):1391–

95; Hines and Peterson, "The Soviet Conventional Offensive in Europe," *Military Review* 64, no. 4(April 1984):2–29.

34. Edward L. Warner III, *Nuclear Operations in Soviet Military Strategy,* unpublished paper, Rand Corporation, Santa Monica, Calif. (June 1983).

35. Raymond L. Garthoff, "BMD and East-West Relations," ch. 8 in Ashton B. Carter and David N. Schwartz, eds., *Ballistic Missile Defense* (Washington, D.C.: Brookings Institution, 1984), pp. 275–329.

36. Robert P. Berman and John C. Baker, *Soviet Strategic Forces: Requirements and Responses* (Washington, D.C.: Brookings Institution, 1982).

37. Feldman, *Israeli Nuclear Deterrence,* pp. 178–79.

38. Bracken, *Command and Control of Nuclear Forces,* pp. 54–65.

39. A limited objectives attack would be similar to the Arab attack on Israel in 1973, in which the attackers' objective was not to destroy the state of Israel but to regain respect for Arab military power as a basis for subsequent negotiations. See Mearsheimer, *Conventional Deterrence,* pp. 53–55.

40. Feldman, *Israeli Nuclear Deterrence,* pp. 242–43 and passim.

41. Ibid., p. 133.

Chapter 10
The Armageddon Factor: Terrorism and Israel's Nuclear Option

1. See Leonard S. Spector, *Nuclear Proliferation Today* (New York: Vintage Books, 1984), pp. 117–48, 369–80; Robert J. Pranger and Dale R. Tahtinen, *Nuclear Threat in the Middle East* (Washington, D.C.: American Enterprise Institute, 1975), pp. 11–18; Steve Weissman and Herbert Krosney, *The Islamic Bomb: The Nuclear Threat to Israel and the Middle East* (New York: Times Books, 1981), pp. 105–28. For a different view, see chapters 3, 4, 5, 6, and 8 in this book.

2. See Spector, *Nuclear Proliferation,* pp. 70–110, 165–91, 359–68, 384–91; Tina Rosenberg, "Bumbling Bomb Squad," *The New Republic,* December 17, 1984, pp. 18 and 20; Robert S. Dudney, "Superpower Goal: Keeping Nuclear Club Exclusive," *U.S. News & World Report,* December 3, 1984, pp. 29–30; Jack Anderson, "Mixed Message to Pakistan," *The Blade* (Toledo), March 25, 1985, p. 11; Eric Rozenman, "The Spread of the Bomb," *Near East Report,* November 12, 1984, p. 16.

3. Edward Teller, "Defense as a Deterrent of War," *Harvard International Review* 7, no. 4(January-February 1985):11.

4. George W. Rathjens, "The Dynamics of the Arms Race," in Herbert F. York, ed., *Arms Control* (San Francisco: W.H. Freeman, 1973), p. 184.

5. Shai Feldman, *Israeli Nuclear Deterrence: A Strategy for the 1980's* (New York: Columbia University Press, 1982), ch. 2.

6. Freeman Dyson, "Reflections (Nuclear Weapons—Part IV)," *The New Yorker,* February 27, 1984, p. 54.

7. See the terse comment of Spector, *Nuclear Proliferation,* p. 149.

8. One exception, in addition to several in this book, is *U.S. News & World*

Report, December 3, 1984, p. 29, which lists Israel as having the capability "within 5 years." The "official" nuclear powers remain the United States, the Soviet Union, Britain, France, and the People's Republic of China.

9. Robert Powell, "The Theoretical Foundation of Strategic Nuclear Deterrence," *Political Science Quarterly 100,* no. 1(Spring 1985):83.

10. Dyson, "Reflections," p. 99.

11. Jonathan Schell, "Reflections (Nuclear Weapons—Part I)," *The New Yorker,* January 2, 1984, p. 60.

12. Alvin Z. Rubinstein, "The Changing Strategic Balance and Soviet Third-World Risk-Taking," *Naval War College Review 38,* no. 2(March-April 1985):11–12.

13. Scott D. Sagan, "Nuclear Alerts and Crisis Management," *International Security 9,* no. 4(Spring 1985):122–28.

14. Rubinstein, "Strategic Balance," p. 13.

15. Strobe Talbott, "Living with Mega-Death," *Time,* March 29, 1982, p. 25.

16. Powell, "Strategic Nuclear Deterrence," pp. 83–90.

17. See the analysis in ibid., p. 92.

18. *The Blade* (Toledo), April 13, 1985, p. 2.

19. Editorial, "Bad Ideas and Good," *The New Republic,* December 3, 1984, p. 7.

20. Cited by Sydney Harris, "Strictly Personal," *The Blade* (Toledo), December 10, 1984, p. P-1.

21. U.N. Secretariat, *Nuclear Weapons: Report of the Secretary-General of the United Nations* (Brookline, Mass.: Autumn Press, 1980), p. 159, hereinafter cited as *Report of the Secretary General.*

22. Quoted by Talbott, "Mega-Death," p. 25.

23. *Report of the Secretary-General,* pp. 172–73. See also Avi Beker's chapter (8) in this book.

24. Amos Perlmutter, Michael Handel, and Uri Bar-Joseph, *Two Minutes over Baghdad* (London: Corzi Books, 1982), pp. 17–18, 132–37, 161–66, 173–77; Robert A. Friedlander, "Might Can Also Be Right: The Israeli Nuclear Reactor Bombing and International Law," *Chitty's Law Journal 28*(December 1980):355.

25. Ibid., pp. 352, 355, 356, fn. 2.

26. *U.N. Chronicle 18,* no. 8(August 1981):68.

27. G.A. Res. 39/14 (XXXIX), 39 U.N. GAOR, U.N. Doc. A/RES/39/14 (November 21, 1984). The vote was 106 in favor and 2 against (Israel and the United States). There were 33 abstentions, mainly Western countries.

28. *U.N. Chronicle 18,* no. 8(August 1981):7.

29. Certain Expenses of the United Nations [1962], I.C.J. 152, 168.

30. Quoted by Noyes E. Leech, Covey T. Oliver, and Joseph M. Sweeney, *Cases and Materials on the International Legal System* (Mineola, N.Y.: Foundation Press, 1973), p. 106.

31. Perlmutter, Handel, and Bar-Joseph, *Two Minutes,* pp. 78–84.

32. Anthony D'Amato, "Imagining a Judgment in the Case of Iraq v. Israel," *Washington Star,* June 15, 1981, p. A-8. On that general principle, see also, Julius Stone, *Conflict through Consensus: United Nations Approaches to Aggression* (Bal-

timore, Johns Hopkins University Press, 1977), pp. 47–50, and Ian Brownlie, *International Law and the Use of Force by States* (Oxford: Oxford University Press, 1963), pp. 258–61.

33. Anthony D'Amato, "Israel's Air Strike upon the Iraqi Nuclear Reactor," *American Journal of International Law 77*, no. 3(July 1983):585.

34. See Robert A. Friedlander, "The *Mayaguez* in Retrospect: Humanitarian Intervention or Showing the Flag?," *Saint Louis University Law Journal 22*, no. 4(1979):601–10.

35. D'Amato, "Israel's Air Strike," p. 588.

36. See the Security Council debate of June 1981 in *U.N. Chronicle 18*, no. 8(August 1981):5–9, 61–71, and the General Assembly debate of November 1984, in U.N. General Assembly Provisional Verbatim Record of the Fifth-fifth Meeting, (November 10 and 19, 1984), U.N. Docs. A/39/PV.55, A/39/PV. 56, and A/39/PV. 65.

37. See, for example, *Time,* June 22, 1981, p. 38; Perlmutter, Handel, and Bar-Joseph, *Two Minutes,* pp. 177–78.

38. On the Israeli domestic political implications, see ibid., pp. 167–71.

39. Harry V. Summers, Jr., "How We Lost," *The New Republic,* April 29, 1985, p. 20.

40. Louis René Beres, *Reason and Realpolitik: U.S. Foreign Policy and World Order* (Lexington, Mass.: Lexington Books, 1984), p. 67. Weissman and Krosney, *The Islamic Bomb,* p. 291, after a detailed examination of the available evidence, feel that "the Iraqi nuclear threat was real."

41. Shai Feldman, "The Bombing of Osiraq Revisited," *International Security 7,* no. 2(Fall 1982):123.

42. TRB, "The Reagahnev Doctrine," *The New Republic,* April 29, 1985, p. 41.

43. Brian Jenkins, "The Consequences of Nuclear Terrorism," in John Kerry King, ed., *International Political Effects of the Spread of Nuclear Weapons* (Washington, D.C.: U.S. Government Printing Office, 1979), pp. 85 and 95, hereinafter cited as *Nuclear Weapons Spread.*

44. Geoffrey Kemp, "A Nuclear Middle East," in ibid., p. 76.

45. See Louis René Beres, *Terrorism and Global Security: The Nuclear Threat* (Boulder, Colo.: Westview Press, 1979); Robert A. Friedlander, "The Ultimate Nightmare: What If Terrorists Go Nuclear?" *Denver Journal of International Law and Policy 12*, no. 1(Fall 1982):1–11; Richard C. Clark, *Technological Terrorism* (Old Greenwich, Conn.: Denvin-Adair, 1980), pp. 7–103. For a more skeptical approach, see Augustus R. Norton and Talia Ben-Gal, "Terror by Fission: An Analysis and Critique," *Chitty's Law Journal 27* no. 8(1979):268–78.

46. Ovid Demaris, *Brothers in Blood: The International Terrorist Network* (New York: Charles Scribner's Sons, 1977), p. 424.

47. Private information discussed with the author by high-level British security personnel, London, England, February 20, 1980.

48. For the PLO trail of blood in the 1960s and the 1970s, see Lester A. Sobel, ed., *Palestinian Impasse: Arab Guerrillas and International Terror* (New York: Facts on File, 1977).

49. *New York Times,* June 16, 1984, p. L-5.

50. Klaus Knorr, "Controlling Nuclear War," *International Security 9,* no. 4(Spring 1985):95.

51. Leonard S. Spector, "Silent Spread," *Foreign Policy* 58(Spring 1985):57.
52. Spector, *Nuclear Proliferation*, p. 3.
53. George F. Kennan, *The Nuclear Delusion: Soviet–American Relations in the Atomic Age*, updated ed. (New York: Pantheon Books, 1983), p. 71.

Chapter 11
Israel's Choice: Nuclear Weapons or International Law

1. See generally: Uri Bar-Joseph, "The Hidden Debate: The Formation of Nuclear Doctrines in the Middle East," *Journal of Strategic Studies*, Vol. 5, No. 2(June 1982); Shai Feldman, *Israeli Nuclear Deterrence* (New York: Columbia University Press, 1982); Rodney W. Jones, *Small Nuclear Forces*, The Washington Papers/103 (New York: Praeger Publishers, 1984); Stephen M. Meyer, *The Dynamics of Nuclear Proliferation* (Chicago: University of Chicago Press, 1984); and Steven Weissman and Herbert Krosney, *The Islamic Bomb* (New York: Times Books, 1981).

2. See The Antarctic Treaty, arts. I & V, signed Dec. 1, 1959, entered into force June 23, 1961, 12 U.S.T. 794, T.I.A.S. 4780, 402 U.N.T.S. 71 (ratified by 26 states as of December 31, 1982); Treaty for the Prohibition of Nuclear Weapons in Latin America, signed February 14, 1967, entered into force for 24 states as of December 31, 1982, 634 U.N.T.S. 281; Treaty on Principles Governing the Activities of States in the Exploration and Use of Outer Space, Including the Moon and Other Celestial Bodies, art. IV, signed January 27, 1967, entered into force October 10, 1967, 18 U.S.T. 2410, T.I.A.S. 6347, 610 U.N.T.S. 205 (ratified by 81 states as of December 31, 1982); Treaty on the Prohibition of the Emplacement of Nuclear Weapons and Other Weapons of Mass Destruction on the Seabed and the Ocean Floor and in the Subsoil Thereof, signed February 11, 1971, entered into force for 70 states as of December 31, 1982, 23 U.S.T. 701, T.I.A.S. no. 7337.

3. Treaty Banning Nuclear Weapon Tests in the Atmosphere, in Outer Space and Under Water, signed August 5, 1963, entered into force October 10, 1963, 14 U.S.T. 1313, T.I.A.S. no. 5433, 480 U.N.T.S. 43 (ratified by 110 states as of December 31, 1982).

4. Declaration on the Prohibition of the Use of Nuclear and Thermo-nuclear Weapons, para. 1(a), G.A. Res. 1653 (XVI), 16 U.N. GAOR Supp. (no. 17) at 4, U.N. Doc. A/5100 (1961).

5. Ibid. at para. 1(b).

6. Ibid. at para. 1(d).

7. Declaration on the Non-use of Force in International Relations and Permanent Prohibition of the Use of Nuclear Weapons, para. 1, G.A. Res. 2936 (XXVII), 27 U.N. GAOR Supp. (no. 30) at 5, U.N. Doc. A/8730 (1972).

8. See *The Shimoda Case*, Judgment of December 7, 1963, District Court of Tokyo, translated into English and reprinted in full in 1964 *Japan Yearbook International* L.759 (1965).

9. [1927] P.C.I.J., ser. A., no. 10.

10. Thus, in this spirit, does U.S. Army Field Manual No. 27-10 provide: "The

use of explosive 'atomic weapons', whether by air, sea, or land forces, cannot *as such* be regarded as violative of international law in the absence of any customary rule of international law or international convention restricting their employment." U.S. Department of Army, *The Law of Land Warfare,* para. 35 (Field Manual no. 27-10, 1956) (emphasis added).

11. See e.g., Stowell, "The Laws of War and the Atomic Bomb," *American Journal of International Law* 39(1945):784; Thomas, "Atomic Bombs in International Society," ibid., p. 736; Thomas "Atomic Warfare and International Law," *Proceedings of the American Society of International Law* (1946):84. Cf. Baxter, "The Role of Law in Modern War," *Proceedings of the American Society of International Law* (1953), p. 90.

12. Consider, for example, the emphasis added to the U.S. Army Field Manual quotation in note 10.

13. *Trial of the Major War Criminals Before the International Military Tribunal,* vol. 22 (1948), p. 464.

14. See, e.g., article 23 of the 1907 Hague Regulations, Respecting the Laws and Customs of War on Land (hereinafter cited as "1907 Hague Regulations"), Annex to the 1907 Hague Convention (IV), Respecting the Laws and Customs of War on Land, October 18, 1907, 36 Stat. 2277, T.S. no. 539, 1 Bevans 631, which provides in part:

> In addition to the prohibitions provided by special Conventions, it is especially forbidden . . . (b) To kill or wound treacherously individuals belonging to the hostile nation or army; . . . (e) To employ arms, projectiles, or material calculated to cause unnecessary suffering . . . , [and] . . . (g) To destroy or seize the enemy's property, unless such destruction or seizure be imperatively demanded by the necessities of war . . . ." For similar language, see article 35(2) of Geneva Protocol I Additional Relating to Victims of International Armed Conflict, adopted December 12, 1977, entered into force, December 7, 1978, U.N. Doc. A/32/144, Annex I, reprinted in *International Legal Materials* 16(1977); p. 1391, which prohibits weapons and methods causing "superfluous injury or unnecessary suffering."

In addition, see Hague Draft Rules of Aerial Warfare, arts. 22-26, reprinted in *American Journal of International Law* 17 (Supp. 1923):245; Declaration of Brussels, August 27, 1874, arts. 12–13, reprinted in Friedman, *The Law of War: A Documentary History* (1972) pp. 194–96; Declaration on the Prohibition of the Use of Nuclear and Thermo-nuclear Weapons, G.A. Res. 1653, 16 GAOR Supp. (no. 17) at 4, U.N. Doc. A/5100 (1961); Resolution on Respect for Human Rights in Armed Conflicts, G.A. Res. 2444, 23 U.N. GAOR Supp. (no. 18) at 50, U.N. Doc. A/7218 (1968); Resolution on Basic Principles for the Protection of Civilian Populations in Armed Conflicts, G.A. Res. 2675, 25 U.N. GAOR Supp. (no. 28) at 76, U.N. Doc. A/8028 (1970); Fundamental Rules of International Humanitarian Law Applicable in Armed Conflicts, Rule 6, *International Review of the Red Cross* 206(1978):249.

15. See, e.g., 1977 Geneva Protocol I Additional, supra note 14, art. 48 which states: "In order to ensure respect for and protection of the civilian population and civilian objects, the Parties to the conflict shall at all times distinguish between the civilian population and combatants and between civilian objects and military objectives and accordingly shall direct their operations against military objectives."

See also Geneva Convention (IV) Relative to the Protection of Civilian Persons in Time of War, August 12, 1949, 6 U.S.T. 3516, T.I.A.S. no. 3365, 75 U.N.T.S. 287; 1907 Hague Regulations, supra note 14, arts. 25 and 27; Resolution on Respect for Human Rights in Armed Conflicts, G.A. Res. 2444, 23 U.N. GAOR Supp. (no. 18) at 50, U.N. Doc. A/7218 (1968); Resolution on Basic Principles for the Protection of Civilian Populations in Armed Conflicts, G.A. Res. 2675, 25 U.N. GAOR Supp. (no. 28) at 76, U.N. Doc. A/8028 (1970); Fundamental Rules of International Humanitarian Law Applicable in Armed Conflicts, Rule 7, supra note 14, at 249.

16. See, e.g., 1977 Geneva Protocol I Additional, supra note 14, arts. 20, 51, 53, 55. See also 1954 Hague Convention for the Protection of Cultural Property in the Event of Armed Conflict, May 14, 1954, art. 4(4); 1949 Geneva Convention (IV), supra note 15, art. 33; Geneva Convention Relative to the Treatment of Prisoners of War, August 12, 1949, art. 13, 6 U.S.T. 3316; T.I.A.S. 3364; 75 U.N.T.S. 135; Geneva Convention for the Amelioration of the Condition of Wounded, Sick and Shipwrecked Members of Armed Forces at Sea, August 12, 1949, art. 47, 6 U.S.T. 3217; T.I.A.S. 3363; 75 U.N.T.S. 85; 1949 Geneva Convention for the Amelioration of the Condition of the Wounded and Sick in Armed Forces in the Field, August 12, 1949, art. 46, 6 U.S.T. 3114; T.I.A.S. 3362; 75 U.N.T.S. 31.

17. 1977 Geneva Protocol I Additional, supra note 14, art. 35(3) states: "It is prohibited to employ methods or means of warfare which are intended, or may be expected, to cause widespread, long-term and severe damage to the natural environment." See also ibid., art 55(1); Stockholm Declaration of the United Nations Conference on the Human Environment, Report of the U.N. Conference on the Human Environment, Principles 2 and 26, U.N. Doc. A/Conf./48/14 (June 5–16, 1972), reprinted in *International Legal Materials 11*(1972):1416.

18. See Hague Convention (V) Respecting the Rights and Duties of Neutral Powers and Persons in Case of War on Land, October 18, 1907, arts. 1, 2, 3, 4, and 10, 36 Stat. 2310, T.S. no. 540, 1 Bevans 654. Article 1 states the basic rule: "The territory of neutral Powers is inviolable." See also Hague Convention (XIII) Concerning the Rights and Duties of Neutral Powers in Naval War, October 18, 1907, arts. 1 and 2, 36 Stat. 2415, T.S. no. 545, 1 Bevans 723.

19. Protocol for the Prohibition of the Use in War of Poisonous or Other Gases, and of Bacteriological Methods of Warfare, June 17, 1925, 26 U.S.T. 571, T.I.A.S. no. 8061, 94 L.N.T.S. 65, states:

> Whereas the use in war of asphyxiating, poisonous or other gases, and of all analogous liquids, materials or devices has been justly condemned by the general opinion of the civilised world; and
> Whereas the prohibition of such use has been declared in Treaties to which the majority of Powers of the world are Parties; and
> To the end that this prohibition shall be universally accepted as a part of International Law, binding alike the conscience and the practice of nations;
> Declare:
> That the High Contracting Parties, so far as they are not already Parties to Treaties prohibiting such use, accept this prohibition, agree to extend this prohibition to the use of bacteriological methods of warfare and agree to be bound as between themselves according to the terms of this declaration.

See also Hague Declaration 2 Concerning Asphyxiating Gases, July 29, 1899 reprinted in A. Roberts and R. Guelff, eds., *Documents of the Laws of War* (1982), p. 36; L. Friedman, ed., *The Law of War: A Documentary History*, vol. 1 (1972), p. 249; 1907 Hague Regulations, supra note 14, art. 23(a); Resolution on the Question of Chemical and Bacteriological (Biological) Weapons, G.A. Res. 2603A (XXIV), 24 U.N. GAOR Supp. (no. 30) at 16, U.N. Doc. A/7630 (1969).

20. M. McDougal and F. Feliciano, Law and Minimum World Public Order—

The Legal Regulation of International Coercion 523(1961). See e.g., *United States v. List, Trials of War Criminals* 11(1948):759, 1243–44; *Law Reports of Trials of War Criminals* 8(1948):65–66:

> Military necessity permits a belligerent, subject to the laws of war, to apply any amount and kind of force to compel the complete submission of the enemy with the least possible expenditure of time, life, and money. In general, it sanctions measures by an occupant necessary to protect the safety of his forces and to facilitate the success of his operations. It permits the destruction of life of armed enemies and other persons whose destruction is incidentally unavoidable by the armed conflicts of the war; it allows the capturing of armed enemies and others of peculiar danger, but it does not permit the killing of innocent inhabitants for purposes of revenge or the satisfaction of a lust to kill. The destruction of property to be lawful must be imperatively demanded by the necessities of war. Destruction as an end in itself is a violation of international law. There must be some reasonable connection between the destruction of property and the overcoming of the enemy forces. It is lawful to destroy railways, lines of communication, or any other property that might be utilized by the enemy. Private homes and churches even may be destroyed if necessary for military operations. It does not admit the wanton devastation of a district or the willful infliction of suffering upon its inhabitants for the sake of suffering alone.

21. See Weston, "Nuclear Weapons Versus International Law: A Contextual Reassessment," *McGill Law Journal* 28(1983):542. See also Weston, "Nuclear Weapons and International Law: Prolegomenon to General Illegality," *New York Law School Journal of International and Comparative Law* 4(1983):227.

22. For a formulation somewhat different but nonetheless paralleling and complementing the six prohibitory rules summarized above, see Fundamental Rules of International Humanitarian Law Applicable in Armed Conflicts. supra note 14.

23. See, e.g., article 22 of the 1907 Hague Regulations Respecting the Laws and Customs of War on Land, supra note 14, which provides: "The right of belligerents to adopt means of injuring the enemy is not unlimited." See also 1977 Geneva Protocol I Additional, supra note 14, art. 35(1); Resolution on Respect for Human Rights in Armed Conflicts, supra note 14, para. 1(a).

24. Accord E. Castren, *The Present Law of War and Neutrality* (1954), p. 207; M. Greenspan, *The Modern Law of Land Warfare* (1959), pp. 372–73; N. Singh, *Nuclear Weapons and International Law* (1959), pp. 162–66; Falk, Meyrowitz, and Sanderson, Nuclear Weapons and International Law, *Indian Journal of International Law* 20 (1980):563; H. Meyrowitz, "Les juristes devant l'arme nucleaire," *Revue General International Public* 67 (1963):820, 842.

25. Article 36 of 1977 Geneva Protocol I Additional, supra note 14, extends this inquiry to the longer term, with obvious implications for defense policymakers and operators: "In the study, development, acquisition or adoption of a new weapon, means or method of warfare, a High Contracting Party is under an obligation to determine whether its employment would, in some or all circumstances, be prohibited by any other rule of international law applicable to the High Contracting Party."

26. For another exploration along similar lines, see Arbess, "The International Law of Armed Conflict in Light of Contemporary Deterrence Strategies: Empty Promise or Meaningful Restraint? *McGill Law Journal* 30(1984):89. For related inquiries, see *Nuclear Weapons and Law*, A.S. Miller and M. Feinrider, eds. (Westport, Conn.: Greenwood Press, 1984).

27. Resolution on the Definition of Aggression, December 14, 1974, G.A. Res.

3314 (XXIX), 29 U.N. GAOR Supp. (no. 31) at 142, U.N. Doc. A/9631.

28. Treaty Providing for the Renunciation of War as an Instrument of National Policy, August 27, 1928, 46 Stat. 2343, T.S. no. 796, 2 Bevans 732, 94 L.N.T.S. 57.

29. U.N. Charter art. 2, para. 4: "All Members shall refrain in their international relations from the threat or use of force against the territorial integrity or political independence of any state, or in any other manner inconsistent with the Purposes of the United Nations."

30. CEP is defined as "the radius of a circle around the target at which a missile is aimed within which the warhead has a 0.5 probability of falling." *U.S. Arms Control and Disarmament Agency, SALT Lexicon* (rev. ed. 1975), p. 5.

31. Genocide, the crime of *deliberately* bringing about the destruction, in whole or in part, of a national, ethnical, racial, or religious group as such, could well be listed among the prohibitory rules listed in the first section of this chapter. Punished at Nuremberg, it since has become institutionalized in the Convention on the Prevention and Punishment of the Crime of Genocide, adopted by the U.N. General Assembly, December 9, 1948, entered into force, January 12, 1951, 78 U.N.T.S. 277. Of course, genocide can be perpetrated without nuclear weapons, and Israel might well interpret a concerted Arab assault against it with only conventional forces as genocidal. Because the stated *intent* of Israel's adversaries has often been the total destruction of Israel, such an interpretation may be entirely justified. But even this would not legitimize preemptive nuclear genocide by Israel.

32. Congress of the United States, Office of Technology Assessment, *The Effects of Nuclear War* (Washington, D.C.: U.S. Government Printing Office, 1979).

33. See e.g., Cockburn and Cockburn, "The Myth of Missile Accuracy, *New York Review of Books,* November 20, 1980, p. 40. In the Middle East, delivery systems would most likely be fighter bomber aircraft, surface-to-surface missiles (SSMs), and short-range ballistic missiles (SRBMs).

34. See *Documents on the Laws of War,* supra note 19, pp. 138–39.

35. 1977 Geneva Protocol I Additional, supra note 14, art. 51(6).

36. See, e.g., M. McDougal and F. Feliciano, Law and Minimum World Public Order, The Legal Regulation of International Coercion, 522 (1961), pp. 652–59.

37. See F. Kalshoven, *Belligerent Reprisals* (1971), pp. 375–78; N. Onuf, *Reprisals: Rituals, Rules, Rationales,* Princeton University Center of International Studies, Research Monograph no. 42, Princeton, N.J., July 1974, p. 22.

38. R. Fisher, "Getting to 'Yes' in the Nuclear Age," in *Toward Nuclear Disarmament and Global Security: A Search for Alternatives,* B. Weston, ed., (Boulder, Colo.: Westview Press, 1984).

39. Supra note 2.

40. Supra note 3.

41. Treaty for the Prohibition of Nuclear Weapons in Latin America, supra note 2, art. 1(1) and (2).

42. Treaty on Principles Governing the Activities of States in the Exploration of Outer Space, Including the Moon and Other Celestial Bodies, supra note 2, art. IV.

43. Treaty on the Prohibition of the Emplacement of Nuclear Weapons and Other Weapons of Mass Destruction on the Seabed and the Ocean Floor and in the Subsoil Thereof, supra note 2, art. I.

44. Draft Agreement Governing the Activities of States on the Moon and Other

Celestial Bodies, art. III, Report of the Committee on the Peaceful Uses of Outer Space, 34 U.N. GAOR, supp. (no. 20) 33, U.N. Doc. A/34/20 Annex II (1979).

45. 1977 Geneva Protocol I Additional, supra note 14, art. 36.

46. Charter of the International Military Tribunal, October 6, 1945, art. 6(c), 59 Stat. 1555, 1556, E.A.S. no. 472, 13, 14 (1945).

47. Supra note 31.

Chapter 12
Deterrence, Holocaust, and Nuclear Weapons: A Nonparochial Outlook

1. Since Israel has never officially revealed the nature of its nuclear program, all factual claims come through journalistic reports in various foreign press (often said to be relying on intelligence sources). See, for example, "How Israel Got the Bomb," *Time,* April 12, 1976, pp. 39–40. For a good survey of this literature see Alan Dowty, "Nuclear Proliferation: The Israeli Case," *International Studies Quarterly* 22 (1978):79–120; Robert E. Harkavy, *Spectre of a Middle Eastern Holocaust: The Strategic and Diplomatic Implications of the Israeli Nuclear Weapons Program,* Monograph Series in World Affairs, vol. 14 (Denver: University of Denver Press, 1977), pp. 5–19; Robert J. Pranger and Dale R. Tahtinen, *Nuclear Threat in the Middle East* (Washington, D.C.: American Enterprise Institute, 1975), pp. 7–21. For a good outline of the origins of the Israeli nuclear program see Fuad Jabber, *Israel and Nuclear Weapons* (London: Chatto and Windus, 1971); also Sylvia K. Crosbie, *A Tacit Alliance: France and Israel from Suez to the Six Day War* (Princeton, N.J.: Princeton University Press, 1974).

2. Though Israel has not signed the NPT, it did claim to endorse the spirit of the treaty by its approval of the June 12, 1968, U.N. resolution commending the text of the NPT. On the details of Israel's policy toward international agreements on nuclear weapons, including its particular objections to the NPT, see the following: Dowty, "Nuclear Proliferation," pp. 105–8; Avigdor Haselkorn, "Israel: From an Option to a Bomb in the Basement?" in Robert M. Lawrence and Joel Larus, eds., *Nuclear Proliferation: Phase II* (Lawrence, Kansas: University Press of Kansas, 1974), pp. 149–82; Yair Evron, "Israel and the Atom: The Uses and Misuses of Ambiguity," *Orbis* 17(1974):1324–43; George Quester, "Israel and the Nuclear Non-proliferation Treaty," *Bulletin of the Atomic Scientists* 25(1969):7–9, 44–45; and Avi Beker, chapter 8 in this book.

3. This formulation was put forward first by Prime Minister Eshkol in 1964, and has been repeated ever since by many Israeli leaders. Of course, a "bomb in the basement" can be developed and maintained without being "introduced" publicly. For more on its ambiguous aspects see "Israel and the Atom," and chapters 3, 4, 5, 6, and 8 in this book.

4. The term *possession* is quite ambiguous. In the past, testing of a nuclear device was considered a technical requirement for genuine nuclear status. But since testing is no longer seen as a necessary condition for actual possession of the bomb, the question of possession becomes in certain circumstances just a matter of definition. As Dowty in "Nuclear Proliferation," asks, "Is an assembled or almost-assembled, but untested, primitive nuclear 'device' a weapon?" (p. 105).

5. This stance was added to the Israeli nuclear lexicon by the late foreign minister Yigal Allon, and it has since held as Israel's official policy on the nuclear issue. See Evron, "Israel and the Atom," Haselkorn, "Israel," and chapter by Efraim Inbar (5) in this book.

6. See Amos Perlmutter, "The Israeli Raid on Iraq," *Strategic Review* 10(1982): 34–43; and Shai Feldman, "The Bombing of Osiraq Revisited," *International Security* 7(1983):114–42.

7. On the role of the nuclear dimension in the Yom Kippur War there are opposing views. See Yair Evron, "The Relevance and Irrelevance of Nuclear Options in Conventional Wars: The 1973 October War," *Jerusalem Journal of International Relations* 7(1984):143–76; Shlomo Aronson, "The Nuclear Dimension of the Arab–Israeli Conflict: The Case of the Yom Kippur War," *Jerusalem Journal of International Relations* 7(1984):107–42. Evron presents the accepted view denying the significance of the nuclear factor in the 1973 war, while Aronson proposes a radical (and highly speculative) interpretation of that war based on the centrality of the nuclear issue for both sides.

8. On actual uses of the Israeli nuclear option as a political bargaining card with the United States, see Lawrence Freedman, "Israel's Nuclear Policy," *Survival* 17(1975):114–20; Robert W. Tucker, "Israel and the United States: From Dependence to Nuclear Weapons?" *Commentary* 60(1975):29–43; Evron, "Israel and the Atom," pp. 147–49; and Alan Dowty, "Israel and Nuclear Weapons," *Midstream* 22 (1976):7–22. See also the literature mentioned in note 1.

9. This point was made clearly in Evron, "Israel and the Atom," pp. 164–65.

10. The existence of a secret nuclear program creates problems for the Israeli democratic system. This is, perhaps, the only matter of public policy in Israel which is completely under the control of military censorship. If modern democracy means *public accountability* of office holders before voters for their policies and actions, this democratic principle has been sharply violated insofar as the nuclear issue is concerned. For a country like Israel, so proud of its democratic tradition and free press, the nuclear issue represents an anomaly. It also exemplifies the general claim that nuclear weapons negate the very ideal of western democracy. On this matter see Richard Falk, "Nuclear Weapons and the Renewal of Democracy," in Avner Cohen and Steven Lee, eds., *Nuclear Weapons and the Future of Humanity* (Totowa, N.J.: Rowman and Allanheld, 1985), pp. 527–50.

11. Dowty, "Nuclear Proliferation," makes some interesting first-person historical observations on this matter (pp. 84–85).

12. First and foremost among these publications is Shai Feldman, *Israeli Nuclear Deterrence: A Strategy for the 1980's* (New York: Columbia University Press, 1982). For a theoretical pro-proliferation argument see Kenneth Waltz, *The Spread of Nuclear Weapons: More May Be Better,* Adelphi Papers, no. 171 (London: International Institute for Strategic Studies, 1981). See also Shlomo Aronson, "Israel's Nuclear Options: A Dovish View," *Jerusalem Quarterly* 4(1979); Steven J. Rosen, "Nuclearization and Stability in the Middle East," *Jerusalem Journal of International Relations* 1(1976):1–32; also by the same author, "A Stable System of Mutual Nuclear Deterrence in the Arab–Israeli Conflict," *American Political Science Review* 71 (1977):1367–83.

13. Feldman, in *Israeli Nuclear Deterrence,* ends the introduction of his book with the hope that his study will contribute to stimulate a national debate in Israel

on Israel's nuclear strategy, "a debate that might . . . help to persuade influential opinion-makers to adopt a more balanced attitude toward a prospect of a nuclear Middle East." (p. 6). So far this has not happened.

14. See Yair Evron, "Some Effects of the Introduction of Nuclear Weapons in the Middle East," in A. Arian, ed., *Israel: A Developing Society* (Assem: Van Gorom, 1980), pp. 105–26. For recent statements of the general antiproliferation argument see Lewis A. Dunn, *Controlling the Bomb: Nuclear Proliferation in the 1980s* (New Haven, Conn.: Yale University Press, 1982); Joseph S. Nye, "Nonproliferation: A Long-term Strategy," *Foreign Affairs* 56(1978): 601–23. For the classical nonproliferation argument, see Karl W. Deutsch and David J. Singer, "Multipolar Power Systems and International Stability," *World Politics* 16(1964):390–406.

15. Feldman expresses quite openly his general endorsement of the theory of nuclear deterrence as an instrument to preserve peace, in *Israeli Nuclear Deterrence*, pp. 33–52, and elsewhere.

16. For a more comprehensive account of the moral aspects of nuclear deterrence, see Avner Cohen and Steven Lee, "The Nuclear Predicament," in Cohen and Lee, eds., *Nuclear Weapons and the Future of Humanity* (Totowa, N.J.: Rowman and Allanheld, 1985). Much of my general argument here is based on that essay. See also Douglas Lackey, *Nuclear Weapons and Moral Principles* (Totowa, N.J.: Rowman and Allanheld, 1984).

17. I use the term *emergent* here in rough analogy to its current use within the philosophy of biology.

18. This point is thoroughly developed in Berel Lang, "Genocide and Omnicide: Technology at the Limits," in Cohen and Lee, *Nuclear Weapons and the Future of Humanity*, p. 131.

19. Otto Nathan and Heintz Norden, eds., *Einstein on Peace* (New York: Schocken, 1968), p. 376.

20. This point is one of the central themes in Michael Walzer, *Just and Unjust Wars* (New York: Basic Books, 1977). See also chapter 11 by Burns Weston in this book.

21. Since the recent studies of the "nuclear winter," this claim appears stronger than ever before. See note 27 of the introduction to this book.

22. On the rationality of war in terms of corporate activity see Joseph Margolis, "The Peculiarities of Nuclear Thinking," in Cohen and Lee, *Nuclear Weapons and the Future of Humanity*, pp. 177–96.

23. See Lang, "Genocide and Omnicide."

24. See George H. Quester, "Substituting Conventional for Nuclear Weapons: Some Problems and Some Possibilities," *Ethics* 95(1985):619–40.

25. The military branches of both the United States and the Soviet Union entertained the idea of a preemptive strike when their countries faced the rise of a newcomer nuclear power. The United States considered it against the Soviet Union in the early 1950s; the Soviet Union against China in the late 1960s. On the U.S. proposals see David Alan Rosenberg, "The Origins of Overkill: Nuclear Weapons and American Strategy," *International Security*, 7(1983):3–71. As to the Soviet plans to strike China, the information is more circumstantial. In late August 1969, the Central Intelligence Agency spread reports that the Soviets were exploring the possibility of a preemptive conventional strike against Chinese nuclear facilities. On this issue see also Henry Kissinger, *White House Years* (Boston: Little, Brown, 1979), pp. 184–5.

26. Stephen M. Meyer, *The Dynamics of Nuclear Proliferation* (Chicago: University of Chicago Press, 1984). Meyer argues convincingly that nuclear proliferation decisions are politically motivated decisions, and technological capabilities are subordinate to political motivations.

27. Carl von Clausewitz, *On War,* translated by J.J. Graham and edited by Anatol Rapoport (Baltimore: Penguin Books, 1968), p. 263.

28. Thomas Donaldson, "Nuclear Deterrence and Self-Defense," *Ethics* 95 1985:537–48.

29. The argument about the vulnerability of C³I is well presented in Paul Bracken, *The Command and Control of Nuclear Forces* (New Haven, Conn.: Yale University Press, 1983). See also Ashton B. Carter, "The Command and Control of Nuclear War," *Scientific American* 252(January 1985): 20–27; and Desmond Ball, *Can Nuclear War Be Controlled?* Adelphi Papers, no. 169 (London: International Institute for Strategic Studies, 1981).

30. For a development of this argument, see Jennifer Leaning and Langley Keyes, eds., *The Counterfeit Ark* (Cambridge, Mass.: Ballinger, 1983).

31. See, for example, Colin S. Gray and Keith Payne, "Victory Is Possible," *Foreign Policy* 59(1980): 14–27; see also by the same author, "Nuclear Strategy: The Case for a Theory of Victory," *International Security* 4(1979):54–87.

32. For a good historical survey of the concept of LNW see Ian Clark, *Limited Nuclear War* (Princeton, N.J.: Princeton University Press, 1982).

33. See Robert E. Goodin, "Nuclear Disarmament as a Moral Certainty," *Ethics* 95(1985): 641–58. Goodin's argument on the idea of "moral certainty" in this context is an "argument from ignorance." His complaint against nuclear deterrence is that it amounts to "playing the odds without knowing the odds. That constitutes recklessness par excellence."

34. McGeorge Bundy, "A Matter of Survival," *New York Review of Books,* March 17, 1983, p. 3.

35. For a good theoretical discussion of deterrence in the context of international politics, see Patrick M. Morgan, *Deterrence: A Conceptual Analysis* (Beverly Hills, Calif.: Sage Publications, 1983). Much of my discussion here is derived from Morgan's analysis.

36. See, for example, Robert Jervis, *Perceptions and Misperceptions in International Politics* (Princeton, N.J.: Princeton University Press, 1976); see also by the same author, "Deterrence and Perception," *International Security* 7(1983): 3–30.

37. Jonathan Schell, *The Fate of the Earth* (New York: Alfred A. Knopf, 1982), p. 202.

38. For this claim see Michael Mandelbaum, *The Nuclear Question* (New York: Cambridge University Press, 1979), p. 279; see also Stephen Kaplan, *Diplomacy of Power* (Washington, D.C.: Brookings Books, 1981), pp. 667–77.

39. See, for example, the Harvard Nuclear Study Group, *Living With Nuclear Weapons* (New York: Bantam, 1983).

40. I rely here on Morgan's distinction between two types of deterrence: general deterrence and special deterrence. While general deterrence is the ever-present regulatory mechanism of war avoidance in the international arena, special deterrence is a specific threat, an infrequent occurrence. The former is a matter of long-term military capabilities and political intentions, the latter is a matter of responding to particular aggressive intentions. The context of special deterrence typifies situations of actual

crisis, when the option of resorting to military force is a very real one, not just hypothetical. See Morgan, ibid., ch. 1–2.

41. For a development of this argument see, Patrick Morgan, "New Directions in Deterrence Theory," in Cohen and Lee, *Nuclear Weapons and the Future of Humanity* (Totowa, N.J.: Rowman and Allanheld, 1985), pp. 197–222.

42. For this suggestion see Barrie Paskins, "Proliferation and the Nature of Deterrence," in Nigel Black and Kay Pole, eds., *Dangers of Deterrence* (London: Routledge and Kegan Paul, 1983), pp. 112–31.

43. This perception is crucial to understand the Israeli position at the eve of the Six-Day War. The Arabs did not adequately appreciate this Israeli sensitivity. See Janice Stein, "Calculation, Miscalculation, and Conventional Deterrence: The View from Cairo," in Robert Jervis and Richard Ned Lebow, eds., *Psychology and Deterrence*, forthcoming.

44. For a psychohistorical account of Israeli national perceptions that stress similar points see Jay Y. Gonen, *A Psycho-History of Zionism* (New York: Mason J. Charter, 1975). On the Holocaust fixation in determining Israel's foreign policy see also Michael Brecher, *Decisions in Israel's Foreign Policy* (New Haven, Conn.: Yale University Press, 1975), pp. 333–35, 342–43, 514.

45. Michael Handel, "The Yom Kippur War and the Inevitability of Surprise," *International Studies Quarterly* 21(1977):461–502; see also Yair Evron, *Problems of Arms Control in the Middle East,* Adelphi Papers, no. 138(London: International Institute of Strategic Studies, 1977).

46. See Steven Rosen and Martin Indyk, "The Temptation to Pre-empt in a Fifth Arab-Israeli War," *Orbis* (1976):265–85.

47. See Michael Brecher, "The Middle East Subordinate System and Its Impact on Israel's Foreign Policy," *International Studies Quarterly* 13(1969):117–40.

48. For a similar analysis see Evron, "Israel and the Atom."

49. Leonard Beaton, *Must the Bomb Spread?* (Baltimore: Penguin Books, 1966); Frank Barnaby, *Preventing the Spread of Nuclear Weapons* (New York: Humanities Press, 1969); Alastair Buchan, ed., *A World of Nuclear Powers* (Englewood Cliffs, N.J.: Prentice-Hall, 1966).

Index

About the Contributors

Avi Beker, currently assistant professor of political science at Bar-Ilan University in Ramat Gan, received his Ph.D. in political science from the Graduate Center of the City University of New York in 1982. A member of the Permanent Mission of Israel to the United Nations (1977–1982) and a delegate to five General Assemblies, he was a delegate to the U.N. Disarmament Commission and to the two Special Sessions of the General Assembly dedicated to Disarmament (May-June 1978, June-July 1982). Professor Beker has published numerous articles and is the author of the book *Disarmament Without Order: The Politics of Disarmament at the United Nations* (Greenwood Press, 1985).

Stephen J. Cimbala is associate professor of political science at Pennsylvania State University, Delaware County. He received his Ph.D. in political science in 1969 from the University of Wisconsin-Madison. Professor Cimbala's contributions to the field of defense and national security studies have included writings on deterrence, arms control, nuclear and conventional war, and other related issues. His recent publications include *National Security Strategy* (Praeger, 1984).

Avner Cohen, currently lecturer in philosophy at Tel Aviv University, received his Ph.D. from the University of Chicago in 1981. He has written on skepticism, philosophy, and psychiatry and metaphilosophy. In recent years he has worked on philosophical issues raised by the nuclear predicament and co-edited (with Steven Lee) *Nuclear Weapons and the Future of Humanity* (Rowman and Allanheld, 1985). Dr. Cohen has held several visiting appointments in the United States.

Alan Dowty, professor of government and international studies at the University of Notre Dame, received his Ph.D. from the University of Chicago in 1963. Prior to 1975, when he began teaching at Notre Dame, he served for twelve years on the faculty of the Hebrew University in Jerusalem. During that time he also served as executive director of the Leonard Davis Institute for International Relations and as chairman of the Department of International Relations. Professor Dowty has published many articles on international relations, U.S. foreign policy, and the Arab–Israeli conflict. Among his books are *The Limits of American Isolation* (New York: University Press, 1971) and *Middle East Crisis: U.S. Decision-Making in 1958, 1970 and 1973* (University of California Press, 1984).

Zeev Eytan, currently a senior research associate at the Jaffee Center for Strategic Studies at Tel Aviv University, received his Ph.D. at the University of Chicago in 1974. A colonel in the Israeli Defense Forces (IDF) until 1980, Dr. Eytan specializes in military forces in the Middle East. He is co-author, with Mark Heller, ed., and Dov Tamari, of *The Middle East Military Balance* (1983) and *The Middle East Military Balance* (1984), both published by The Jaffee Center for Strategic Studies, and he has written extensively on the Yom Kippur War in *Ma'arachot*, the IDF Journal.

Robert A. Friedlander, professor of law at Ohio Northern University College of Law, received his J.D. from De Paul University in 1973 and a Ph.D. in history from Northwestern University in 1963. The author of many books and articles dealing with terrorism, his most recent books are *Terror-Violence: Aspects of Social Control* (Oceana, 1983) and a four-volume documentary analysis of terrorism: *Terrorism: Documents of International and Local Control* (Oceana, 1979–1984). Professor Friedlander has testified before the U.S. Senate Committee on Foreign Relations and other committees of the Congress.

Robert Harkavy, professor of political science at Pennsylvania State University, received his Ph.D. in international relations from Yale University in 1973. He is the author of several books, most recently *Great Power Competition for Overseas Bases: The Geopolitics of Access Diplomacy,* and the co-editor of several others, most recently *The Lessons of Recent Wars in the Third World* (Lexington Books, 1985). He has served tours with the U.S. Atomic Energy Commission and U.S. Arms Control and Disarmament Agency. Professor Harkavy was recently a visiting research professor at the U.S. Army War College, and he was a Humboldt Fellow at the University of Kiel, Germany, and a Fulbright research fellow in Sweden.

Efraim Inbar teaches political science at Bar-Ilan University in Ramat Gan. He received his Ph.D. from the University of Chicago in 1981. The author of many scholarly publications dealing with national security issues in the Middle East, Professor Inbar has written extensively on the subject of Israeli strategy and foreign policy. His most recent work is *Outcast Countries in the World Community*, a volume of the University of Denver Monograph Series in World Affairs (1985).

Gerald M. Steinberg is a member of the political science faculty at the Hebrew University in Jerusalem and also teaches international relations at Bar-Ilan University. His current research focuses on the interaction between technology and politics, and his book *Satellite Reconnaisance* was published by Praeger in 1983. Some of his many other works have appeared in the *Bulletin of the Atomic Scientists, Technology Review, The Journal of Peace Research*, and *Policy Sciences*. Professor Steinberg's extensive analysis of the Israeli defense industry will soon be published by the Stockholm International Peace Research Institute. His Ph.D. is from the Department of Government of Cornell University (1981).

Burns H. Weston is the Bessie Dutton Murray Professor of Law at the University of Iowa. He received his A.B. degree from Oberlin College (1956) and his LL.B. and J.S.D. degrees from the Yale Law School (1961, 1970). A Senior Fellow of the World Policy Institute and a Fellow of the World Academy of Art and Science, his professional affiliations also include the Board of Directors and Consultative Council of the Lawyers Committee on Nuclear Policy, the Lawyers Alliance for Nuclear Arms Control, the American Bar Association's Standing Committee on World Order under Law, and the American Society of International Law. He is a member, in addition, of the editorial boards of the *American Journal of International Law*, the *Bulletin of Peace Proposals*, and the *Journal of World Peace*. The author of many books and articles, including articles in the *American Journal of International Law*, the *Encyclopedia Britannica, The Human Rights Quarterly*, and an award-winning coursebook, *International Law and World Order* (West, 1980), his most recent book is titled *Toward Nuclear Disarmament and Global Security: A Search for Alternatives* (Westview, 1984).

Avner Yaniv received his Ph.D. from Oxford University and is currently a senior lecturer in political science at the University of Haifa. A frequent lecturer in many countries throughout the world, he has been a visiting fellow at the universities of Hamburg and Oxford; a visiting professor at the Department of Government, Georgetown University; and a visiting professor at the Department of Government and Politics, University of Maryland, College Park. His many published writings include articles in such periodicals as *International Affairs, International Security, Journal of Politics, International Interactions, Armed Forces and Society, The Washington Quarterly, The British Journal of Political Science, The Jerusalem Quarterly*, and the *Middle*

East Review. Professor Yaniv is co-editor and contributor to *Syria under Assad* (Croom-Helm, 1985; St. Martins, 1985) and the author of *Deterrence without the Bomb: Israeli Strategy in Perspective* (Lexington Books, 1986) and *Dilemmas of Security: Politics, Strategy, and the Israeli Experience in Lebanon* (New York; Oxford University Press, 1986).

About the Editor

Louis René Beres, professor of political science at Purdue University, received his Ph.D. at Princeton University in 1971. A noted specialist in foreign affairs and international law with particular reference to strategic studies, he is the author of many major books and articles in the field. A frequent lecturer in the United States and abroad on matters concerning nuclear weapons and nuclear war, he is recognized internationally as one of the world's leading scholars in the movement for a durable and just peace. In preparing *Security or Armageddon* for publication, Professor Beres has made several journeys to Israel.